The Lelewer Legacy:
Traditions of a Loving Family

The Lelewer Legacy
Traditions of a Loving Family

Nancy Lelewer

Ivy House Publishing Group
www.ivyhousebooks.com

PUBLISHED BY IVY HOUSE PUBLISHING GROUP
5122 Bur Oak Circle, Raleigh, NC 27612
United States of America
919.782.0281
www.ivyhousebooks.com

ISBN: 978-1-57197-503-4
Library of Congress Control Number: 2009942560

Cover Design by Suzanne Heiser

Printed in The United States of America

I was an only child, but my world was rarely lonely as it was filled with stories about my forebears told to me by my father, a fascinating family—my own—and a multitude of friends.

I dedicate this book to:

Great-grandfather David Lelewer (3/21/1843–3/1/1912)

Grandpa SS, Selig Seward Lelewer (10/1/1872–5/25/1947)

With a special "hats off" to my father,
"Papa" Joseph David Lelewer (3/30/1906–11/26/2004)

CONTENTS

Remember that there's nothing higher, stronger, more wholesome and more useful in life than some good memory, especially when it goes back to the days of your own childhood, to the days of your life at home. —Dostoevsky

PREFACE

I recorded my parents' memories for five years, from 1988 to 1993. The first time I handed the microphone to my father he smiled at me and said,

> In the beginning there was man. And sometime later came great Gross Papa Lelewer, who was better known as Selig Lelewer, my great-grandfather. He was born in Lissa, Province Posen, Germany, which is now Poznan in Poland. Selig's family was very poor in spite of his being hard working and one of the most skilled fur tanners in the city. In 1847, there was a great famine in Germany and business was at a standstill. When he learned that compensation for his class of work was being reduced below living wages, he quit and left on a sailing vessel to seek his fortune in America. He was never heard from again. It is my opinion that he probably landed in Tahiti and if by chance you go there and see any long-nosed Tahitians it's because of his stay in the islands.

At that point, I knew I was on my own when it came to writing this book.

My father knew how to live fully, how to love deeply, and how to die gracefully. He was my best friend for nearly seventy years. We were together almost every minute the last year of his life and, during that time, we talked about everything—his youth; his parents, grandparents, and brother; his schooling; his classmates; his days in the family business; his early loves; my mother; sex; politics; sports; changes in the world; finances; the fact he was dying; his obituary; his cremation and my mother's; and the newspapers and friends he wanted notified.

As he grew closer to death during that year, he asked me to call his friends and invite them to visit. I was to be honest and to say he was dying and wanted to share some time with them. His friends came. Some came tentatively at first, yet, by the end of a visit, each left feeling better. My father's words were upbeat, never grim. Even in the last weeks of his life, he made the people around him feel comfortable—it was his way.

My father, grandfather, and great-grandfather were creative, charismatic men of business. The Lelewer business succeeded because of their intuition, resilience, quirky problem solving, stick-to-itiveness, and deep devotion to one another. But even more, they were men who knew right from wrong, who gave help without expectation of return, who radiated goodness, got satisfaction from seeing other people happy, gave back to society, and much more.

The stories here are a composite of what I recorded and my memories of a wonderful family.

ACKNOWLEDGMENTS

I'd like to thank Ashley Hardin, Anna Howland and Stephanie Wetzel at Ivy House Publishing for their input and guidance and the following people for their help along the way: Kay Brigham, Michael Erickson, Mary Hadley, Suzanne Pemsler, Christina Polo, Meredith Rutter. And a special thanks to my fabulous editor, Pat Carda.

PARTIAL LELEWER FAMILY TREE

Moses Lelewer died in Lissa, Germany in 1818. He was the great-grandfather of David Lelewer who was my great-grandfather. He had one son, Isaac Michael, born in 1730, who was married to Deborah. They had seven children whose names are listed below. Also listed are the descendents of the seventh child, Selig M., who was my great-great-grandfather.

I. Muidel m. Kalish
II. Esther m. Wiener
III. Moses
IV. Gottschalk
V. Hinde m. Schnapp
VI. Shiffere m. Schnapp
VII. **Selig M. (died at sea)** 1827–1847 m. Zelda Rothgiesser 1823–1898
  A. Isador m. Melissa Fissher
  B. Rike m. Morris Posner
    1. Henry Posner
      a. granddaughter–Hannah Posner
  C. Shifferene ?–1853
  D. Muidel 1847–?
  E. **David** 3/21/1843–3/1/1912
    (Joseph Lelewer's Grandfather)
    1 m. Hannah Newman 1848–1884
      1. Sadie m. Albert Hoefeld
      2. **Selig Seward** 10/1/1872–5/25/1947
       (Joseph Lelewer's father)
      3. Blanch m. Arthur Feilchenfeld
      4. Nellie m. Abe Monheimer
      5. Sylvia m. Herman Goodfriend
    2 m. Matilda Hoefeld
      6. Harriet m. Sigmund Robbins

PARTIAL LELEWER FAMILY TREE *(continued)*

VII, E, 2. Selig Seward
       m. 12/29/1904 Myrtle Schnadig 1/3/1883–4/18/1967
a. **Joseph David Lelewer** *(my father)* 3/30/1906–11/26/2004
  m. 3/2/1932 **Mina Clara Ullman** *(my mother)* 1/24/1911–2/11/2005
    1a. **Nancy Ullman Lelewer** 3/2/1935–
      1m. 9/15/1957 Stephen Sonnabend
        1b. **Kathy** 6/11/1958–
          1m. 8/30/1981 Tom Rowe 9/23/1956–
            1c. **Mina Caroline** 11/5/1994–
            2c. **Hattie Ullman** 6/4/1998–
        2b. **Wendy** 10/14/1959–
          1m. 3/25/1984 Michael Erickson 2/3/1962–
            1c. **Kelly Sonnabend** 1/14/1989–
            2c. **Brett Lelewer** 4/22/1991–
        3b. **Eric Sonnabend** 4/25/1962–
          1m. 3/27/1990 Donna Patti 6/20/1964–
            1c. **Rachel Lauren** 7/17/1990–
            2c. **Olivia Hanna** 5/2/1992–
        4b. **Patti** 9/30/1963–
          1m. 12/31/1989 Steven Wagner 2/21/1961–
            1c. **Kristina Sonnabend** 1/25/1993–
            2c. **Joseph Sonnabend** 10/12/1994–
      2m. 1/1980 Dr. David Kohn

b. **David Herbert Lelewer** 4/13/1911–12/31/1973
   (Joseph Lelewer's brother)
   m. 7/6/1935 Madeline Kann 2/24/1914–10/28/1995
    1a. **Stanley Lelewer** 6/2/1937–
      1m. Bonnie Cossman 3/12/1961–
        1b. **Joanne** 1/4/1964–   m. 4/13/1997 John Harpel
            1c. **Lexa** 6/7/1998
            2c. **Zander** 4/10/2001–
        2b. **Stephen** 8/25/1966–7/25/1993
      2m. 1/2/1971 Brenda Ringwald
        3b. Kristin 6/3/1974–
      3m. 6/23/1990 Mary Reinhart
    2a. **David Kann Lelewer** 8/4/1940–2/23/1997
    3a. **Jan Lelewer** 7/18/1944–
      1m. 6/11/1966 Mark Lipschutz
        1b. **Matthew David** 4/26/1975–
          1m. 5/28/2006 Sheri Wittson
        2b. **Suzanne** 9/23/1985–
          1m. 9/01/2009 Joseph Flynn

THREE GENERATIONS OF LELEWER MEN

Left to Right: Selig Seward (SS) Lelewer (10/1/1872–4/1/1947)
Joseph David Lelewer (3/30/1906–11/26/2004)
David Lelewer (3/21/1843–3/1/1912)

CHAPTER 1
The Lelewer Stores

Long before I remember neon signs lighting up stores along Lincoln or Belmont, a Lelewer sign hung at the corner of these two Chicago streets. The letters in the Lelewer logo were black except for a brilliant red *E* in the middle. The background was stark white. The sign tilted, swung the black letters to the left and to the right, paused, and repeated the process. The movement of the sign and the red *E* were eye-catchers and much admired when I was growing up. Business poured in.

It was my great-grandfather who began the Lelewer family business. David Lelewer arrived at the age of 18 in New York City from Germany in 1861 just before the start of the Civil War. He walked off the boat and, after waiting for his cousin who did not show up, began to search for the address written on the paper that he held tightly in his hand. He needed a place to stay and a job. Despite little education, no knowledge of English, and only $2.10 in his pocket, he managed to find his way in the immigrant-filled city. Two years later, he stopped just long enough to determine how far he had come.

"On March 21, 1863, my 20th birthday," Great-grand-father David wrote many years later, "I took inventory of my wealth, which consisted of $15 in the bank, $3.45 cash in pocket, totaling $18.45."

After two more years, Great-grandfather David knew he would have to leave the city to realize his long-held dream of owning his own business. In 1865, at the end of the Civil War, Great-grandfather David moved to Indianapolis, Indiana, and founded the Lelewer Fur Store. It was, as it has always seemed to me, an act of considerable courage. "To make the first step in business is the hardest. Same as it is with a child trying his first step to walk. It is scared for the fall, by instinct," he wrote.

The store sold fur hats and coats for men. Women, in this period, did not wear furs, but long Cossack fur coats with little spiral fur hats were popular among men of substance. Times were hard after the Civil War, however, and there weren't many men who could afford furs. Great-grandfather David's fur busi-ness only lasted three months. Undaunted, he tried the fur busi-ness again and then again. In time, he brought his brother, Isador, over from Germany, changed the name of the store to D. Lelewer & Brother, and started the first fur factory in the state of Indiana. He even employed women, which was unheard of at the time.

In an effort to keep his business afloat when fur was not in demand, Great-grandfather David tried adding other kinds of hats to his stock, but the effort was not successful. For fifteen years, Great-grandfather David suffered repeated failures, but he never gave up. In 1880, when word got out that Chicago was booming, he left Indianapolis, the one place he had felt secure, and, at the age of 37, moved to Chicago with his wife and five children. Once the family was settled, he opened a fur store on State Street next to a well-known clothing store. It was an ideal location, but the furs Great-grandfather David brought from Indianapolis did not sell in Chicago. Once again he added hats to the inventory. "There is no use wasting time or thought about furs exclusively without ready funds," he wrote, "so I fell back on the hat business which goes without interruption most of the year." Fortunately, he also managed to sell a few furs to wealthy customers.

As things began to look up, Great-grandfather David opened a second store. He advertised regularly in the newspapers. Fur repairs began to pour in and the sales, both retail and wholesale, of furs began to increase. "By January 1, 1886," Great-grandfather David wrote, "everything we owed was paid off. We made a living and netted about $6,000. I patted myself on the shoulder and began to get a good opinion of myself to become the Napoleon of the fur trade. Who would not at the first success of a business venture?"

It was while Great-grandfather David's son, Selig Seward, was working as a furrier apprentice in the State Street store that Grandpa SS (as we would eventually call him) decided hats might be more profitable than furs. From the store, he could see men lined up outside other stores waiting to get their hats. In the late 1800s, men's hats were important year round. Straw hats were worn in the spring and summer, and derbies and felt hats in the autumn and winter. At Easter, men would don their best clothes and hats and promenade in the Easter Parade. Great-grandfather David used hats to supplement the income from furs. Grandpa SS believed becoming known as a store that specialized in men's hats as well as furs could lead to greater profitability.

Having thought things over carefully, Grandpa SS approached his father and presented his business plan. Great-grandfather David gave the plan careful consideration.

If the Lelewer stores were going to begin emphasizing hats, he concluded, the Lelewers needed to know a great deal more about hats than they did. Great-grandfather David told SS to find the most knowledgeable hat man in the area and hire him, take the man to Yonkers, New York, which was then the heart of hat manufacturing, and buy hats for the store directly from manufacturers, not from middlemen or jobbers. That way, Great-grandfather David explained, Lelewer stores could compete with anyone.

Grandpa SS asked everyone he knew, and even people he didn't know well, for the name of the best hat man. It took some time, but eventually he came up with a name, Clyde De Grant. De Grant was acknowledged to be the best hat man in the entire Midwest. There was, however, a disadvantage to working with Clyde—he was always drunk. Grandpa SS may have wondered if drunkenness was one of the hallmarks of hat men. It seemed as though most hat men of that time were either drunks or mad. The expression "mad as a hatter" was born in the 1800s. Hat makers frequently suffered from slurred speech, shaking, and blackened teeth, all symptoms of mercury poisoning. At the time, mercury nitrate was used to soften the felt used in hat making. On the plus side, at least as far as Grandpa SS was concerned, Clyde was presently jobless because he was always drunk.

Grandpa SS hired Clyde, got him sober, cleaned him up, and took him to New York. There he and Clyde bought hats. A sober Clyde De Grant knew just how and what to buy. He outfitted the stores with all the furniture necessary to display and sell hats. For the next two years, as he learned the ins and outs of hat making, Grandpa SS did not let Clyde out of his sight day or night. It couldn't have been an easy life for Grandpa SS, but he was dedicated to the Lelewer stores and to making the hat business succeed. At the end of the two years, Grandpa SS had learned enough to give up baby-sitting Clyde, who promptly went back to his old habits.

Years later, my father described the hat-making process to me. The plushy part of rabbit fur was fed into a machine somewhat similar in looks to a cotton-candy machine. An exhaust fan blew air from underneath until the pieces of fur stuck together in a large cone. The fur was then removed, pounded, and shaped into a smaller cone about half the size of the original cone. This cone of fur, my father explained, was sent to the hat manufacturer where a multi-roller was used on it. The roller shrank the fur cone by injecting steam into it, then twisted, dipped, and turned the cone continuously.

Trimming and sizing came next. Every hat size required its own sizing block, and each block was made from the smooth American Poplar tree. Finally, the manufacturer would choose fine leather for the hatband. For the man who bought the hat, the fit and color were important, but, according to my father, the true personality of the hat resided in the band where there might be a bow or even a feather. The bow or feather was always on the left side. This placement came about, according to tradition, because swords were held most frequently in the right hand, and you did not want the feather to get in the way of spearing your opponents.

When Grandpa SS learned the hat business from Clyde, hats were selling for $3.00 to $3.50 in Chicago stores. The fine felt hats Grandpa SS bought sold for $2.00 each in the Lelewer stores. The business was an instant success. One of the State Street stores sold 100,000 hats one year—a phenomenal number. In time, caps, selling for $1.00 to $1.50, were added to the inventory. Still later, Grandpa SS went to Gloversville, New York to buy gloves to sell in the stores.

It was soon evident that the hat business was indeed more profitable than the fur business. Great-grandfather David and Grandpa SS phased out the fur business, changed the name of the store to D. Lelewer & Son, advertised as Chicago's largest hatter, and opened store number three. Grandpa SS proved to be a shrewd businessman. He paid no rent for the State Street store because he negotiated a ninety-nine year lease on the property and then rented half of the property to the Melville Shoe Company for a Thom McAn store at a price that covered the rent for the property. He hired the best publicist available, chose an excellent bookkeeper, and kept a perpetual inventory—unheard of in those days. He also hired a window trimmer whose sole job was to create displays of hats, caps, and gloves in the windows of each Lelewer store. The window trimmer made signs that were exquisite works of art. Shoppers would stop to admire them, then look at the hats, go in, and buy.

As Edison's invention of the electric light came into use, Grandpa SS again proved himself an innovator. While some re-tailers installed a few light bulbs in their stores but continued to use kerosene lamps as their primary source of light, Grandpa SS put light bulbs in exclusively. He even had a single incandescent bulb in the window of the State Street store. It wasn't brilliantly lit, but it was the first light in the window of a commercial prop-erty in Chicago.

In the early 1920s, Grandpa SS seized on yet another inno-vation—the radio. Thinking that it ought to be possible to use the one-and-a-half-minute song that was played at the beginning and end of a program to promote the stores, he hired Marvin Frank to create a jingle (one of the first) advertising the Lelewer stores. It was possible in those days to change the words to an already composed song and use it without paying royalties. Grandpa SS and Marvin Frank selected "You Were Meant For Me" as the music they wanted to use. Frank then hired a singer and pianist, Clem and Harry, to record the song, which was played on KYW, Chicago's first radio station:

When you want a hat for wear
Call on Lelewer
They have three stores in town
And growing every day.
Best hats in the world
You'll hear people say.
They have all styles and colors too.
Their clerks will gladly wait on you.
Your money is well spent
And you will be content
When you wear a Lelewer.

What I still remember from my childhood is my grandfather's way with words. I loved it. He was a born advertising man. The Lelewer stores sold Knox hats, an expensive brand of hat. The manufacturer of Knox hats claimed that when a man put on a Knox hat, it gave him a sense of added prestige. At the same time, all hats make a man look taller, so Grandpa SS promptly coined a slogan for Knox hats that was used in all the Lelewer stores: "Every Knox a boost." One of his other slogans, "For a hat becoming to you, you should be coming to us," also worked well.

My father's entry into D. Lelewer & Sons was humble and in keeping with Great-grandfather David's belief in learning the business—he wrapped hats. In fact, my father wrapped hats, bagged them, and acted as a porter. His entry marked the departure of Henry Posner, a cousin of Grandpa SS. At the turn of the century, Grandpa SS had hired Henry who had been raised in a Cleveland orphanage, taught him the hat business, and had made him a partner in D. Lelewer & Sons, which, by the 1920s was on its way to becoming a chain of stores. Henry was successful in the hat business, but when my twenty-year-old father joined the business in 1926, Henry realized that he would never be sole owner of Lelewer's and chose to leave. SS bought Posner's half of the store leases and his portion of the premises at 310 South State Street.

My father always loved the hat business although, during the 1920s and 1930s, some of the clientele at the store at 32 North Dearborn Street may have given him pause. It seems Al Capone, also known as "Scarface," was a Lelewer hat fan. According to my father, Capone's Chicago office was above the Dearborn Street store, and it wasn't unusual for Capone to come in, lay down a hundred dollar bill, and say, "Take care of my boys when they come in."

"We would select one of the finest hats we had when one of his boys came in," my father recalled, "and make sure it was a perfect fit. At the end of the day, if there was money left over, you can bet we returned the change to Scarface."

At the beginning of the Great Depression, my father's brother, David, joined the company and began in the same way as my father had—as a hat wrapper. Still, times change, and in the 1940s, Dad and his brother, working together, successfully changed the merchandising format from hats to men's clothing.

It was the automobile industry that literally, if slowly, lowered the roof on hats. As new car models were introduced, it became increasingly difficult for men to get into or out of a car without having their hats knocked off. When JFK gave his inaugural speech in 1960 without a hat, it was the final nail in the coffin of the men's hat industry.

Neither my cousins nor I were interested in going into the men's clothing business. When I was old enough, I worked for my father before Father's Day and at Christmas. I started as a sock sorter. My job was to sort the socks and put them back into pairs. In case you have never noticed, navy blue socks and black socks look almost identical, and no sooner would I get the pairs in order than someone would come along and mess them up again. As I grew older, I graduated to shirts. To try on a shirt, a man removes the collar cardboard and the flat piece that, along with many straight pins, gives the shirt its shape. It was my job to restore the shirt to its original folded beauty after it had been tried on.

Eventually, I became a saleslady. I still clearly remember the time a large man selected a floral shirt, a plaid blazer, and a very bright and busy necktie. "How do I look?" he asked. I gulped and then suggested that he might want a plain tie. He looked pained. Overhearing our conversation, my father came over and said to him, "You look great." The man beamed, and I could see him standing with shoulders back, admiring himself in the mirror. After the man left, my father said with consummate tact, "Some people dress differently from what you are accustomed to. You can't judge people on their taste. They want to hear they look great. That's what you need to tell them."

I opted to be a cashier. I didn't like that much either.

In the capable hands of my great-grandfather, his son, and

his grandsons, the Lelewer business thrived for over a hundred years. During this time, D. Lelewer & Son grew from one fur store to three fur and hat stores to thirteen hat stores, and, by the 1950s, to thirteen men's clothing stores. I can recall ten. There were eight stores in downtown Chicago: State Street, Lincoln and Belmont, 79 West Monroe (the main store and office), 63rd and Halstead, Madison and Crawford, Madison corner Wells, LaSalle corner Washington Street, and 32 North Dearborn. The two other stores I remember were in Racine, Wisconsin, and on Lake Street in Rockford, Illinois.

In the late 1960s, my father and his brother, David, divided the stores between them and ran them for a few more years. David took 63rd and Halstead, the most successful of the stores, and my father had the rest. When David died, the bank appointed someone to run his store. Within a year, the store failed and was sold for very little. My father continued, but found it difficult to compete with the large discount stores. As his leases ran out, he didn't renew them. In 1978, he closed the last store and, on July 18, 1985, he received a copy of the Articles of Dissolution of D. Lelewer & Son from the Secretary of State of Illinois. As of that date the corporation ceased to exist.

The Lelewer logo

CHAPTER 2
The Three Grands:
Great-Grandfather David, Grandpa SS, and Grandma

It was in my grandparents' apartment that I had my first look at a copy of Great-grandfather David's autobiography and first heard stories about him. Great-grandfather David's father had left his home and family to seek a better life for them in America. He had died at sea. Great-grandfather David's description of his family's life after his father's death is wrenching. His mother, he wrote in his autobiography, worked day and night to support the family:

> . . . I doubt if I am able to describe the great suf-
> ferings and heartaches Mother had to endure
> when she realized the unfortunate and helpless
> condition she was in. I can only imagine them
> and I am surprised that some scenes in connec-
> tion therewith made such a deep impression on
> me—at the tender age of five—that they are like
> a picture before my mind . . . Mother worked

from early morning till late at night, her only moments off, to cook our meager dinners. . . and I doubt if her earnings amounted to more than twenty-five cents per day . . . if that much. She was mostly employed plucking geese and other poultry. In this, she had the "unfortunate monopoly." Most poor women were too lazy and too unclean to do the work. I think for carrying the poultry to the rabbi for slaughter, picking the feathers, opening and cleaning the interior, she received in American money, about 2 and-a-half cents. Her fingers were worked almost out of joint. This was the best she could get to do. She also assisted caterers for weddings, helping in the kitchen, watching the dead before burial, and nursing the sick. We had three times weekly market days, and mother sold on the market square to farmers, goose wings, instead of feather dusters, old bottles, pots, some of the former of questionable use, anything to earn a few pennies . . .

Great-grandfather David himself endured loneliness, harsh teachers, and as he grew older, long working days. When he was ten years old, his beloved younger sister died. Eight years later, at the age of eighteen, like his father before him, he left home, seeking money for his mother and family. Having scraped together enough money to buy passage in steerage, Great-grandfather David left Germany for America. As a child, I was in awe of his courage. I still am.

He arrived in the United States on May 29, 1861 with a wooden shoe case, a carpetbag holding his few possessions, a little over two dollars in his pocket, and his cousin's address written on a piece of paper. He had been told she would meet him at the steamer's landing at Castle Island, New York. She did not show up. He eventually found her apartment on the fourth floor of a tenement on Orchard Street. At first, she and her husband told him he could not stay with them, but finally they gave him permission to sleep on the kitchen floor.

Great-grandfather David's arrival couldn't have been at a worse time. Abraham Lincoln had just become president, the South had seceded from the Union, and everything was in chaos. There were no jobs. Everyone was asking, "Will there be war?"

Eventually, because he knew how to sew, Great-grandfather David moved in with a couple who finished cloth caps. In return for his work, they gave him board and a sofa to sleep on. The springs stuck into him, and bedbugs bit him. Realizing he needed cash for necessities, he took a second job and worked from 6:30 P.M. until 10:00 P.M. or later for ten cents per night. His first American purchase was a pair of boots for sixty cents, but since he had been barefoot most of his life, he had no idea how to shop for them. It wasn't until his feet began to hurt that he realized he had bought two left boots two sizes too small for his feet.

It took Great-grandfather David two months to earn his first dollar. He did so by making himself indispensable to a furrier. He cleaned the store, ran errands, and did anything else that would be helpful. The furrier eventually made him a cutter with a wage of $4.50 a week. Gradually, great-grandfather's wages rose to $7.50 a week and he was able to send money to his mother in Lissa, Germany. Still, the hard work took its toll. Great-grandfather David soon became so ill, he seriously considered returning to Germany. A friend recommended a doctor, who, Great-grandfather later learned, was considered to be the best doctor in New York. After examining him, the doctor said: "You need good food, fresh air, and exercise. Change your habits." Seeing how little money Great-grandfather had, the doctor refused payment and wished him well. The doctor's advice was undoubtedly good, but it was not practical. To survive, Great-grandfather David had to keep working, and the working conditions and tenements of New York City in the 1860s didn't offer much in the way of good food, fresh air, and exercise.

Years later, after opening his Chicago store, Great-grandfather ran into (quite literally) another impractical cure for a medical problem. For years, he suffered from severe migraine headaches. One day, he bounded up the stairs to a balcony that was used as an office in the State Street store. As he reached the top of the stairs, he accidentally smashed his head on the balcony's ceiling. Some time thereafter he noted in surprise that his migraine was gone. He never had another migraine, but, even so, the remedy was not one that he recommended to anyone.

In his later years, I was told by Grandpa SS that Great-Grandfather David was a tall, thin, well-groomed gentleman who proudly sported a mustache and beard. Although he had little formal education, he was clearly well read. His autobiography reflects knowledge of the classics and a familiarity with the speeches of presidents and other dignitaries. Like Grandpa SS, he had a way with words. "Man creeps into childhood, bounds into youth, sobers into manhood and softens in age," he wrote, "which makes you, Sadie [his daughter], crow that you belong to the old fighting stock. With me it is the fighting stock which was." He used his hard-wrought English skills in his autobiography to thank all who helped him and to pass on what he had learned, including the value of saving money in good times. In hopes of drilling that point home, he included a poem entitled *Live Within the Dollar's Rim* by Dr. W. A. Blackwell.

Live Within the Dollar's Rim
For age and want save while you may,
No morning sun lasts all the day,
Life's evening shadows like a pall
Soon o'er each pilgrim's path must fall;
And O, how dark those clouds will seem,
Whose linings show no silver gleam
To him who satisfied each whim –
Lived not within the dollar's rim.

Lay up against that rainy day
A little from your weekly pay
And by and by with great surprise
A goodly sum will greet your eyes;
Gold put on interest does not shrink,
But for you daily it will work;
Then heed this warning call with vim
And live within the dollar's rim.

A bank book is an upward lift,
A sign of industry and thrift,
That gains respect from young and old
For him whose saving there is told;
'Twill lighten all the cares of life,
Make happy children, husband, wife;
No shylock e'er will worry him
Who lives within the dollar's rim.

In my copy of his autobiography is the following letter from his eldest daughter, Sadie:

My dear father:

> *I took great pleasure today in purchasing the best book [journal] McClurg's carries for my copy of your memoirs.*
>
> *It is asking a great deal to expect you to write several copies of the reminiscences of your eventful and highly interesting life, but I hope at the same time the task will be a labor of love and I know your own handwriting will greatly enhance the value of your book to each one of your six children.*
>
> *I look forward to the time that my copy will be complete and in my own home, always for me to treasure as a sacred souvenir of the best father that ever lived.*

> *Your loving daughter,*
> *Sadie*

Family always came first to Great-grandfather David. Family meetings were held at his home Friday evenings, and everyone was expected to be there to discuss family matters and to say prayers. Great-grandfather was a religious man and, as such, one of the major fund-raisers for Sinai Temple in Chicago. While Grandpa SS and other family members were less religious than their father, they were dutiful, so they all went to Great-grandfather David's on Fridays. I am sure one of Great-grandfather's proudest days was the day the Temple opened. On that day, my

David Lelewer
3/21/1843–3/1/1912

*Left to Right: Great-grandfather David's second wife Matilda
with Daughter Harriet*

grandfather remembered, Great-grandfather David stood outside greeting members and accepting accolades for his remarkable accomplishment. When most of the people were inside, he walked down the aisle, waved to his friends, took his seat, and the moment the service began, died.

Great-grandfather David's only son, Selig Seward Lelewer, was born in Indianapolis, Indiana on October 1, 1872. He was the second child of Great-grandfather David and his wife, Hannah Newman. In 1880, when he was eight years old, Grandpa Selig Seward, known as SS because he didn't like his name, moved with his father, mother, and four sisters to Chicago. A few years later his mother died. At some point, Great-grandfather remarried and had a daughter, Harriet, by his second wife, Matilda.

As a young man, Grandpa SS, who began working for his father at the age of fifteen, had a very high-pitched voice, which he found quite embarrassing. He took voice lessons and learned, with a great deal of practice, to speak at a normal pitch, which he used to tell great stories. Although he only attended school through eighth grade, he was knowledgeable and intuitive with beautiful penmanship.

On December 29, 1904, in Oak Park, Illinois, Grandpa SS, who was thirty-two, married my grandmother, Myrtle Schnadig, who was a twenty-one-year-old, five-feet, six-inch, brown-eyed piano teacher. When I knew her, she kept her hair short and wore beautifully tailored, long, dark blue or black dresses that set off her carefully chosen jewelry. "Pearls or a perfect pin are sufficient," she would say.

They honeymooned in California, and Grandpa SS, noting the increase in population on the West Coast, debated buying property in what later became downtown Los Angeles. Grandma convinced him that it would be difficult to manage California property from Chicago, and they returned home to begin their married life.

Although grandma didn't have a college degree, she did have street smarts. She learned early in life what it meant to go without. Her father had been employed and was also a noted baritone, but, after his death, her mother opened a china shop to support the family. Her only helpers were her two little girls, my grandmother and her sister, Elsa. Life was not easy for them.

In 1907, three years after they were married, Grandpa SS, who had been working eighteen-hour days to build the Lelewer hat business, fell ill. His doctor told him, just as a doctor had told his father years before, "Your life style is unhealthy. You need fresh air, exercise, and, to cut down on your workload." Unlike his father, Grandpa SS felt he could act on his doctor's advice, and thus, two family traditions were begun—going south for two months in the winter and sleeping outside year round.

At the time, my father, who was a year old, Grandpa SS, and my grandmother were living in a third-floor apartment[1] with a porch on Chicago's south side. The porch had no roof but that did not deter my grandfather.

Grandpa SS, my father, as soon as he was deemed old enough, and later, my father's brother slept outside on the porch year round except for the months of January and February when the family went south. The boys and Grandpa SS bundled up in Dr. Denton pajamas with feet, but my father once claimed he had had a sore throat from September 1 to June 1. "If it rained, we got wet," he said. "If it snowed, we were covered in white. We got so used to it we weren't bothered in the least. It was a wonderful experience if you were an outdoorsman. To get into bed, we had to climb through the window as the porch floor was too cold and

[1] 5042 Drexel Boulevard

Top: Joseph Schnadig & Lizzie Heller Schnadig
(Myrtle Schnadig Lelewer's parents, my great grandparents)
Bottom: Young Myrtle Schnadig (Joseph Lelewer's mother)

damp to walk on." My grandmother did not join them. Later, the family moved to an apartment[2] with a porch that had a roof but was open on three sides. The men continued to sleep outside. In fact, my father slept on the porch until he married my mother. I've always suspected my grandmother never bothered to decorate the bedrooms in their apartment because they were rarely used.

Fortunately, the January and February trips south were a tradition that my grandmother, indeed, the entire family, enjoyed. Because Grandpa SS had hired his cousin, Henry Posner, a few years earlier, he knew the stores would be fine while he was away. My father was three when the family first went to Florida. Early on, they went to Jacksonville, St. Augustine, and Green Cove Springs in the northern part of Florida. Later, they vacationed in Deland, Daytona Beach, and finally, Palm Beach and Miami. Miami Beach had not yet been developed when they began to go to Florida, and, in the early 1900s, there were hotels that posted signs on their lawns—"No Jews, no dogs."

On some of their annual trips to Florida, two of Grandpa SS's sisters and their families, the Goodfriend and Feilchenfeld families, would join them. The children were close in age to my father and his brother, and they all had a good time together except when they were sent to the local schools. Because anti-Semitism was rampant at the time, my father, his brother, and his cousins were not welcomed at the schools. They couldn't make friends, were frightened by the relentless atmosphere of hate, the cruel words spoken to them, and the rocks thrown at them as they raced home. Their parents had no choice but to take them out of school and have them privately taught. My father once noted, "This worked much better." Then he paused, grinned, and

---

[2] 5053 Drexel Boulevard

said, "I guess," leaving me to wonder how hard he had studied.

One year, the families went to Green Cove Springs, ten miles from Jacksonville. The children loved to fish for crabs from the pier there, and, on one memorable day, Violet, one of my father's cousins, suddenly cried out, "Oh! my ring, my ring. It fell into the water. Mommy gave it to me."

Almost collectively, the cousins replied, "Don't worry, we'll find it. We'll feel for it in the sand."

"No. You'll get pinched by a crab. Help me look in the water. Maybe we can see the ring down there. It isn't that deep."

"It won't work," my father said. "The water's too murky to see anything."

Later that day, Stanley, one of the cousins, found himself staring at the crab he had caught because there seemed to be a sparkly something on its claw. His mouth flew open in astonishment when he realized he had discovered the lost ring.

Another year, Grandpa SS decided to take the family to Eustis, Florida, which had not yet become a popular vacation spot. The opulent Waterman Hotel with a bath in each lovely room and a roof garden was Grandpa SS's destination. What he did not realize was that the hotel policy was anti-Semitic. The family with their three wardrobe trunks—no suitcases in their day—rode by train to Jacksonville and then transferred to a bus for the trip to Eustis. The bus trip from Jacksonville to Eustis was six hours with many stops en route. They arrived at 6 P.M., and their luggage was placed on the boardwalk—there were no concrete or cement sidewalks. As the bus pulled out, Grandpa SS went in to register.

"My name is Lelewer. I have a reservation," he said to the clerk behind the front desk, trying not to let his weariness show. He wanted to register and get everyone settled quickly.

"We don't have a reservation for anyone by the name of Lelewer." My grandfather pulled out his confirmation letter and handed it to the clerk, who barely glanced at it.

"No," said the clerk firmly. "It's obviously a clerical error. I told you we don't have a reservation for you or your family." He stared icily at my grandfather. Grandpa SS got the point. Perhaps the hotel allowed dogs, but it certainly didn't allow Jews.

Grandpa SS left the hotel and looked up and down the street. There were about a half dozen houses and a grocery store. That was it. He tried to explain to the family exactly what had happened, but how do you tell your family there is no place to go and no more buses that day? He was at that point in his explanation when someone said, "Hello, Mr. Lelewer." Thoroughly startled, Grandpa SS looked up to see a gentleman who had worked as an accountant for Albert Hoefeld, a relative of my grandfather. The gentleman had moved from Chicago to Eustis, Florida when he had become a certified public accountant (CPA). He hadn't, however, forgotten my grandfather, and he hadn't stopped just to say hello.

He could see something was wrong by the expression on my grandfather's face. Grandpa SS turned to him and explained their dilemma.

"Don't worry, Mr. Lelewer," Mr. Hoefeld said. "My house is your house. My wife and I will be handling accounts all over Florida for the next three months. We leave tomorrow and won't be back until April."

The generosity of the offer and the fact that neither Mr. Hoefeld nor his wife were Jewish helped to soften the blow of the hotel clerk's words. After a moment of speechlessness, Grandpa SS accepted the incredibly kind offer, and the family stayed in the gentleman's home until he and his wife returned. My father

Selig Seward (SS) Lelewer
10/1/1872–5/25/1947

Myrtle Schnadig Lelewer
1/3/1883–4/18/1967

was very young at the time but he never forgot the unexpected kindness and loved to tell the story.

I never saw Grandpa SS without a white shirt and necktie. He had a long, lanky frame and dark brown hair when he was young, a large nose, and wore round glasses. Adults loved his quick wit and agile mind. When someone told him, "Lelewer is difficult to spell," he would quip, "No it isn't, Lelewer is spelled with ee's [ease]." Because the cardboard lids that were inserted in the openings of milk bottles were almost impossible to remove, Grandpa SS wrote the milk processing company, "Why don't you put a small folding tab on the bottle-top, so a person can pull the top off the bottle?" They did. When he noticed that all the matches in a match book could ignite and burn the user because the striking surface was on the front cover, he wrote the manufacturer of folding match covers, suggesting they put the striking surface on the back cover. They did.

For seventeen years, Grandpa SS was treasurer of and very involved in the Chicago Home for Jewish Orphans, a charity begun in 1893, which later merged with the Jewish Home Finding Society. Grandpa SS believed that every child they placed in a private home had a chance at a better life.

I always looked forward to visiting my grandparents' city apartment. When Grandma played the piano, I sat on the bench right next to her, enchanted by the music. She could play anything as long as she had the music before her. Elsa, her sister, sang for us occasionally in a rich, beautiful, contralto voice. Grandma loved opera. Unfortunately, Grandpa SS did not. Still, that did not deter my grandmother who took my father in Grandpa SS' place. At a time when many women did not drive, my grandmother was the official family driver. When my father was in high school, Grandma drove an Electra. My father remembered turning the crank in the front of the car to get it started. Later, they bought an electric car, but, when they went to the opera in Ravinia, there were times they had to push the car the last few blocks home as there was no place to charge the battery along the route. Years later, it was Grandma who would drive Grandpa SS from the south side of Chicago to Highland Park[3] when they came to visit us.

Sometimes when we visited them in the city, Grandpa would ask, "Would 'Fancy Nancy' like to come for a walk with me?" I always said yes. I thought he was fun, and I liked the name he gave me. He held my hand and chatted as we went along. I would have to run to keep up with his long-legged strides. When we went to the drugstore, Grandpa would pick up a newspaper for himself and buy a toy for me. He would hold it for me as I pulled myself up the high ice-cream parlor stool so that we could sit together at the counter. It was a hot fudge sundae[4] for me, every time, while he drank a chocolate soda. Between sips, he recited poems and stories to me. I loved the way he tossed rhymes he invented on the spot into the middle of the stories.

I was twelve when Grandpa SS died, but I have vivid memories of him to this day. My father always said that his father was the best father he knew—a great teacher, mentor, and friend. "He taught me golf, the hat business, finance, dealing with people, and I always felt loved," my father once said. When my father went through his father's safety deposit box, he found two IOUs from men to whom Grandpa SS had lent money. A note was attached to the IOUs: *At my death, destroy these IOUs, don't ask these*

---

[3] One of several affluent towns on the north shore of Chicago

[4] Evanston, just to the north of Chicago, was one of the first locations to pass a blue law against selling ice cream sodas in 1890. Some drug store operators and ingenious confectioners there, obeying the law, served ice cream with the syrup of your choice without the soda. Thereby they complied with the law. This sodaless soda was called the Sunday soda. As sales of the dessert continued everyday day of the week, local leaders objected to naming the dish after the Sabbath so the spelling was changed to Sundae.

men for a penny and don't speak of these loans to anyone. That, I think, says everything there is to say about my grandfather.

My grandmother lived to be eighty-four. Nine years before her death, she flew from Chicago to Boston over Thanksgiving weekend for her first visit with my daughter, Kathy, her first great-grandchild. My husband, Stephen, and I lived in a two-bedroom apartment in Hancock Village, and Grandma happily shared our small second bedroom with our five-month old daughter. Grandma got up when Kathy cried at night and rocked her or changed her, each time cooing a gentle sound to calm her. My grandmother spent the whole weekend

Thanksgiving 1958, Hancock Village
Kathy and her great-grandmother, Myrtle Lelewer

in the role of cheerful helper. I wondered if she was exhausted when she returned home. If she was, I was never privy to that information. She spoke only about how beautiful Kathy was.

Grandma was a master at socializing, a storehouse of information, and a great card player, even in her eighties. She was always surrounded by friends who gathered in her room at the Shoreland Hotel, a retirement residence on the south side of Chicago. For the last three years of her life, she was unable to walk because of gangrenous feet, so she held court sitting in a chair night and day with her legs outstretched and her feet hanging off the end of an ottoman. Eventually my father designed a contraption that allowed her to be in bed. It raised her feet slightly off the bed and held the sheets and blankets off them as any pressure on her feet caused tremendous pain.

Grandma paid all her bills up to a few days before she died. She kept her own books, but my father was in charge of her money. Once when I was visiting her, she asked my father, as she did from time to time, to put another $1,000 in her account as she had some bills to pay. "Well, if it's that easy," I said, "put $1,000 in my account, too." He laughed.

When the gangrene problem first arose, Grandma's doctors asked permission to amputate her toes. She responded with an unequivocal, "No." Some time later, when the problem grew worse, the doctors asked my father's permission to amputate her legs. He replied, "My mother said no to your taking her toes. I'm certainly not going to give permission to remove her legs."

During the last year of her life, she told my father on several occasions that she wanted to die. My father spoke to her doctor who said, "Joe, your mother may tell you that she wants to die, but she is very bright and alert. She is managing all her medications herself, and they are right next to her on the table.

If she truly wanted to die, she could end her life any time she wanted. She knows that."

I think the hardest thing for any adult/child to do is to watch a loved parent fade away. My father visited Grandma often, as did my mother and my cousin, Stanley. When Grandma took a turn for the worse in April of 1967, my father raced her to the hospital where she was fitted with an IV, a catheter, and another tube. He was told that all they could do was to try to make her "comfortable." Although he knew that she had never thought much of hospitals, he felt he had no other choice until she looked up at him and, in an almost inaudible voice, said, "I want to go home to die."

My father took a deep breath, bent down, and said to her, "I'll take you home in my car. Give me just a few minutes."

"My mother knows how ill she is. She has asked to be in her own home, in her own bed, when the moment comes." he said to her doctor. "We need to abide by her wishes."

After a thoughtful pause, the doctor acquiesced. He gave her an injection to alleviate the pain of the drive and sent her back to her home with my father. Grandma fell asleep secure in the knowledge she was going home. My father carried her to her bed, and she never awakened.

Eight years earlier, in December 1959, a little less than a month after Grandma had visited us over Thanksgiving, Stephen, Kathy, and I had spent a week with my parents in Highland Park. Grandma had come out from Chicago to be with us. I like to remember her in the photo we took that week, a photo of four generations together—my grandmother, my father, my daughter, and me.

December 1958, Highland Park, Illinois.
Standing: Joseph Lelewer
Seated in chair: Myrtle Lelewer holding her
great-granddaughter, Kathy Sonnabend
Seated on arm of chair: Nancy Lelewer Sonnabend

CHAPTER 3
Joseph David Lelewer

No one who ever met my father forgot him. In the fall of 1999, when my father was close to ninety-three years old, a man stopped him as he, my mother and I came out of a restaurant. "Hi Joe," the gentleman said. "It's been a long time. I'm Mickie Guggenheim."

My father said, "Oh, sure, I remember you very well from long, long ago."

After a bit of conversation, Mickie and my father determined they hadn't seen each other in seventy-one years!

I suppose I shouldn't have been surprised that my father could leave a restaurant and run into a friend he hadn't seen in seventy-one years. Throughout his life, he had many friends. In fact, he never stopped making friends. While many of us have a few childhood friends who are best forgotten, among my father's childhood friends, all but one became worthwhile citizens. Of course, that one friend was, in his own way, famous. Between the ages of twelve and thirteen, my father became friends with

Dickey Loeb, the Richard Loeb of the infamous Leopold and Loeb duo. In 1924, Nathan Leopold and Richard Loeb tried to commit the perfect murder.[5] My father and Dickey Loeb, as he was known when my father knew him, never attended the same school but did live a few blocks from each other. My father used to go to Dickie's house. They both enjoyed talking, climbing fences, and walking on the tops of walls. "He was brilliant and fun to be with," my father told me. "No one would have guessed he would become a murderer."

My father, Joseph David Lelewer, was born on March 30, 1906. It was the same year the American Jewish Committee, which my father devoted many hours to as an adult, was founded—a fact that gave him great pleasure.

At the age of eighty-eight, when I recorded his words, he still could remember his youth clearly. With twinkling eyes, he recited for me the beginning text of his first book in first grade: "My name is Ned. I have a sled. I can run. I can jump. Can you run? Can you jump?"

"I wasn't a howling success as a student in school," he said. "When I was supposed to go from high first grade to low second, I flunked. To pass your grade at Comiskey Grammar School, the principal, Mr. Lewis, gave you a spelling test. He was a very imposing figure, tall, elderly, with great bearing and a beard to match.

'Spell the word *away*,' Mr. Lewis said.

'A-y-a-w-,' I answered.

'You flunk,' he said.

"Mrs. Buttondorf, my teacher, said I was a good student

---

[5] On May 21, 1924, Richard Loeb and Nathan Leopold kidnapped and then murdered fourteen-year-old Bobby Franks. They were defended by Clarence Darrow who succeeded in having them sentenced to life imprisonment plus ninety-nine years rather than death. Both young men were brilliant and came from well-to-do families. The only motive ever given for the kidnapping and murder, which papers called the "crime of the century," was the desire to commit the perfect crime.

Joseph David Lelewer
Top Left: Six months old
Top Right: 9/1/1907, Age 1 & ½ years
Bottom: 7 years, 2 months (6/1/1913)

Myrtle Lelewer in 1915 with sons:
David, age 4 years (on left) and Joseph, age 9 years (on right)

and felt I should be put into low second on probation even if I couldn't spell *away*. I think she wanted to get rid of me—which was the same as 'away.' So, that was my beginning in school."

"In sixth grade," my father continued, "our teacher, Miss Oakley, wanted us to sit up straight. All the students slouched in their seats. She would take a pencil, stand it up on her desk with the eraser down and the point up, and say, 'Sit up straight like the pencil.' We all would straighten up, but, as soon as she lay the pencil down on her desk, we would go back into our slouch."

When it was time for my father and his brother to go to high school, my grandmother decided they should attend the University of Chicago Laboratory School. She wanted the best for her sons, and the school, which was founded on the learning principles of John Dewey, was then known (and still is) for its academic excellence and progressive theories. My father learned to think both critically and creatively there and developed a life-long passion for learning. He once told me, "I was in the bottom ten percent of my class but loved the academic program and the friends I made at the Lab School."

I've often thought nothing more clearly indicated my grandmother's determination that her sons move up in the world than her choice of the Lab School and the fact that she hired a piano teacher for my father. For whatever reason, even though she was a piano teacher, she did not believe she could teach my father successfully. It seems, however, that the teacher she hired couldn't teach him either, so he never learned to play.

"I think I got as far as scales, which I didn't do well. The closest I came to being a musician," my father said, "was during my years at the University of Chicago's Lab School when my mother took me with her to the opera on Monday nights in the winter time. She wanted company, and my father complained that opera disturbed his sleep. I enjoyed opera so much that later, during my college years, I enrolled to become a supernumerary [a nonsinging extra] at the Opera Company in Chicago."

The operas that my father and grandmother attended were performed in Sullivan and Adler's famous auditorium, which was built between 1886 and 1889. The auditorium occupies half a city block and, back then, housed a hotel, restaurants, an enormous bar, an office building, and an opera house with 4,300 seats (the largest in the world at the time of its construction). The opera house has no obstructed views and perfect acoustics. Today, the hotel is occupied by Roosevelt University, and the bar is gone; removed when the street was widened. The building, which has been restored, was the first multi-use edifice constructed in the United States.

My father once told me he had met all the renowned opera singers of the time while working on stage. "I was a spear bearer," he told me. "We had to put on costumes and were supposed to look like soldiers when we walked in and out carrying the spears. The costumes didn't fit too well and were filthy, but I thoroughly enjoyed that experience."

I can remember his eyes twinkling as he spoke, "One of the stars I loved most was Rosa Raisa. When she played the role of Rachel, a Jewess in La Juive, I was selected, with three others, to carry her on stage in a chair to be held up by the four of us. 'Don't drop me, boys,' she said when she got into the chair. So, we tilted the chair a little bit but were careful not to drop her when we put her down on center stage."

Although he always admired his mother's foresight in selecting the Lab School for him, he found it difficult, at least at the time, to accept her thoughts on the women he cared for. My father didn't get the growth spurt that helped turn girls' heads until his late teens, but even early in life, he had an affinity for women. I don't think that ever changed. Beautiful women always caught his eye. His two early loves were women my grandmother liked but felt he should not marry. The first was Bobby Brill. She was so beautiful, his friends were jealous of him. Unfortunately, Bobby's parents lacked money and position, and Grandma wanted my father to marry well. With some reluctance, my father listened to her and stopped seeing Bobby Brill. Bobby called him the day after her wedding. Although he was the one who had broken off the relationship, he could still remember years later how devastated he had been by that phone call.

His other love was Louise Landsman, nicknamed Lovely Lou. She lived on the south side of Chicago and came from Jewish society. He was so crazy about her that he went to Boston to visit her when she was a student at Wellesley College. "I thought she was the nuts—I guess I was the nut," he told me.

To see Lovely Lou, my father had taken the train from Chicago to Boston, and Lou had come into Boston from Wellesley. They met at the bus stop at Copley Square.

"I've made a reservation for dinner at the Copley Plaza Hotel," my father said. "C'mon, let's walk."

"No, I don't walk. I ride," answered Lovely Lou.

A horse and carriage was nearby. My father hailed it, and they got in.

"Copley Plaza Hotel, please" my father called out. There was a long pause.

"Where?" asked the driver with a look on his face that my father accurately read as are you out of your mind?

"Copley Plaza Hotel, please," my father repeated. Lovely Lou, ensconced in the carriage, smoothed her dress, made herself comfortable, and smiled.

The horse and carriage rolled twenty feet and stopped.

"Here it is—Copley Plaza Hotel," said the driver.

My father wanted to marry Lovely Lou, but my grandmother said, "No, you are too young, too immature to make this life decision." Once again my father bowed to his mother's wishes. "Looking back," Dad said years later, "I *was* too immature to have married at that time. I've been lucky. Your mother and I have had close to seventy-three wonderful years together. It was fortunate that I listened to my mother."

My father wasn't usually so contemplative when he reminisced. Most of the time he described happy, funny, or piquant events. He loved to describe the Sunday dinners his family enjoyed at a restaurant when he was a child. For $5.50, the family sat at a table with white-cloth tablecloths and napkins and had soup, beef or chicken, potato, vegetable, coffee, tea or milk, and dessert. Grandpa SS's 10 percent tip of 55 cents was considered very generous in the days when ice cream cones cost one penny.

Even after seventy years, my father clearly recalled the wisecrack he made when he was five years old and out for a walk with his father. On the walk, Grandpa SS had run into a friend and had introduced my father to him. My grandfather's friend smiled down at my father, patted his shoulder, and said, "You look just like your dad." My father responded, "That's my tough luck," which Grandpa SS never let him forget.

Another walk my father remembered occurred when he was ten and his brother was five. The boys were sent to pick up their father's shoes at the shoemaker's. My father carried the shoes halfway home and then said to his brother, "It's your turn to carry them."

"No, you are the eldest, so you have to carry them."

My father, who had a bit of a stubborn streak, put the

shoes down on the side of the road, and the two boys walked home without them. Needless to say, both boys were sent back to get the shoes, and luckily, they were still there. Each boy got only half a whipping for what they had done when they got back home. Whipping, or "stropping" in my father's case, was the mode of teaching children to do the right thing when he was young. My grandfather had a leather razor strop that was about two feet long, three inches wide, and 1/4 inch thick. Grandpa SS used it to sharpen his open blade razors, but when he thought the boys had done something naughty he would give them a whipping, or stropping, with it. My father would run around the dining room table hoping to avoid Grandpa SS, but eventually he would be caught and his bottom would hurt for a few days.

Although Grandpa SS was strict, my father always said that he was also fun and a great teacher. He made a deal with my father that if my father didn't smoke or drink until the age of twenty-one, Grandpa would give him $1,000, a great deal of money then. My father collected. My father then made the same deal with me, and I collected. I offered the same deal to my children, and one collected. Now, I have told each grandchild that he or she can collect $1,000 at the age of twenty-one if he or she doesn't smoke, another $1,000 for not drinking, and a final $1,000 if there are no tattoos or body piercings other than for a single earring in each ear for the girls. I rather doubt Grandpa SS realized he was beginning a family tradition when he made the offer to my father.

Grandpa SS seems to have been one of the first to recognize my father's natural athleticism. When my father was six, Grandpa SS began to teach him how to play golf. Right from the beginning, my father loved the sport, and he and Grandpa SS spent many happy years playing golf together at Idlewild Country Club.

In fact, my father so enjoyed the game that, when he was twelve, he would ride his bike to Jackson Park after school to play a round. He paid twenty cents for nine holes and carried one club, the equivalent of today's two iron. Since everyone else had finished playing by the time he got there, he would hit off the first tee, run after the ball, and use the same club to approach and to putt. It usually took him less than an hour to complete the course, and if there was time, he'd play more than nine holes.

By the late 1920s and early 1930s, golf had a large following. There were no televisions, web casts, or iPhones but people listened to the major matches on radio, and the sports pages of the major newspapers usually featured the top golfers. Local club championship matches were a common occurrence.

In 1928, my father won the golf championship at Idlewild Country Club. At the time, he had a three handicap and, according to him, that particular day he played well and got lucky. In the final match for the championship, he played 36 holes against Johnny Jones, who was a good golfer. At the noon break, my father was five down. It was match play in those days, so each hole counted. After lunch, Johnny and my father played the tenth and eleventh holes and my father was still five down with seven holes to go when it began to pour. The rain became torrential. Johnny Jones wore glasses and it was raining so hard that he couldn't see through them. My father didn't wear glasses. He wrapped a towel around the club handle so it wouldn't slip and banged the ball down the fairway as well as he could. He won the last seven holes and the championship. The following year, he joined Ravisloe Country Club and won the club golf championship there in 1929.

A year later, in 1930, Bobby Jones (no relation to Johnny Jones) won all four majors (the open and amateur championships) in both the United States and Great Britain. To this day, he is the only golfer to have ever done so.

Although my father never competed above the club level, he was a superb athlete. His best sport was golf, but he was also good at tennis, handball, baseball, bowling, and horseback riding. He was ambidextrous, so one year when he was in a bowling league and his right shoulder gave out, he bowled with his left hand. He ended up with a 142 average bowling left-handed, which was not that far off his lifetime right-handed average of 162.

After Dad married, he and his friends decided to have what they called Fathers' Spring Training, a weekend in the Ozarks playing softball. Despite its name, the weekend took place in the fall. The men had jerseys made with FATHERS' SPRING TRAINING CLUB on the back and a number on the front. My father's number was 7. The first year, the Fathers' Spring Training Club was made up of fifteen men who headed to the Ozarks to play softball. The second year, the weekend turned into two weekends with a week in between and twenty-five men. Some of the men played golf, some played tennis and everybody played softball.

Each evening they would have elaborate dinners, and various participants would give speeches. One of the most eloquent speakers was Louis Behr, a friend of my father who was in the insurance business. Mr. Behr loved to talk, and people usually enjoyed his speeches. One year when he was due to make the opening speech at the banquet, Albert Pick of Pick Hotels went to each participant and said, "Now when Lou Behr finishes his speech tonight, I don't want anyone to applaud. Don't look at him, just talk to each other as though nothing happened." Lou Behr finished his speech, and everyone simply ignored him. Not used to such a reaction, the poor man just stood there with his mouth open until finally everyone began to laugh.

During Fathers' Spring Training, three or four men would inevitably have some kind of injury that would later confine them to bed. Many had sprained ankles because they weren't in shape. In fact, my father spent most of one year in bed with a bad back as a result of Fathers' Spring Training. Even so, Dad said, "All in all it was terrific and the camaraderie was wonderful. Wives never came because they were never invited. The final year, I remember particularly because we went down in a private Pullman car since there were so many of us. That was a pretty good brawl in itself."

The men's friendships lasted throughout their lives. Many years later, one sunny afternoon, a couple of Fathers' Spring Training friends were sitting in the Hassler Hotel in the center of Rome playing bridge. Another friend came along and said, "How can you play bridge on a sunny day in Rome when there is so much to see here?" Whereupon one of them turned and said, "What's so great about Rome? Everything here is broken!"

My father's love of sports was not limited to the games he actually played. He loved to attend the Chicago White Sox games and Northwestern football games and often spoke about the first two great Jewish athletes to gain prominence, Benny Friedman whom my father watched when Michigan played Northwestern, and Hank Greenberg of the Detroit Tigers whom he saw many times when the Tigers played the White Sox.

"Benny Friedman," my father once said, "helped change the game from a straightforward running game to the modern pass-and-run game. He led the league in 1928 in both passing and rushing touchdowns; something no one else in the NFL ever has accomplished, but was kept out of the NFL Football Hall of

Fame probably because he was Jewish. He finally was admitted posthumously on August 7, 2005, over twenty years after his death."

What has always fascinated me is just how eclectic my father's interests were. He loved cars and started driving his family's Electra when he was very young. For his twenty-first birthday, Grandpa SS gave him a red Chevrolet Cabriolet with a rumble seat. The seat, which was also known as the mother-in-law's seat, was located on the outside of the car where the trunk usually is and faced backward. My father found it very *cool*.

He also loved anything to do with communication. At the age of seven, he built a radio known as a "crystal detector set." He could still explain how it worked many years later; "In order to pick up a station I needed a needle and an extension of a wire attached to the rest of the radio set. I fiddled around on the surface of a round piece of metal called the 'crystal,' until I found the spot that located the station I was looking for." When he was ten, he built another radio called a "honey comb" set. He had to listen to it through a headphone since there was no loudspeaker. He recalled being thrilled to get Arlington, Virginia; a big achievement at that time.

I suppose from crystal radios, it was only a short step to Morse code. My father was fluent in Morse code when I was a child, and he worked hard to pass his knowledge on to me. To help me learn, he drew the alphabet on a sheet of paper and showed me how the long (dash) and short (dot) sounds were derived from the shape of the letters. Portions of each letter were darkened in dashes or dots, he explained. A, for example, is represented by a dot and a dash because the letter A has a point on top (the dot) and a line between the vertical sides (the dash). The sound of the dot and the dash in Morse code is di dah. I was fascinated by the concept, but the memorization was too much for me. Worst of all, at least for me, is the fact that Morse code is based on spelling out every word. Unfortunately, I still can't spell.

Given his interest in communication, it is not surprising that we had the first television in our neighborhood. On a family trip to Chicago one weekend, I had noticed a large crowd at a store window almost a block away, "Mom, Dad," I had called out. "Look at all those people in front of that store window. Can we see what's going on?"

My mother and father said yes, and when we reached the store, my father, who was taller than most of the people there and on tiptoes, could see over the heads in front of us and into the store.

"Its television", he said. "Remember all we heard about 'radio with pictures'? That's it." My father slipped inside, and my mother and I saw him talking to a salesman. The next thing we knew the television, I think it was a DuMont, was in the trunk of our car. From the trunk of the car it went to the den.

We were delighted with what we saw in the early days, but the heyday of television did not really begin until I was in my teens. My father and mother especially loved zany, saucer-eyed Imogene Coca and the brilliant monologist Sid Caesar who talked gibberish but, with his extraordinary timing, made the audience understand exactly what he meant. Always, as we sat in the den watching them, someone would start to laugh and the entire room would explode in hilarity.

My father never tried to be funny, but, like Groucho Marx[6], he made people laugh and then smile at the memory. Like his father before him, he was a master at playing with the English language. He could combine two words that weren't usually put together, create new words, slur a word to sound like something else which gave it a different meaning or double meaning or just state a fact in an obvious way: "If I felt better, I'd feel better." In doing so, he made people feel good. He had pet expressions, such as "please douse the glimmer" in place of "turn off the light" when we left a room or went to bed. Upon leaving for a business trip, Dad would give Mom and me a hug and say: "Hold the Fort." On returning from a trip or coming back to Highland Park or Boston from Florida, he would always say as he opened the front door, "Be it ever so bum, there's no place like hum." If an event turned out to be less than its build up my father would confide in me, "It was a big nothing."

Frequently, Dad left messages on my answering machine that ended "Love, Hiam Yankle" (a country bumpkin). He called St. Louis "St. Lousy" because of the heat and terrible humidity he'd endured on visits there before air conditioning became common. He loved to watch the pelicans along the canal that abutted the house in Sarasota, Florida. As he watched them, he frequently would recite the Dixon Lanier Merritt limerick from 1910:

A wonderful bird is the Pelican
His bill will hold more than his belican
He can take in his beak
Food enough for a week
But I'm damned if I see how the helican!

---

[6] Groucho Marx (1890-1977) was the most famous of the Marx brothers, a comedy team that began in vaudeville and later made a successful transition to the movies. The Marx brothers' witty word play and clever physical gags made them among the world's biggest movie stars in the 1920s. From 1950 to 1961, Groucho had his own quiz show, *You Bet Your Life*. The show rarely gave away more than $1,000 to be split between two contestants, but its trademark line, "Say the secret word and win $100," is still remembered. My parents and I enjoyed all the Marx brothers' movies, especially *A Night at the Opera*. I still recall two of Groucho's one-liners: "I must confess I was born at a very early age" and "Anyone can get old. All you have to do is live long enough."

Joseph David Lelewer,
age 37 (1943)

There was in my father's humor, wisdom. When someone coughed, he would say, "It's not how often you're coughin' but the coffin they're carrying you off in." If things were pretty much equal, he would say, "It's a horse a piece." Many times he told me, "You can't get ahead getting even" and "Learn from the mistakes of others, you can't live long enough to make them all yourself." As he grew older, the wisdom became tinged with acceptance. Shortly after moving to Lasell Village, a retirement facility, he began to refer to the residents there as "inmates." One night he and my mother were dining with another couple. The service that evening was very slow, and the gentleman suffered from severe back pain. To ease his discomfort, he would lift himself out of his chair and then lower himself back down. His wife became embarrassed by his actions and finally said, "Stop jumping up and down." "What do you want him to do?" my father asked. "Jump sideways?"

He knew people often respond to a person's demeanor rather than his or her words. Because this concept amused him, we never quite knew what he was going to say when someone spoke to him.

"How are you?" someone would ask.

"Terrible," he would say, smiling broadly and looking happy.

"That's good," was always the response.

At other times, a waiter might say, "Do you want your check?" My father would reply, "Not especially, I'd prefer a pillow." Sure enough, the waiter would answer, "I'll bring it right away" and bring the check, never the pillow.

Of course, if my father saw people were confused by his comments, he would immediately stop and usually get everyone laughing.

There was also my father's devilish side. My daughter Patti is Jewish. Before she married Steven Wagner who is Catholic she agreed to raise their children as Catholics. When Patti and Steven learned Patti was carrying a boy, they decided to name him after my father. Patti called my father to ask his permission because in the Jewish religion one usually doesn't name a child after a living relative.

"Great Papa, I'm pregnant with a boy and we'd like to name him Joe after you. Would that be alright?"

"I'd be honored if you name your son after me. Have you thought of a middle name?"

"No."

"What about Edward?"

"Who is Edward? I've never heard of anyone in the family named Edward."

"I just thought it would make interesting initials for a Catholic kid."

"Oh Great Papa you're naughty."

"That's true."

He had a rule that he wouldn't discuss anything upsetting after dinner—it could wait 'til morning. He also believed firmly in making plans before taking action and thinking things through before making decisions. To my father's way of thinking, the time to slow down, take a few deep breaths, and make a plan was whenever one was anxious, tired, or upset. "Rushing in an upset or anxious state," he said, "often leads to accidents compounding the original problem."

He practiced what he preached. If we were behind in a tennis game, he would walk me to the back of the court, take an extra few seconds, and then come up with a play for the next point. I still recall his description of his first MRI. He felt, he said, claustrophobic, nervous, and tense. "I wasn't helping myself, so I decided to use the time to relax and go to sleep."

"Did you fall asleep?" I asked.

"Yes, I got awakened when they started rolling me out."

When I had my first MRI, I remembered his comments and, like any obedient daughter, did as he had done. It worked, of course.

CHAPTER 4
Peoria Days: Nana, Popeye, and Mina Clara Ullman

I was thirteen years old when my maternal grandfather died. Mother's father was born Clarence Aaron Marks, the fourth child of a family named Marks, which originally was from Stuttgart, Germany. Clarence Aaron was born in Bloomington, Illinois on February 29, 1880. The joy of his birth was short lived. His mother died when he was ten days old. As his father couldn't manage a baby and three older children—Julius, Joseph, and Clara—Clarence Aaron was adopted by his father's sister who was married, but had no children. With the adoption, Clarence Aaron Marks became Clarence Aaron Ullman known as "Father" to my mother, Mina Clara Ullman, and as "Popeye" to me and my cousins. It was my cousin, Dick, who dubbed our grandfather "Popeye" because Dick loved the cartoon character Popeye the Sailor when he was a toddler. Although he was not raised with his brothers and sisters, Popeye and his siblings remained close throughout their lives.

When he was young, Popeye didn't take school seriously.

One afternoon, when asked by his father where he'd been, he replied, "At school." Since he was sunburned and reeked of sulfur from the quarry he had been swimming in while playing hooky, he didn't fool anyone. He dropped out of school after eighth grade and worked as a liquor salesman until the passage of the Eighteenth Amendment (Prohibition) in 1920, which left him out of a job, but not out of ideas. He knew Peoria didn't have a warehouse and, recognizing the city's need for one, convinced a close friend, Arthur Lehman, to form a partnership with him and put up most of the money for a fireproof warehouse. It still stands on the corner of Oak and Adams Street and continues to be used.

Their company, Federal Warehouse, was expanded over the years to include many companies.[7] Sometime before the partnership was formed, Popeye decided he needed more education to run a business, and attended business school.

Mother's mother, Hattie—"Nana" to me—was born February 19, 1882 in Detroit, Michigan. I remember Nana as giving, very bright, and quite literal. Her mathematical mind, as I discovered when I went to the store with her, rivaled the speed of any cash register then and probably even now. While the clerk was still punching numbers into the cash register, Nana would have already totaled her purchases and determined what she should receive in change. Like other women of her day, she lived with her mother and stepfather from the time she was a toddler until

---

[7] Clarence, his son Jerome and my cousins, Dick and Don Ullman continued expanding the Federal Companies until March 4, 2009 when the Ullman family sold it. At the time of the sale, the Federal Companies had grown to include:
- Household Goods Relocation & Storage
- Warehousing, Transportation and Distribution (Logistics)
- Records Management & Computer Media Storage Services
- Motorcycle Transportation & Storage
- Auto Transportation & Storage
- Office & Industrial Relocation
- International Relocation
- Trade Show & Exhibit Transportation
- Sensitive Electronics Transportation
- Retail Delivery (Appliances & Home Furnishings)

Aaron Ullman—Clarence A. Ullman's adopted father

Clarence Aaron Ullman
Top Left: age 4 years, 1884.
Top Right: age 20 years, 1900.
Bottom: Clarence Aaron Ullman (2/29/1880–10/2/1948)

Top: Selig Seward (SS) Lelewer on left, Clarence Aaron Ullman on right
Bottom: November 1935, Peoria, Illinois. Left to right:
Hannah Holland Zohn Goldberg (my great-grandmother)
Nancy Ullman Lelewer (3/2/1935–   )
Mina "Sis" Ullman Lelewer (1/24/1911–2/11/2005)
Hattie Zohn Ullman (2/19/1882–11/21/1955)

Hattie and Clarence Ullman, Peoria, Illinois

age twenty-two when she married Popeye in 1904. After their wedding in Spokane, Nana and Popeye went to live with Popeye's adoptive parents in one of the first houses built in Peoria, a small, two-story home. When Popeye's adoptive father died, Popeye inherited the house. He sold it in 1913 to a gentleman who was anxious to own it, but didn't have sufficient cash. A friend advised Popeye to accept the gentleman's Standard Oil of Indiana stock in lieu of some cash. The stock, through its many mergers and name changes, has been in the family for over ninety years. It's now known as BP PLC.

Popeye and Nana were Reform Jews with deep feelings for their religion. Popeye was president of Anshai Emeth Temple, a reform temple in Peoria. My great-grandmother, Hannah Zohn Goldberg, Nana's mother, had kept a strictly kosher home, but Nana did not. Still, Nana never bought bacon even though she would eat beef tenderloin wrapped in bacon when she dined out. On those occasions, she would remove the bacon and eat the beef. It didn't matter to her that the bacon fat had gone into the meat she was eating.

My mother, whose given name was Mina, but who was called "Sis" by her brother, friends, and my father, was born on January 24, 1911, two years before Popeye sold his house. Mother was a darling little girl who grew into a lovely woman, but she was not always perfect. She once asked her older brother, Jerome, to help her with the dishes. When he said, "No, I'm a boy," she threw a knife at him. Fortunately, Mother was always terrible at sports, so, even though she aimed, she missed.

Although the cutoff for entrance into first grade was January 1 and Mother's sixth birthday was January 24, when the time came for her to attend school, Nana convinced the school authorities to accept her. It was a serendipitous decision for it was in first grade that Mother made a lifelong friend who happened to have the same unusual name, Mina. At the age of eighty-five, long-time friend Mina visited my mother and father on Longboat Key in Florida, much to their delight.

Mother and Mina attended Washington Grade School on Moss Avenue. It was typical of the grade schools of that period—orderly and structured. Students didn't have backpacks or wear sneakers, and they were expected to use what are now called indoor voices most of the time. Even on cold days, they waited in line outside school, giggling quietly with friends. Most girls, including Mother, wore woolen coats with velvet collars, a bow in their hair, long stockings, and Mary Jane shoes. At 9 A.M., when the school's doors were opened, they marched in together to a John Philip Sousa's march played on the school's Victrola.

Everyone in 1917 knew the Victrola, made by the Victor Talking Machine Company, was the most popular brand of phonograph available. Advertisements showed Nipper, a small dog, with his head cocked listening to "his master's voice" as it emanated from the Victrola. Buyers were urged to "look under the lid, look on the label" to be sure they were getting a Victrola.

Perhaps it was those early morning John Philip Sousa marches that encouraged my mother's love of music. As an adult, she recalled loving the music to "In the Hall of the Mountain King" in second grade.

Even when she was in her nineties, Mother remembered her early school days. "My first grade teacher, Miss Matson," she told me, "printed the word 'Animals' on the blackboard and listed 'cat,' 'dog,' 'kitten' and 'bird' below it. In second grade," she said, "my teacher was Miss Saul." Mother's memory was truly phenomenal. She could name twenty of the twenty-five classmates who attended school with her from first grade through

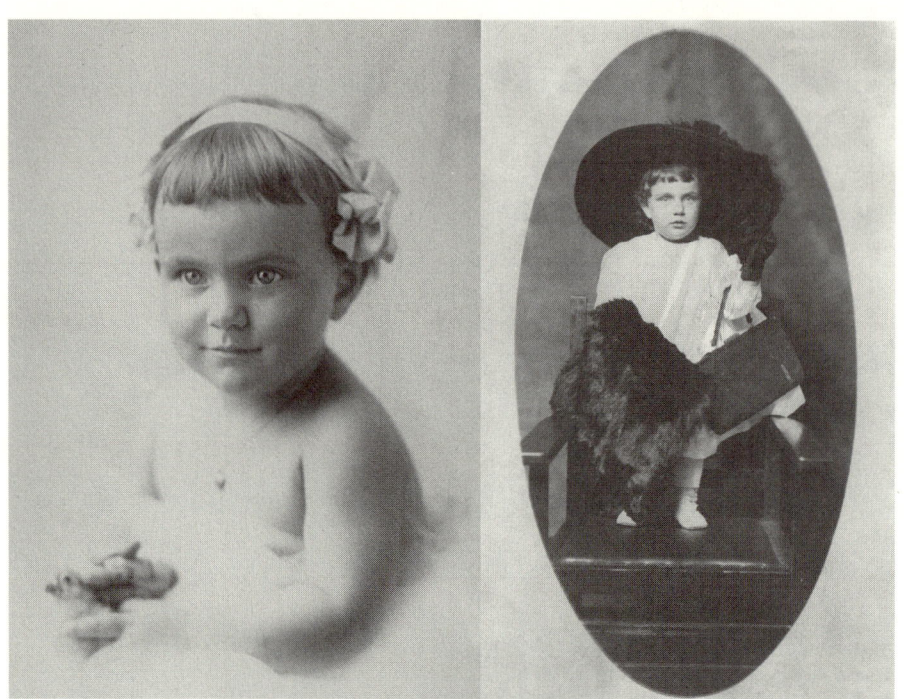

Mina Ullman, Peoria, Illinois
Top Left & Right: Almost 2 years old, end of 1912
Top Right: Dressed in her mother's hat, muff and purse
Bottom: Mina Ullman, almost 15 years old (12/25/25)

high school. The ones I often heard about were Ted Page, Jack Elliot, Jack First, Charles Adam, and Bob Owen, who was the love of her school days. Whenever she spoke of him, she would smile, and her head would tilt in a shy pose.

Unlike boys and girls in first and second grade when I was in school, Mother was never taught to print. Instead, she was instructed in the Palmer writing method. In fourth grade, she learned the parts of speech and how to diagram a sentence, something I didn't learn until high school.

It seems to me, as I look back now on my schooling, that the early foundation for my mother's education was better than mine. Other than struggling somewhat with Latin and chemistry, Mother did well throughout her school years. In high school, she completed two years of Latin with the help of ponies (translations of her Latin readings), and was greatly relieved when her parents didn't insist that she take third-year Latin, which would have been Cicero. When her struggles with chemistry became too great, her parents hired a young rabbi who loved the subject to tutor her and get her through the exam.

While Mother was in high school, she volunteered at Neighborhood House, a facility for underprivileged children in Peoria. In that period, social work, particularly on a volunteer basis, was considered acceptable work for a young woman. Given that, it is not surprising that while working for her college degree in Chicago, she again chose to work with underprivileged children at Chicago's Hull House, which had been founded by Jane Addams. Addams was a member of the first generation of college educated American women who dedicated their lives to social service and reform. Mother's job at Hull House was to cut the clothes off the children who arrived there,

1928, Mina Ullman at graduation from Peoria High School, age 17 years

bathe them, and comfort them with clean, new clothes and a nutritious meal.

In those days, poor parents would often sew clothes on their children so the clothes couldn't be lost. It was a practical solution to a problem that could be expensive, but not one conducive to frequent bathing. When they arrived at Hull House, the children's smell was terrible.

As high school came to an end, my mother dreamed of attending the college of her choice and applied to Connecticut College for Women. Several years earlier her brother Jerome had applied to the University of Michigan and, when accepted, had attended school there. Popeye, however, did not feel Mother should be 1,200 miles from home. He believed she had been protected at home and needed to be brought into the real world gradually. He may well have been right. The consequences of entering the real world too quickly for women back then could be grim.

In any case, at home, Popeye's word was law. He was strict with his family but not with others. Nana could not wear fingernail polish, yet he had no objections to other women wearing nail polish. My mother's rouge (today's blush) would disappear when she was at home. "Stop looking for it," Popeye would say. "I've thrown it out."

At age sixteen, Mother had to be in the house by 11 P.M. When there were high school dances, her curfew was midnight. One night, when she got home twenty minutes late, she found Popeye standing at the top of the stairs in his nightgown. "Where have you been?" he called down to her. "It's about time you got home." Looking at her date in embarrassment, she answered, "Well, I'm home now." She never came home late again.

As a result of Popeye's objections, and even though Connecticut College had accepted her, Mother went to Ferry Hall, a prep school and two-year college that had been founded by an Episcopal minister. The school was close to Peoria and the Peoria Superintendent of Schools sent his daughter there allaying Popeye's concerns. For her part, Mother learned about life every morning at chapel, which was required, and at the obligatory 5 P.M. vespers every Sunday. Miss Tremain, the headmistress, would stand ramrod straight before the assembled students, drop an empty teacup and saucer on the floor for attention, and begin her announcements. She was most eloquent when she told of expulsions.

I don't mean to suggest that Popeye was some kind of petty household tyrant. His word was law in his home, but there were almost always good reasons and love behind his actions.

I still remember the time that Popeye forbade me to climb a ladder from the basement to the second floor of the house my father was having built on Sheridan Road. I was six years old at the time, and my father would take me with him when he went to inspect the progress of the house.

After the second story was added, an unsecured ladder ran from the basement to the second floor. One could grab a beam and swing off at the first floor or go all the way to the second floor. My father and I had done it many times.

When I started up the ladder with Popeye and my father, however, Popeye promptly said the climb was too dangerous for me. Even when my father told him I had done it before and was careful, Popeye said, "Well, she's not doing it in my presence." I started to cry, and Popeye said firmly, "Better you should cry than I." Dad gave me a chore to do, and he and Popeye went up the ladder, leaving me in the basement crying. It took several years before I understood the wisdom of Popeye's statement.

At least twice a year when I was young, always on Thanksgiving and once in the summer, my parents and I would drive or board the Peoria Central train to see Nana and Popeye, my mother's brother, Uncle Jerome, his wife, Elsie, and my two cousins, Dick and Don. I looked forward to these visits and enjoyed the train ride. That's when we played games and when I learned about my mother's family.

When we arrived, we always piled out of the car or train loaded with heavy suitcases and shiny gifts that Mother had wrapped in pretty papers and silk ribbons. We would go first to see Nana and Popeye in their two-story home with its porch in front and small grass backyard. Unlike Grandma's home in Chicago with its small rugs on hardwood floors, no drapes, and baby grand piano in the living room, Nana's home had heavy drapes and carpet so deep I could see my footsteps in it. I still recall her large dining-room table. I don't think we ever ate at it.

Nana was not demonstrative. I can remember seeing Popeye's arms around her, but I don't remember seeing her return the embrace or ever offer an embrace to others. Still, I loved her dearly, and she and my mother were quite close. Before I left for my junior year in Spain, I went to Peoria to spend a weekend with her. I remember peppering my speech with many exclamations as I described my plans. By her smiles I knew she understood and shared in my excitement.

Peoria always seemed to greet us with extreme heat in summer and extreme cold at Thanksgiving. I have never been hotter or colder in my life than during those visits.

In the summer, I had a tiny room on the top floor of my

Top Picture (L to R): Dick Ullman, Don Ullman & Nancy Ullman Lelewer
Bottom Picture (L to R): Top row, Clarence Ullman & Jerome Ullman
Middle Row (L to R): Dick Ullman and Nancy Ullman Lelewer
Bottom Row: Don Ullman

Top: Nancy Lelewer on one of the ladders
Bottom: 508 Sheridan Road under construction

cousin's house. Despite the dormer window, not a breath of air entered the room. There was no air conditioning, so I would lie in a puddle of sweat waiting for the night to end. The only relief from the heat came in the form of a swim in the backyard pool of my cousin's friend.

When I was older, Nana and Popeye went to Mackinac Island in Michigan during the summer for a couple of weeks as a vacation. They always would invite us to join them, which we did.

On Thanksgiving Day in Peoria, we watched the Peoria Central High School football team on which my cousin, Don, played. There were years when the wind would howl and the snow beat against my face as I stood on the sidelines. It seemed to be a form of torture, but it didn't keep me from becoming a lifelong football fan.

I shouldn't complain too much about Peoria's weather. After all, the town, and particularly Popeye's warehouses, made our lives easier throughout World War II. While there was rationing during the war and we did need coupons for sugar, meat, shoes, coffee, tires and gasoline, the area's farmers were sometimes short on cash and would pay in commodities for the use of Popeye's warehouses. Popeye and my uncle would then share these goods with us.

During this time, we also got cream directly from a farm. It was not pasteurized and had the consistency of sour cream. It was so thick we needed a spoon to get it out of the jar.

Since butter was unavailable, we bought white oleo, which came with a packet of deep yellow-orange dye. My mother would have me roll up my sleeves, wash my hands, and mix the oleo and the dye together in a large bowl. My hands would turn orangey-yellow, but it was great fun squishing the stuff together.

The last time I heard from Nana was on August 24, 1955, when I left on the SS Independence for my junior year in Spain. Nana sent me a farewell telegram, which I still have in my scrapbook. "Write when you can," it said. I did. In one long letter, which she received November 20, I told about my voyage across the Atlantic, the classmates in my Smith group, my many adventures to date, and the wonderful woman in Madrid with whom I was living.

The last words in my letter were, " . . .There's hardly time to sleep, I guess I'll do that when I'm older. At the moment I couldn't be happier and am having the time of my life. I think about you and hope you are well."

I never received an answer. Nana was found dead in her bed with the letter open in her hands. She had found time for a long sleep but not until, I believe, she knew I was safe and happy. I think about Nana now—how she might have loved to use that amazing mathematical mind of hers in other ways, perhaps as a working woman. She was born a little too early for that.

CHAPTER 5
The Early Years

During Mother's first year at Ferry Hall, my father was invited to a school dance there by Millicent Jacobs, one of my Mother's friends. Millicent talked Mother into exchanging dance cards, and thus swapping partners, for one dance. When it came time to dance with the man whose name was on her card, however, Mother was nowhere in sight. Mother's card said Joe Lelewer, but Mother confused that name with the name Joe Lederer, a man whom she had already met. To my mother's eyes, Joe Lederer was a short, far less handsome man than her own date that evening. She, therefore, followed the age-old tradition of fleeing to the bathroom.

A year or so later, when Mother was at a restaurant with her date for the evening, she was introduced to a group of her date's friends who also were at the restaurant. My father just happened to be one of the people to whom she was introduced. He asked her to dance, and she agreed, happily. After all, he was tall, had dark brown hair, and hazel eyes with a twinkle in them.

While they were dancing, he asked, "Where were you when my name was on your dance card? You never showed up." Suddenly Mother realized her mistake. Joe Lelewer was certainly not Joe Lederer. Joe Lelewer was handsome and a fabulous dancer—an irresistible combination.

From that point on, my mother and father went out with each other regularly, often dancing to the Big Band music of Tommy Dorsey, Glen Miller, Count Basie, and Louis Armstrong. In time, the song, "I Can't Give You Anything But Love, Baby" with music by Jimmy McHugh and lyrics by Dorothy Field, became their song.

The swing beat and Ella Fitzgerald kind of lyrics made for sensuous, yet lively dancing. Daytime dating also had its moments, but they were often slightly less romantic. At one point, when my father drove around a corner too fast, his car flipped on its side and fell onto a mailbox. The window on my mother's side of the car was open, and my mother found herself lying on her side with the mailbox next to her face. Even though she was shaken, she was undeterred and went on dating my father.

Sometime later, my father and his friend, Howie Kahn, visited Mother at her home in Peoria. The two friends, horsing around, broke one of the twin beds in the guest room. Penitent and more than a bit nervous, my father confessed the deed to his future father-in-law who accepted his apology. (I've often wondered if Mother did some pleading for him before he confessed.) While her father may have had some qualms about this newcomer, his qualms didn't seem to bother Mother. She kept right on dating my father.

At Christmas, my father sent her what many years later she described as "pale blue, lacy pajamas." At the same time, and definitely more on the Emily Post line, another beau sent her a pair of leather gloves with the note, "I hope these gloves keep your hands as warm as you make my heart." Popeye heartily approved of the gloves. "What is the meaning of the pajamas?" he asked. Not knowing what to say, Mother simply shrugged her shoulders and kept right on dating my father.

My father loved to ride horses and, wanting to share his pleasure with her, took my mother horseback riding. When she fell off three times while the horse was only walking, he concluded she would not be a good riding partner, but he kept right on dating her. And Mother, probably relieved that she wouldn't have to try riding again, kept right on dating him.

One night in early February when the two were at a restaurant, my father, instead of chatting the way he usually did, spent considerable time running numbers. "What are you doing?" my mother asked.

"I'm trying to decide if it's cheaper to buy a horse or marry you." I doubt it was cheaper, but on Valentine's Day he proposed.

When my father asked Popeye for my mother's hand, he brought along an accounting of his finances, and told Popeye that he planned to take Mother to Florida and Cuba for their honeymoon. Popeye took a quick look at the paper and smiled. "You two are starting way ahead of where Hattie and I started when we got married. I didn't have money for a honeymoon. We got married, walked down the railroad tracks, and went home."

The one condition Popeye had was that Mother finish college after she was married. In some ways, it was an unusual condition for the time. Certainly Popeye had learned from experience the importance of an education. Even so, there were probably few women whose families expected them to complete their degrees once they married. After all, at that time, a woman's place was considered to be the home; marriage and motherhood, some thought, should be the primary goal of all women. Unlike many women of her era, however, my mother did get her degree and did work for a while after she married.

At the time of my parent's engagement, Popeye gave my father a 50th anniversary edition of a small, sterling-silver pocket watch with my father's initials on the back. The watch, which I still have along with the box it came in, is a family treasure. My father and Popeye grew to think the world of each other.

Joseph David Lelewer and Mina Clara Ullman were married March 2, 1932 at the Hotel Père Marquette in Peoria, Illinois. The hotel, which had opened five years earlier, is now listed in the National Register of Historic Places. Somehow, my grandmother managed to put together a wedding for seventy-five in a couple of weeks just so my father and his bride could go south for the month of March—a Lelewer family tradition.

March 2, 1932, Wedding of Mina Ullman and Joseph Lelewer
Hotel Père Marquette, Peoria, Illinois

310 SOUTH STATE STREET
CLARK CORNER MONROE
LA SALLE CORNER WASHINGTON
32 NORTH DEARBORN STREET
MADISON CORNER WELLS

EST. OVER 60 YEARS

D. LELEWER & SON

Chicago's Largest Hatter

KNOX HATS

OFFICES
310 SO. STATE STREET
WABASH 4124

JOSEPH LELEWER

Top: 1931, Joseph Lelewer's business card
Bottom: 1928, Central Park, New York, Joseph Lelewer, age 22, on horse. Heimie
Friedman, hat manufacturer and owner of horse, standing on left.

Top: Mina "Sis" Ullman and Joe Lelewer dating on horseback
Bottom: Sis and Joe Lelewer, August 1932

75

Mina Ullman Lelewer
Peoria, Illinois
March 2, 1935

Mina and Joseph Lelewer
Peoria, Illinois
March 2, 1935

"It was one of the most elaborate affairs of the winter," the newspaper account states. "The main dining room was decorated in the form of a sunken garden. The tables were laid in a hollow square against the outer edges of the room and arranged with seats on one side only. The inside was draped completely with smilax. A prim box hedge enclosed the garden, which had patches of green lawn and graveled walks. Bright flowering tulips, jonquils and hyacinths bloomed in pots across the borders."

Three rabbis officiated at the service. A chupah framed the wedding couple, and my father, following tradition, broke the glass. They did not, however, dance the hora, nor was my father carried on a chair above the heads of the guests. These were regarded as old country traditions.

After their honeymoon, and very much in love, they moved into a two-bedroom apartment on the south side of Chicago. My father was twenty-five and in the family business. My mother was finishing her college degree and still adjusting to her new name. Her first experience with it came when she heard her gym instructor yelling "Mrs. Washington, Mrs. Washington," over and over while looking directly at her. Finally, it occurred to Mother that she had told the gym teacher that Lelewer rhymed with Delaware, which Washington had crossed during the revolution.

Life was happy for the newlyweds most of the time. In the 1930s, it wasn't unusual for a reasonably well-to-do married woman to have help who either lived in or came in to work on a daily basis. Mother had two maids plus a woman who did the laundry for her. If it seems excessive to us these days, it worked for them. As in every marriage, adjustments had to be made. My mother once told me that on their first anniversary, my father went to work and, after work, played nine holes of golf.

He called and said, "I'm playing well, do you mind if I play another nine?"

"It's our anniversary," she replied tearfully.

"I'll be right home."

Within half an hour, my father had arrived with apologies, a card, and a large bouquet of flowers. Mother said she had been so angry, she might have left him had it not been for the fact she was pregnant and very sick.

She may have been angry when she spoke to him, but my father, who never again forgot an anniversary or special occasion, always could make her smile and forgive him. I can recall one Thanksgiving trip to Nana and Popeye's house when Mother and I took the train from Braeside to Chicago and then boarded the train to Peoria. Usually when we did this, my father would spend the morning in the city and then join us on the train. This time, Mother and I walked through many cars until we found seats in the car just behind the engine. Mother kept looking over her shoulder, trying to spot my father coming through the cars, but he was nowhere in sight. She said nothing, just fidgeted with some papers on her lap. The train left the station, and still my father had not appeared. "Let's play cards," Mother suggested. Her lips were pursed, and her face was white. She dropped a few cards as she dealt.

Ten minutes out of the station, someone tapped her on the shoulder. She turned abruptly, continuing to grip her cards. I can still remember how her whole body softened when she saw her husband standing behind her. He smiled at her, and she smiled in return as if he had handed her a bouquet of flowers.

"Joseph, where have you been?" she asked, without raising her voice or showing any anger.

"I ran a little late, but I'm here," he answered.

My father also made adjustments. My mother was not a morning person, and marriage did not change that. One morning, she poured cream into my father's orange juice instead of his coffee by mistake. He handed her a knife.

"What's the knife for?" she asked.

"To cut your fog," was his wry response.

It was during these early years that my mother became an artist in her own way creating beautiful, serene surroundings first for my father and later for my father and me.

For as long as I can remember, each evening meal was preceded by a cocktail hour with hot and cold hors d'oeuvres served on carefully chosen plates and trays. Plates, trays, and platters were always lined with white, filigreed doilies. On special occasions, candy was served on high-stem silver dishes.

Every night, Mother would be beautifully dressed for dinner no matter what she had been doing during the day. The dinner table would always have fresh flowers and lighted candles. She would make butterballs with two special, thin wooden paddles and place them on individual butter plates with sprigs of parsley. Our plates would be decorated with the radish roses and other vegetable flowers that are usually found only in restaurants. Each place setting would have its own red fingerbowl with a slice of lemon floating in the water.

She chose her menus with care, and, to this day, there are two specialties of hers that my children, their families and I still enjoy, Chicken Divan and roast beef with the politically incorrect name of No Peekie Roast Beefie. It was from my mother's dinners that I learned about beauty, color, and design.

During the first year of their marriage, my parents often double-dated with my father's close friend, Bob Koretz, and his girlfriend, Fran Levi, who was my mother's good friend.

Throughout their lives, my father and Bob bounced one liners off each other in a kind of verbal ping-pong that kept everyone in hysterics. During the early years when they double dated, the quartet would return to my parent's apartment. Knowing Bob and Fran had little privacy, my parents would discreetly leave them in the living room. After doing this for a while, my parents began to urge Bob and Fran to marry. At that time, Bob worked for Foote, Cone, and Belding Communications, a large advertising company. He had little in savings and a small salary. Although it took some work, my parents managed to convince the two that things would work out. Two weeks after the wedding, however, Bob was laid off. Fortunately, just before he took a new job in Milwaukee, Foote, Cone, and Belding hired him back at a higher salary.

It was a wise decision on the company's part for Bob became one of the advertising greats. In those days, men and women used handkerchiefs, not Kleenex, which had been invented in 1924 by Ernst Mahler, a scientist working for Kimberly-Clark. It became Bob's job to change the public's ways and have them use Kleenex, not handkerchiefs, for each sniffle. To do so, he coined the phrase, "Don't put a cold in your pocket." He put the Little Lulu cartoon character in ads for the product and then, in another commercial, he had Harry James put wet Kleenex tissues on the end of his trumpet, when he played, to show the strength of the tissue. Today, handkerchiefs are considered a thing of the past, and most people use tissues. Bob also created Pepsodent's "You'll wonder where the yellow went when you brush your teeth with Pepsodent", Toni Home Permanent's "Which twin has the Toni?" and Hallmark Cards' classic, "When you care enough to send the very best."

My parents and the Koretzes remained friends for years.

In 1937, Fran and my mother formed a play group made up of twelve children in Highland Park. Mother and Fran took the children down to the beach behind Fran's home for one of the group's early outings. As soon as the towels were set out, the children scrambled for the water. Every few minutes, Fran and Mother would count heads. At some point, Mother cried, "Oh no! I only count eleven." The two of them counted again and then again, becoming more and more frantic. Fortunately, before panic truly set in, Fran realized that they weren't counting me. Mother had tucked me into her arms behind a large towel. Fran hadn't seen me, and Mother was so worried she hadn't counted me! The play group continued to meet, but always on dry land.

The Koretzes and my parents together with a number of other families including the Jacobys, Metzenbergs, Foxes, Tausigs, Ottenheimers, and Wells, were members of what was known as The Potluck Club. Every other Sunday members would meet at someone's home for dinner, and each member would contribute something to the meal. On those Sundays when the Potluck Club did not meet, my parents and I occasionally would go to a church where black women served delicious southern fried chicken. We would sit on picnic benches and eat until we were full.

Looking back, I remember my mother as rather reserved and proper when I was young. I suspect many people of my era remember their parents that way. After I became an adult, my father assured me that my mother had had her frivolous, fun-loving side when she was young. He could remember her climbing into a playpen at a party one night and tossing the toys at the guests. I must admit it is still hard for me to imagine, however, when I go through my parents' honeymoon photo album, I catch a glimpse of Mina, not Mother. There she is on a horse and underneath is my father's comment, "On for a second. . ." Underneath

Bob Koretz, age 58

Fran Koretz, age 59

a photo of a wondrously young Mina and my father in front of a tennis court are the words, "Obstructed view of tennis court." My favorite photos, however, are two pictures of a lake, one with my mother standing in the lake, the other with my father sitting on the dock facing my mother with his feet dangling in the water. The pictures are arranged one above the other. In between them is written "Mama 'lakes' Papa." That is a truth that never changed.

CHAPTER 6
Sisters, Brothers Have I None

I believe my mother always knew, deep within, that some element was missing in our relationship, that there seemed to be a kind of distance between us.

There was love.

There was respect.

There was caring without question.

Still, my father and I talked easily with each other. My mother and I were always slightly more formal. When I was younger, I simply viewed myself, rather traditionally, as "Daddy's little girl." Surrounded by my father's love and secure in my knowledge of it, I grew up and made my way in the world for better or for worse. Now that I'm older, however, I've learned more about my mother, and I have had time to think about my childhood. I realize my father wrapped us both in a protective cocoon of love. My mother needed that cocoon, just as she felt she needed some distance between us. I suspect she lived in fear that, if she let down the barrier between us, something dreadful would happen. Of course, fears are not always rational, but they are almost always based on something real. For my mother, I suspect that basis was the loss of two children and the termination of three pregnancies.

A little over a year after my parents were married, my brother John was born. Mother developed toxemia during the pregnancy and blew up like a balloon. From birth, John suffered from continuous projectile vomiting. At that time, there were no drugs or surgical procedures that could help him, and no amount of love could save him. He never developed muscle control. He was never able to roll over or sit up. Before he died at the age of one, he was rushed to the hospital many times. The death certificate listed the cause of death as "unknown." There was no comfort for my mother in that phrase. She lost control of her arms, and everything she tried to hold slipped away just as her child had. The doctors said it was due to her nerves and told my father to take her to a quiet spot to recuperate, which he did.

On my parents' third anniversary, March 2, 1935, I was born—a healthy baby girl. Mother did not develop toxemia during the pregnancy, and I was fine. But, when I was two, my mother delivered her second son, Tom, my parents' third child. Once again, Mother developed toxemia during her pregnancy. Once again, the baby suffered from projectile vomiting, developed no muscle control, and was rushed to the hospital many times. Tom died of pneumonia at the age of thirteen months.

I cannot imagine the pain my parents, particularly my mother, endured from losing two children. She had carried each child for nine months, had felt each move within her. She was at home caring for each of them, rushing first one and then the other to the hospital, bringing each home again, never seeing any improvement, always knowing that death was coming, but never knowing why. It wasn't that my father wasn't supportive, but he could, and did, indeed had to, go to work. He could even play golf sometimes. He didn't live the trauma on an hour-to-hour basis, except on Sundays and when he rushed the babies to the hospital with Mother.

I wonder if my mother ever blamed herself for what was happening. It may not be rational, but some women do when they lose a child. She may have asked herself if there was something, anything, she could have done to prevent it. When you watch the clock tick by the hours, your thoughts can go in many directions.

After Tom's death, Mother, again, lost control of her arms and, once again, my father took her to the forty-three-room stone and log lodge at Starve Rock State Park where they had gone before. The lodge was perched atop a wooded bluff overlooking the Illinois River. There were acres of forest, canyons, and waterfalls. They took long walks, made bookends at the craft shop, and let their grief ease, which helped her heal. Still, while grief can ease, I am sure the pain of such a loss never goes away and scars form deep inside.

Mother was told not to have any more children as there was no way to prevent toxemia, and another pregnancy with toxemia would be life-threatening.

Unfortunately, it was far easier in those days to tell someone not to become pregnant than it was to prevent a pregnancy. Mother became pregnant two more times. Abortions were illegal, but each time my father spoke to a friend of his, an OB/GYN, who performed the surgeries in a hospital. By the time of the second abortion, my mother was frantic. She had lost two children and had had two pregnancies ended. She decided to have a tubal ligation. Unbelievably, after it was performed, she became pregnant again and had to have a third abortion.

I am quite sure these experiences made her worry more about me all through my childhood. She may even have come to believe that, if she revealed how much she cared for me, I would disappear as my brothers had. My father once told me that Mother used to hold Kleenex under my nose when I was a baby to be sure I was breathing. At the time, a doctor told my father to hire a nurse to care for me or "your wife will make Nancy neurotic." I know from photos I had a nurse, but I have no memory of her. I had fun with my father and did everyday things with my mother.

As I grew older, it was my mother who took me clothes shopping, to doctor appointments, to the dressmaker, who helped me with my homework, and who was there when I returned from school.

Although my parents were told not to have more children, it did not put a halt to their desire for more children. On a regular basis—at birthday parties I attended or on our shopping expeditions—my parents were surrounded by children who were the ages their sons would have been. Thus, when I was seven, I traveled with my parents to St. Louis, Missouri to meet two children—a little boy and his sister—whom my parents hoped to adopt. As I recall, we met with a woman in a small room, probably an office at the adoption agency, and were introduced to two adorable children. One was a four-year-old redhead with the requisite freckles named Richard, the other was his sister, Judy, who was two-and-a-half and had long, blonde hair.

We were asked to take them out for a few hours. We may have had lunch together. I know we all had ice cream at

Nancy Ullman Lelewer
Chicago, Illinois
Top: Age 1 year
Bottom: Age 2 years

Nancy Ullman Lelewer with her nurse, "Monkeydo"
Chicago, Illinois
Age 2 years

Top: Nancy Ullman Lelewer with her dad in Chicago, age 2 years
Bottom: Nancy Ullman Lelewer, age 4 years, with her mom in Florida

some point during our time together. They loved the chocolate ice cream they had chosen and even enjoyed the crunch of the cone. Since chocolate was our family favorite, my parents and I viewed their choice as a happy omen that meant they would soon join our family. Heaven knows we had the space for them in our home and in our hearts. I began to imagine the games Richard, Judy, and I could play together, the places we could go together.

Unfortunately it was not to be. It wasn't that we "failed" the agency test. In keeping with the popular belief of the time, a committee at the agency decided it wasn't fair for a family that already had one child to adopt two children when other families had none. The agency found a childless couple to adopt Richard and Judy. I was too young to know how that hurt my parents, particularly my mother.

If my parents made other inquiries into adoption, I was not aware of them. In 1949, however, when I was fourteen, my parents adopted a seven-year-old boy named Bodo through the Jewish Children's Bureau in Chicago. I still remember the day they went to pick him up. I had told my friends all about the adoption, but I was not going with my parents because I had field hockey practice that afternoon. I am sure a number of questions were going through my mind—What was he like? Would he fit in? Would I want to spend time with him? Looking back, I don't recall worrying that I would cease to be the sole focus of my parents' attention, so I suspect I had been well prepared for his arrival and adoption. At the same time, I was a teenager and, thus, almost by definition, self-centered and self-absorbed.

Bodo had lived in a concentration camp in Germany until it was liberated. His mother had been killed in the camp's gas chamber. We didn't know if Bodo had ever known life outside

Bodo

the camp. He had been born around 1942, so, it was possible he had been born in the camp and had never known any other kind of life.

After his mother's death, a woman in the camp looked out for him the best she could becoming his surrogate mother, his lifeline. When the camp was liberated, he left with her, but she had children of her own to feed and clothe with almost no money and little strength. Given her situation and the conditions in postwar Europe, it is perhaps not surprising that she gave Bodo to the Jewish authorities that took him to the Jewish Children's Bureau. The agency arranged for Bodo to travel to Chicago. My father covered the cost of everything before and during the adoption process.

My new brother spoke no English in an era when schools did not offer English as a second language (ESL) programs. I spoke no German. He was starting first grade; I was starting high school. I introduced him to everyone in my own teen world and took him with me to football games and other events on the weekends, but the barriers between us were too great. There was not only an age barrier, but also a language barrier, and an experience barrier. I knew ice-skating, football, hot dogs, hamburgers, ice cream, the Lone Ranger, best friends, and a loving family. And what did Bodo know? I doubt that any of us, including my parents, could completely comprehend what Bodo knew of the world. Perhaps it was inevitable that although we lived side by side we never became sister and brother. My parents understood. I was never forced to "be a good sister." I was never made to feel I wasn't doing my part for the family.

Bodo had serious problems adjusting to his new life. Just to survive, he had learned to steal food for himself and, perhaps, for his surrogate mother. With us, he continued to steal food and hide it under his pillow just in case he needed it at some point. This was understandable and forgivable. After all, Bodo's world had not been marked by great security. Less forgivable, however, was his theft of my father's rare antique coin collection, which he spent. I treasure the two coins he missed.

More troubling than the theft of food or the coin collection was his reaction to women. Perhaps because of his camp experiences and the fact that his surrogate mother had given him up, Bodo hated women, or at least distrusted them. My mother sought advice from the social worker at the Children's Bureau but nothing seemed to help. Mother told me many years later that she found it frightening to be alone with him as he grew older.

Bodo remained with us until he was involved in an incident on the school playground when he was fourteen. It seems that he threatened a younger girl with a knife. I don't know if he actually held the knife to her or if he just showed her the knife or even what he threatened to do. In any case, she was terrified and must have screamed. The police and my father were called. My father came home immediately and, after hearing accounts of the event, called the Jewish Children's Bureau. Much later, as an adult in fact, I learned that Bodo had shown a worrisome interest in knives for some time. He used to like to spend time in the kitchen sharpening them, my mother told me. "I'm bringing Bodo to your agency right now," my father had said. "He cannot spend another night in our home." I was home from my junior year abroad at the time, and I can still remember both my mother sitting very quietly as she told me about the incident and my father's reaction when I came home that afternoon. That day was the last time I ever saw Bodo.

My father and the agency went to work immediately to

find a place for Bodo. They eventually found a school, which my father paid for, in Lenox, Massachusetts. My father continued to pay for everything Bodo needed until he reached the age of twenty-one. At that point my father told the agency he felt his responsibility was over. The agency assumed responsibility for him a while longer.

At some point in the early 1960s, my father discovered that Bodo was not an orphan. The West German government (Germany was divided into East Germany, a Soviet satellite, and West Germany until 1990) had begun paying reparations to war orphans in the 1950s. My father had applied for Bodo and, in the process, discovered that Bodo had a Christian father living in East Berlin. My father managed to get in touch with the man and learned that he was interested in meeting his son. Bodo was given his father's name, address, and phone number and told that his father wanted to see him. Perhaps not surprisingly, Bodo had no interest in going to East Berlin and no desire to see his father. He told my father, "I don't remember the German language and can't speak it." As far as I know, Bodo and his father never met.

Bodo kept in touch with my father for some time but eventually the contact ended. I did learn from my father that Bodo had gotten a job, married, and had had two children. I can't help hoping that he was able to apply some of the warmth and love he saw in my parents' home to his own family. I have no idea where he is now or what he has done with his life. I hope he is happy. There is no magic lamp that grants wishes when it is rubbed, but, if there were, I would wish that my parents, especially my mother, and Bodo himself, had not had to endure so much sorrow as a result of his traumatic early years. Looking back, I am deeply touched by the time and effort my parents put into giving Bodo a warm and loving home and not letting their concerns impinge upon my life.

CHAPTER 7
Hearth and Home

Over the years, I have discovered that we all have our own definitions of home, and that those definitions are the result of many different memories. For some people, the style of a house—ranch, colonial, cape—brings back memories of home. For others, a sound—the roar of the lawn mower—or a smell—burning leaves or soup simmering on the stove when the autumn air is crisp—turns the clock back to childhood and home. For me, the house I grew up in, the Sunday stories as I call them, told to me by my father, my uncle, and my grandfather again and again, the meals we enjoyed together—the platters of cold cuts, coleslaw, potato salad, dill pickles from the deli, and ice cream with pitchers of thick fudge sauce—the games we played, and the neighborhood we lived in, all, spell home to me. My childhood home was Sheridan Road, Braeside Elementary School, Highland Park, and most of Chicago.

Our first home in Highland Park was a rented house on Lambert Tree Road. My room was at the opposite end of the second floor from my parents.

One night, when I was two years old, my mother was woken from her sleep by my crying. She jumped out of bed to go to me, but in her fog, walked into a closet. Hearing both her muffled blows on the closet walls and my cries, my father woke up and called out, "Where are you?" After a puzzled minute or two, he retrieved Mother from the closet, and together, they raced to my room, only to discover I had fallen back to sleep.

When I was six, my father had a house built for us on Sheridan Road. Although an architect prepared the final plans, my father did the preliminary house sketches and outlined the landscaping for our home, which was one of the first built in the neighborhood. He was familiar with the work of Frederic Law Olmstead and located the house on the lot in a way that emphasized privacy and views and also optimized the sun's light. The house, which was set back from the street by a tiny forest of trees and fit comfortably into its surroundings, was located on the northern portion of our land. This allowed for a large, continuous, grassy area behind and to the south side of the house. This area, which we used for croquet, catch, and our victory garden during World War II, received the afternoon sun.

For the victory garden, my father and I planted carrots, peas, corn, asparagus, parsley, squash, tomatoes, and strawberries. We kept it weeded and watered, and I learned that it was great fun to pick a carrot, wash it with the hose, and eat it right out of the garden.

Victory gardens were important during the war years, but vegetables at meal times were a touchy topic for both my father and me. My father used to say, "I like vegetables, I just don't eat them." That wasn't entirely true. He ate peas, corn on the cob, string beans when they were served almandine, asparagus when covered with plenty of buttered breadcrumbs, spinach if it was creamed, and cauliflower and broccoli when covered with hollandaise sauce.

It's fortunate he liked peas because I didn't when I was young. One night I pointed to the peas on my plate and said firmly, "I don't like peas." I was careful not to make a face. Mother stiffened but said not a word, which I knew meant I was to eat them; no discussion. My father used a different approach, "I call the things on your plate, 'peziolas', and I love them." He put a forkful in his mouth, his eyes lit up, and I could see he was savoring the flavor. "Try them," he urged. "'Peziolas' are delicious." I tried two at first. Not bad. In a few minutes, I felt a "peziola" smile, matching my father's, on my own face and ate all of them.

The grassy area on the eastern portion of the lot, between the small forest and our home, got the morning sun. For years, when weather permitted, we had a badminton net set up there. When I was young, my friends and I loved the ravine and brook on our property. We would jump back and forth across the stream, hunt for frogs along its banks, or sit on rocks and feel the bubbly water glide across our naked feet. When the house was quiet, I would open a window to hear the gentle swoosh of the water over the rocks.

The exterior of our home was primarily red brick trimmed with stained wood. The tan-colored slate roof softened the rooflines and provided a certain earthiness that was paralleled in the flagstone entry. There was a built-in barbecue on the porch. Dad and I would stand in front of the barbecue chatting as he broiled thick steaks for Sunday get-togethers with the family. When we did not go into the city for a Sunday get-together, my grandparents, and sometimes my Uncle David, Aunt Madeline, and my cousins from Glencoe, Stanley, David and Jan, would come out to Highland Park. In the summer, the screen porch

Top: My aunt and uncle, Madeline and David Lelewer
Bottom (L toR)My Lelewer cousins from Glencoe: Stan,
Jan (Lipschutz), and David, 1996

would be filled with adults having cocktails and my cousins and me munching on hors d'oeuvres. In winter, cocktails were served in front of the fireplace in the living room, and my father would bundle up in a warm coat before dashing out onto the porch to grill the steaks.

The arrangement of the house on the lot gave us sunlit rooms year round, additional heat in the winter, and great sunsets for viewing. The morning sun would come into the den where it couldn't awaken anyone. The afternoon sun would flood the living room, porch, and my parent's bedroom. The den, where we would gather in the evenings, housed our television, a wooden table and chairs and the Trat sleeper.

The Trat sleeper is a regular sized twin bed (upholstered box spring and mattress), housed in a wooden frame on a track, with wooden arms and cushions attached to the back of the frame, above the bed. Behind the cushions is a storage compartment for blankets, sheets, pillows, etc. and on top a wooden shelf that can hold knickknacks above the cushions. The bed can be slid partially under the storage compartment making it a comfortable seat that is the length of the twin bed, and gives the appearance of a standard sofa. It also can be slid forward for comfortable sleeping.

It was while sitting on the Trat sleeper in the den that I would watch "You Are There," a program hosted by Walter Cronkite. History teachers often asked their students to watch the show. Each program would set up an historical situation and, at different points in the story, Cronkite would stop the action to interview one of the characters. He would close each program with the words, "All things are as they were, except you are there."

Upstairs, there were three bedrooms, the colorful and cheery one was mine, the largest was my parent's, and the smallest was the guest room. Off the landing and directly above the garage was a fourth bedroom and bath, which was used as the maid's quarters.

My room was my world when I was small and filled with things I loved including my train set.

When the train set arrived, my father had single-handedly reenacted the classic story, "Child Gets Train; Dad Is Ecstatic." He set up the train immediately, put an enormous board on the floor of my bedroom, then laid out the track and nailed it down, hooked up the train, and let 'er rip. Shortly thereafter we acquired more cars and engines, bridges that could be raised and lowered, a train station with lights, and a magical coal car. Coal would go up the chute, the chute would swivel, and coal would be dumped into a waiting car. I became proficient in handling the switches and operating the trains at night when the only lights came from the trains themselves, the few signals along the track, and the train station. While the train set was beloved by my father, I often had it all to myself which led to the classic story, "Child Gets Train; Child Is Ecstatic."

When I was older, my father put a long, narrow chart on one of my walls. He told me it represented business and economic cycles, which meant little to me at the time but, like the explanation he gave me, has become more meaningful over the years. There was a line on the chart that went up and down, and one spot on the chart where the line almost fell off the chart. My father explained to me that when the line went up, business and the economy were good, that is, businesses were making money, employment was almost full, and people had money. When the line was down, business wasn't good, people lost jobs, and money was scarce. The steep drop of the line symbolized the crash of the stock market followed by the Great Depression.

My father told me to be sure to put some money away when times were good so that when times were bad I would have money. "History repeats itself," my father said. "You may live to see another market crash and deep depression, but you will be all right if you always live a little under your income and save money." Dad believed in being in the market and felt one would make money in the long run as long as one didn't have to sell when the market went down.

I heard the same speech often, "If you don't have the money for something, don't buy it. Know what your income is, what your fixed expenses are, and set some money aside for the unexpected. In short, have a budget and live within it."

As time went on, he taught me about buying municipal bonds, filling out a ladder so not too many bonds would come due in the same year, to buy general obligations, and always to ask for the underlying value. "The day may come when these insurance companies can't pay, so don't count on them," my father frequently said. And, if he told me once, he told me a thousand times, "Don't put all your eggs in one basket, and never rely on only one adviser. Be informed. No one cares about your money as much as you do."

The basement of our house was finished for a plethora of hobbies and entertainment. To the left of the stairs was the corner bar, which was open to the playroom and the hall. The bar was enjoyed by my parents and later made famous by high school boys at my parties who took swigs of straight Real Lemon to impress my friends and me. To the right there was a large multi-purpose area, a carpentry workshop, and a small, enclosed darkroom.

My father began teaching me woodworking when I was very young. At first, he would ask me to find specific tools as though the tools were hiding and I was hunting for them. Long before I could spell their names, I learned to recognize Phillips screwdrivers, crescent wrenches, and other tools.

Often when we worked together, my father would turn to me and say, "Would you finish this, please?" Foolish question! I learned to hit the nail, target-straight, without gouging the wood. By age seven, I had mastered the miter box, tools, and saws. It was all still a game and nothing was more satisfying than sawing through a piece of wood, following the penciled line. My father taught me to sketch what we planned to build whether it was a bookend or the box that I made with a lid that opened and closed tightly. He taught me how to figure out the number of nails and screws we needed and how to check to see if we had enough glue. I loved going to the hardware store.

The darkroom came about when photography became another of my young loves. I had a Brownie camera, and all I had to do was press the button to take a picture. My father, however, had specific ideas about what we'd shoot. People populated our photos. "If you want a picture of a scene, buy a postcard," he would say. At first, I'd forget not to shoot into the sun. Rarely did I remember that photos taken with strong vertical lines create a sense of grandness, while those with horizontal lines create a feeling of rest. After all, rest wasn't in my vocabulary as a child, nor was a studious application of camera technique. I just shot photos. One click, one photo. Slowly, my father's tutelage began to pay off. I learned there was joy in thinking a second before snapping a picture.

As I learned how to take photographs, I learned how to process and enlarge them. In the darkroom that he built for us, my father and I would stand side-by-side and, working heads together from procedure to procedure, develop the pictures I had taken. I still remember the red light we worked in to keep from overexposing the film and the rather smelly developing chemicals and fixatives we needed. I know we needed a timer and a thermometer as I remember my father saying, "We can't leave photos too long in any solution," and "All liquids must be kept at the same temperature." Those were photograph-processing mantras in our darkroom. Using the thermometer was a favorite chore of mine.

One day when we were working in the darkroom, my father hung a photo on the clothesline and said, "Here's your masterpiece." Somehow, I had done it all—taken time, considered light and angles, and it had worked. There was the photo of Chips, my dog. His ears looked rakish, and I could almost feel his fur.

Chips had arrived at our home and become my dog when I was in second grade. My parents had gone to a formal dinner in the city. I can just remember seeing my father in his tux and my mother in a fitted blue-satin gown with slits up the sides. She wore her favorite diamond and pearl pin with its dangling diamond and matching earrings that evening. As they were going up the stairs to their friend's apartment, they saw a little girl crying her heart out on the stairs. Even her long blonde hair was matted with tears. Next to her was a dog with black fur around one eye. Of course, my parents stopped.

"Why are you crying?" my father had asked.

"I have to get rid of my dog, or my parents will be evicted. I gave him to a friend, but he keeps coming back," she sobbed.

"What's the dog's name?"

"Chips," she answered. "He's part Collie and part Spitz."

"We'll take your dog and give him a good home," my

father said. "We live an hour's drive away. That's pretty far. We have a daughter your age named Nancy who will love Chips. She's very kind to animals."

The child listened intently.

"Tell your parents we'll pick Chips up after our dinner party. What apartment do you live in?"

The girl pointed to a door with the brass number 23 on it. "There."

"We'll be back," my father said. "Don't worry. Your dog will have a wonderful home."

The child slowly stopped crying, waved goodbye, and took Chips into her apartment.

"I'm not happy about having Chips in our home," my mother said.

"Dear," my father replied, "Chips will be no trouble and wonderful company for Nancy." The really touching thing about most fathers, and mine was no exception, is their optimism.

Mother, probably somewhat reluctantly, agreed, and they picked up Chips after the party.

My father put Chips in the front seat between the two of them, but when they were half way home, Chips wanted more air and leaned over Mom to get his nose out the partially opened window.

"Open the window a bit further," my father urged. "Try to move Chips to the other side of you. He wants more air."

Too late, Chips vomited all over Mother. Poor Chips, poor Mother. Her new gown was ruined. My father stopped the car. Mother bent down in the darkness next to the car to avoid being seen in the headlights of the passing cars as she stripped down to her bra and panties without saying a word.

When my mother was annoyed, her face would tighten

and her jaw would clench. I suspect that, at this point, her jaw was in an absolute knot.

My father cleaned up the front seat with a towel he kept under his seat and put poor Chips in the trunk of the car. Chips howled and then he was quiet. Mother got into the back seat and sat perfectly rigid as they drove home in total silence.

"Don't bring that dog in the house," she said when they arrived home. She ran up the stairs to take a shower. My father gave Chips a dish of water and tied him to a tree for the night. Chips lapped some water and then stuck his nose between my father's legs in typical dog style. My father gave him a couple of pats and said goodnight.

Early in the morning, my father told me they had a surprise outside for me. I ran as fast as I could out the door and stopped short when I saw this beautiful white dog with the most amazing mass of black fur around his right eye. While I was petting Chips, my father told me about the girl. In a child's way, I felt sorry for her but happy for me. I raced to school to tell my friends, and my father went to work. After we were gone, Mom slipped Chips into the car, drove to the cleaners and then to the dressmaker. When she was several miles from our home, she let Chips out of the car and drove off to lunch with friends. After lunch she returned home to find Chips sitting on our front step.

I can only imagine the shocked look on her face when she discovered Chips waiting for her. When I returned from school moments later, she was composed, but seemed to be shaking her head over something. Chips slept in the garage until my father built a doghouse for him. Still, it wasn't too long after the doghouse was built that Mother allowed him in the house, and a few months after that, I saw her patting and talking to him.

My father and I taught Chips to roll over, heel, sit, and

1944, Nancy Ullman Lelewer, age 9 years, with her dog Chips
Highland Park, Illinois

lie on command. He even learned to climb the stairs of my slide and then slide down. He would sit in the basket of my bike when I rode it. I felt like Dorothy with Toto in *The Wizard of Oz*. Six years after he arrived, a policeman came to the house, handed Chips' collar to me, told me he had been hit by a truck and killed instantly, and walked away as I stood there in shock. I think my heart broke that day. My parents could not console me. My father promised me another dog, but all I wanted was Chips. A couple of months later, my parents bought a black poodle they named Mortimer. He was a nice dog, but he was not mine.

I lived in a home of order and soft voices, voices as gentle as the colors surrounding us—pale beige carpeting and blue-gray upholstered furniture and our living room fireplace had pale blue and white dutch tiles around the two sides and top. Early mornings in our home did not involve people grabbing toast or a doughnut and running for the door. My father and I would have breakfast together, and then he would take breakfast to my mother on a wooden tray with a glass bottom. By that point, my father had decided it was best for Mother to stay in bed and let her morning fog wear off.

The tray was part of a wooden stand that was used for breakfast in bed. Each side of the stand had spaces that held books and newspapers. The tray fit perfectly into the center. When I slipped into the bedroom with him as he delivered the tray, my mother would be in bed; a vision in her light blue bed jacket over one of her simple, flowing Lucie Ann nightgowns. Her bed jackets were beribboned and decorated with lace along the edges of the sleeves and collar and framed her face. Her hair always seemed perfect, her nails buffed. She looked like a princess or a movie star to me.

On Sundays, either for breakfast or lunch, my father would

make his famous pancakes. They were paper-thin crêpes fried just right in a large, heavy, black skillet. Everyone loved them, and my father would stand for close to an hour making one after another when friends or family were present. Often he had two big, black fry pans going at the same time. Plates and individual containers of maple syrup were warmed in the oven beforehand, and butter and powdered sugar were on the table. Anyone who ate those pancakes was thrilled to be invited back to have them again.

My mother once said our home was the ideal setting for me. She was right. Even the drawers in our home were carefully organized except for the one topsy-turvy junk drawer in our kitchen and the two in the garage. Pictures were always squared off and aligned perfectly. I was taught to clean up my projects as I went along.

All of that neatness was helpful to a child who needed to find "everything in its place," but I never thought about that when I was young. In the same way I never thought about the beautiful moldings within the house or the collection of magnificent antique furniture, some of which held rare pewter that furnished it. My parents had one of the finest private collections of antique pewter in the United States, yet I thought of it as something that had always been there. Pewter, by its nature, does not shout. It has an inherent softness to its patina. Our home seemed to have that same soft patina. Mother was meticulous, yet she maintained a lived-in quality to the house making it comfortable for us and for overnight guests. There was a calm aura and ease within our home that would be broken only by the laughter and occasional high jinks of my father. Mother was right. It was an ideal setting for me.

Mina "Sis" Ullman Lelewer In her mid-thirties

CHAPTER 8
What Do You Do with a Girl?

My father's philosophy for bringing up a daughter came about from a question he put to my mother just after I was born: "But, what do you do with a girl?"

"The same as you do with a boy," she answered.

Her answer was her first gift to me for it determined much of the richness of my early life. It was an extremely generous gift; so generous that, over time, it may have contributed to the distance that seemed to exist between my mother and me. Both my father and I excelled at sports—Mother did not. I wonder now how difficult it must have been for her to be in a family in which sports played an important role. There were probably times when she felt she was standing on the sidelines of our attention. Looking back, I know that, as I got older, she competed with me for my father's attention. At the time, however, all I knew was that my mother had a smile that lit up a room, that my father adored her and she him, and that I was deeply loved by both of them.

Mother's answer to my father's question settled the issue

once and for all and allowed him to be involved in almost every aspect of my childhood. I became a tomboy who preferred pants and knickers to dresses and skirts. I liked climbing trees. I played in pick-up football games at school, as girls weren't allowed on teams. At home there was carpentry, photography, trains, and chores with my father. No one ever asked whether some particular hobby, game, or chore was appropriate for me as a girl. I could participate in any project my father chose. I loved them all. My father shared all the things he knew with me and made me aware of the world as I grew up.

Sunday was our day for yard work, which my father and I wanted completed before company arrived in the form of Grandma and Grandpa SS, Uncle David, Aunt Madeline and my cousins, or my parents' friends. I usually began my chores with my father's roses. They bloomed outside the bay window near our front door and on the side trellis. It was a constant battle to keep the aphids off them, and it became my responsibility to spray the roses with a terribly smelly mixture my father prepared for me. I don't believe the smell was supposed to drive the aphids away, but I'm not sure why not. I had to take care to spray with the wind so as not to fumigate myself, something I learned the hard way. I took my responsibility quite seriously because my father had won prizes for his roses at the garden club shows in Highland Park, and I was his helper. I still have his first and second place ribbons.

While I sprayed, my father mowed the lawn. When I was done with the roses, I took over the mowing, and my father would trim the edges and weed. I remember that I worked hard to make all my lines straight and not miss a blade of grass as I mowed. In the fall, my father and I would rake up the leaves that were falling everywhere. It also was my job to go up the ladder to clean out the gutters. Although I received a weekly allowance, I was never paid for specific jobs, which led me to say one time when the leaves in the gutters were particularly wet and disgusting, "I should be paid for what I'm doing."

"All right," my father called up, "I'll give you a nickel."

"A quarter, or I'm coming down."

"A quarter? That's a lot."

I stood firm on the ladder.

"Well, okay, a quarter is fine."

I cleaned all the gutters for twenty-five cents and thought I had negotiated a pretty good deal. My father always chuckled over my determination to be paid and liked telling the story to my children.

If we didn't have relatives or friends visiting, my father and I would play ball, boy style, with a hardball and gloves after chores. As I grew older, he and I would play tennis or go horseback riding together. In the winter, sometimes my father, mother, and I would go ice-skating.

One of my earliest memories is of my father and me tossing large balls back and forth. By the time I was four, I had graduated to a softball and glove. When I was six, my father and I threw hardballs. I can remember my father telling me, "Don't throw it over your shoulder that way like a girl. Throw it more out to the side, and whip it. You'll get more speed and accuracy."

When I was eight, he said, "I'm going to throw it hard at you, so keep your glove up and give it enough distance from your face." I didn't keep it up enough or give it enough space, so I got a shiner.

"Are you all right?" he asked.

It hurt but I wouldn't admit it. "Yes, I'm okay."

"Then we need to try it again."

That time I was prepared, and my father never threw easy ones after that.

In those days, everyone, except the first baseman, wore gloves that were small versions of a catcher's mitt, which has a pocket in the palm of the hand. This was the kind of glove I had to catch a baseball. Later, gloves changed to resemble the modern fielder's glove. You caught the ball in the section of the glove that extends beyond the thumb and fingers. My father taught me how to throw a fastball and knuckle ball, but when I got older, I had to play on girls' teams where pitching was underhand. Although I was quite good at underhand pitching and did pitch some, I played third base more frequently because, thanks also to my father, I was one of the few girls who could field balls and throw on the run from third to first.

As for batting, well, I had plenty of batting practice too. Some Sundays after chores, my father and I would find an unused baseball diamond and he would pitch endless balls to me.

"Hold the bat up higher."

"You took your eye off the ball on that last one."

"Remember to keep your feet still before you hit the ball."

"Keep watching the ball from the time it leaves the pitcher's hand until your bat hits it."

"Don't forget to follow through."

"Where were you trying to hit that ball?"

It may have the ring of boot camp to some, but I had a wonderful time. After I had hit all the balls, my father would move to first base. It would be my job to pick up each ball and wing each back to him on first base. My father's baseball practice kept me physically fit and healthy and wore me out.

When I was old enough, I joined in the Lelewer tradition

of attending White Sox games at Comiskey Park (now U.S. Cellular Field). My father taught me to keep score by numbers and letters, the way true baseball aficionados do. I filled in little squares and, at the end of the game, recited everything that had happened: "The first batter up grounded out to the short stop (6 - 3), next up got a double (D), then a strike out (K) . . . ." I learned how catchers communicate with pitchers by signaling with their fingers between their legs, and how pitchers respond with a nod if they are going to throw the pitch or shake their head back and forth until the catcher signals a pitch they want to throw. Slowly over time, my father taught me all the rules of the game.

During the height of the men's hat business, vendors at White Sox games in Comiskey Park wore jackets and caps supplied by D. Lelewer & Son. On the back of a jacket was "Wear a Lelewer Hat." Mr. Conahan, head of the concession department, liked my father and, in return for the jackets and caps, gave my father terrific free seats. Mr. Conahan also gave him a White Sox uniform. My father had always wanted a uniform, so when Mr. Conahan was able to procure one for him, my father was thrilled and wore it whenever he could.

A friend of my parents, Isie Policheck, who lived in Milwaukee, invited my parents to a formal dinner party that included the entire Milwaukee Braves team dressed in tuxedos. My father wore his White Sox uniform, and the Braves players thought he really was a White Sox player! My father had great fun at that party, and Isie Policheck never forgot it. Eventually moths got into his uniform and made it unwearable. Fortunately, he acquired another one, which was, again, his pride and joy.

In the fall, my parents and I would attend football games at Northwestern University. Since my parents had season tickets, we went to every game the team played in Evanston. It was at

*1987, Joseph Lelewer, age eighty-one, wearing his
White Sox baseball uniform with his daughter Nancy
Sarasota, Florida*

these games that my father taught me the positions, plays, and penalties, explained the responsibilities of the players, and taught me the scoring of the game. To this day, I have a lot of respect for the intelligence and skill it takes to play professional football. I also have fond memories of the hotdogs we bought at the "Garbage Hotdog Stand," which stood just outside the stadium. The hotdogs were delicious and huge on enormous buns with shredded lettuce, mayo, ketchup, onions, pickles, relish, mustard, and who knew what else piled on top. When it got really cold, we would take along a thermos of hot tomato soup to sip during games. Between the soup and the hotdogs, we had a veritable feast.

My father also introduced me to tennis and horseback riding when I was young. On Sundays and daily during vacations, we would play tennis together anywhere we could find a court— on indoor courts, public courts, at country clubs, and at friends' homes. On Sundays, we would often play on the clay court of the Bensingers, a wealthy Chicago couple who were friends of my parents. We would park in their driveway, walk past the large greenhouse and rows of flower gardens, and arrive at the court. We all wore white, except for Linda Bensinger, who wore wildly colorful skirts and tops and a ribbon in her hair. It seemed to me she was always beautiful, peppy, and fun. After a while, I noticed that whenever she arrived late, someone would give up a place on the court for her, which she would accept with a nod. I finally realized that this vast domain was hers after she invited several of us to stay for a swim and lunch.

Both my father and I loved the freedom we felt when we went horseback riding. We loved the wind in our faces and the beautiful, powerful animals we rode. My father had ridden horses since childhood. One day we had just returned to the stable and

Nancy waiting for her father to mount

were sitting quietly side by side on our horses when a horse and rider trotted into the stable. The horse sharply grazed the rear of my father's horse, which shot into the air. My father grabbed the reins so hard, the horse fell on top of him. My father rolled in one direction, and the horse rolled in the other. I quickly dismounted and held my father's head in my hands as he lay on the ground. His body was motionless. An ambulance was called and people milled about, talking loudly. I was terrified until my father regained consciousness a few minutes before the ambulance arrived. He was okay, but he never rode again.

Sports were not the only thing my father introduced me to. Sometimes, before an afternoon visit with Grandma and Grandpa SS in Chicago, my father would take my mother and me to visit a museum or to look at the city's architecture or to walk, after going into the city, to my father's favorite sculpture.

From the time he was eleven years old until my parents left Chicago, my father loved to visit the sculpture, *The Fountain of Time*. The piece had been designed by the sculptor Lorado Taft and still stands in Midway Plaisance, a strip of land joining Washington Park at its west end and Jackson Park at its east end. The sculpture is a 100-foot long, undulating work that brilliantly illustrates the passage of time by depicting humanity first as an infant, then as middle aged, and finally, as old. In the back of the sculpture, the artist included a self-portrait among the figures. A cloaked figure representing Father Time observes the line of humanity flowing past. The idea for the sculpture came from a line of a poem by Henry Austin Dobsin: "Time goes, you say? Ah no! Alas, time stays, we go."

Many times we would go to the Museum of Science and Industry, the only building remaining from the Columbian Exposition of 1893. When I was a child, I loved to go into the coal mine. I also loved to watch the miniature trains as they whistled and zoomed under bridges and through mountain passes and to visit the street of yesteryear, which had nickelodeons, cobblestone streets, and silent movies. When I was a teenager, the museum unveiled its exhibit of the U-505, a German U-boat captured in 1944. Visitors were allowed to climb into the sub and explore its interior; something I found fascinating. The museum was a wonderland.

Other times, we would go to the Art Institute and wander through the rooms. As a small child, I especially loved the Thorne Rooms, which were miniatures of European and American rooms in different ages and eras. Our explorations of the city usually ended at Snider's where hot fudge sundaes were served in tall, V-shaped metal dishes, and there were individual glass pitchers of hot fudge sauce.

When I was young, seeing what my father pointed out in the city was secondary to the joy I felt walking between my parents and sometimes being swung back and forth like a swing. As I grew older, however, I became fascinated with Chicago's fabulous architectural history. One Sunday as my father pointed out different buildings, I looked long and hard at one particular building—the London Guarantee building, which had been designed by Alfred S. Alshuler, a friend of my grandfather. I recognized the name immediately because we knew Al and Helene Alshuler who lived on our road. My father explained that Al, with whom we often played tennis, was the son of Alfred S. Alshuler. Eventually Al gave me a key to their tennis court, and I was allowed to bring a friend to the court any time. The Alshulers had fabulous annual Fourth of July parties filled with kids of all ages, yummy food, and lots of excitement.

When we did not go into the city, my parents and I loved

to walk along the Lake Michigan shoreline. The beach was only two blocks from our home. I would zigzag from the high bluff down the sandy path to the beach avoiding the many large tree roots. My parents would take the wooden stairs. In autumn, when the leaves had turned to high color, we would go to a nearby forest preserve. One year my father had me collect leaves from many different trees and bushes, mostly maple and oak but also a few elm leaves. Later, we made scrapbooks. I can still remember the streams we passed, the lovely large beds of green moss—as pretty as any lawn—mushrooms sprouting all around, and chipmunks and squirrels dashing into shrubs and hollowed out tree trunks.

On some of our outings, we would take a blanket and food, and my father would cook hamburgers over a fire. My father was always careful about campfires in a forest. Once after lunch, however, my father thought he had put out our campfire, and we went off to another trail, but, when we got back, we found the area and nearby bushes ablaze. There were no cell phones then. My father tossed the car keys to my mother: "Please find a phone, and call the fire department." Mother rushed to the car as my father and I tried to contain the fire. It was a long time before he could forgive himself for somehow leaving a spark alive from our campfire.

For all of our outdoor adventures, my father was again my educational tour guide, "The oak tree sheds all its broad leaves and reproduces by making thousands of acorns once a year in the fall…" "They don't start making acorns until they reach the age of twenty, and they live for over 200 years…" "Trees take in water through their roots. A mature oak can drink more than fifty gallons of water in a day."

He told me the elms were dying from a fungus called

Dutch-Elm Disease, and that made me treasure the elm leaves I found. "They die of a rapidly spreading disease," he said, "that starves the leaves of water." He told me about squirrels, and, to this day, I am fascinated that their bushy tails are about the same length as their bodies. I still remember that their front teeth grow throughout their lives, but that gnawing nuts files them down. "Tell Mom or me immediately if a squirrel or any other little creature should scratch or bite you as they may have rabies," my father warned me, and, in time, I passed those words on to my children.

My mother's response to my father's question—her gift to me—opened the world to me. Under my father's tutelage, I learned to enjoy adventures, to try new things, to never give up, to ask any question I wanted, and to never let someone tell me I couldn't do something because I was a girl. No matter what my question, my father always made me feel it was important, and gave me an answer I could understand.

CHAPTER 9
Elementary Daze

Braeside Elementary School, which ran from kindergarten through eighth grade, was very different from the cold, foreboding, factory-like exteriors of most elementary schools in my youth. Braeside had been designed in 1928 by John Van Bergen, a Highland Park resident and associate of Frank Lloyd Wright. The school, with its low-pitched, hipped roofs, horizontal bands of windows, wide overhangs, and stone and stucco walls, seemed to nestle into its site. So well designed was it that it was listed in the National Register of Historic Places in 1982.

My mother was my guide to school when I entered Braeside as a kindergartener. Each morning for the first month, she would escort me all the way to school and then walk me home. By the time the second month rolled around, my father insisted Mother go only a block and a half with me to help me cross the intersection where cars came together from two roads and Sheridan Road curved left. "It's a straight shot and she can walk it herself from there. Besides, there will be other children walking on the sidewalk she can join," he said. Mother worried, but did as Dad wished. At the end of my school day, I would find her waiting for me so we could cross the intersection together.

The summer after kindergarten, my parents watched me cross the intersection alone several times. Once they were certain I would be careful crossing the street, I was on my own getting to and from school. I was about to be on my own in the first grade classroom too, but I fortunately didn't know that. With the creative play of kindergarten behind me, my academic career was about to face its first big hurdle.

As I wrote in my book, *SOMETHING'S NOT RIGHT*, Braeside Elementary School, like other schools of the time, followed the "look and say" or whole-word method of teaching reading. Phonics were not taught. Students were expected to recognize individual words, not to sound them out slowly. Every day, flash cards were held up before my first grade class. Each card had a single word printed on it, and the class would read the word in unison. Unfortunately, the cards meant nothing to me. Even after several weeks, the black lines on them were not words to me, just mysterious black squiggles. Since the black squiggles seemed to mean things to my classmates, but not to me, I concluded, in short order, there was something wrong with me. Given my age, it was a perfectly logical conclusion and, I think, speaks well of my intelligence. I knew a person could have a broken arm or leg, so I concluded that a part of my brain—the part that should be able to read—was broken. Once I reached that conclusion, I began to lip-sync whatever the class seemed to be saying. It was pure self-defense. After all, no one can laugh at you or give you pitying looks or call you names if you are saying the same thing everyone else is saying. It also helped that our first-grade reading books had limited vocabularies, short sentences, and simple, colorful pictures. The pictures allowed me to decode the stories: "Oh, Dick! See Spot run. Run, Spot, run."

One morning, my first grade teacher, Miss Meyers, told us we were going to have a reading test, our very first. It was to be a true or false test. I felt myself begin to shake inside. I was absolutely certain everyone in the class knew how to read except for me. I can still remember watching Miss Meyers hand out papers to everyone. I was sure she could see how scared I was. "You can get started as soon as you receive your paper," she said matter-of-factly. We were a small class, perhaps twenty children. I watched the other students, one after another, some even smiling, plunk the test down on their desks, pick up their pencils, and begin to write. Write what? I wondered. What did the words on the page mean? I remember looking up in panic, and there, right in front of me, was the test paper of Stephen Rubin, the best reader in the class. I was tall and didn't even need to stretch to see everything on his desk. I mean everything. Stephen even pressed hard on his pencil so his markings were easy to see: T, F, F, T, F. Thankfully, I knew my letters. T had to mean true; F had to mean false. I paused for only a moment. If I didn't write what I saw in front of me, I'd be a failure. My friends would know I was dumb. My teacher would think so, too. My parents would look at me with make-believe kindly faces, but they would be disappointed too, and I would be able to read their disappointment on their faces.

Given that scenario, I copied Stephen's paper and found myself trapped. I couldn't stop. Fear gripped me daily. Would my teacher catch me cheating? Would Stephen's seat be changed? Would he turn around one day and see me staring at his paper? Would he be out sick when we had a test? That, as well as the pain of being commended on HIS good work, occupied my mind day after day. I was one scared little girl, but still I copied every single reading test that year. They were all multiple choice or true/false exams, all easy on the eyes.

At the end of the year, although we didn't know it when we scattered for summer fun, Miss Meyers was promoted along with the rest of us. When September arrived, she was our second grade teacher and had new teaching methods. At the beginning of the term, she called each second grader in alphabetical order to her desk. When she reached the L's, I trembled.

"Come up and read to me, Nancy," she said pleasantly. I walked to the front of the room, looked at the open book, then glanced at her, wanting to weep. I knew my moment of reckoning had arrived. I had to confess. "I can't read any of the books," I said. To her credit, she didn't even wince. Perhaps she had known all along. I didn't ask.

"Here, dear," she said, "here's a book for you to try." I looked down at an easy picture book. "It's babyish," I thought, "but maybe I'll be able to figure out the words from the pictures." I knew it wouldn't be easy. The other children were given real books and seemed to be busy understanding them as they read. Now I know that at least some of them were faking it, but, back then, I didn't know it. I was sure I was the only one in the entire class who could not read.

Miss Meyers' goal was to individualize our reading instruction so we could go at our own speed. My speed went from unbearably slow to slightly less slow. Following my original plan, I read by memorizing a couple of easy books using the pictures as my guide. Miss Meyers encouraged me to memorize words to keep in my "stockpile" as she called the list of words I could recognize. I plodded along learning a few more words each time and even a few word attack skills, but I was unsure of myself when it came to reading and remained so as I completed the upper grades. It took me hours to complete an assignment, but at least cheating was a thing of the past.

I certainly did not know the condition that made me feel different from all my friends and made it difficult for me to learn reading skills had a name, dyslexia. Today, most people are familiar with the term. In those days, however, almost no one spoke of dyslexia or of differences in how children learn.

Although the whole–word method for learning to read was used in almost every school system, the whole-word method did not, and does not, work for dyslexics. Indeed, it does not work well for most children. Ironically, my mother, who had been trained as a primary school teacher and had been taught letter sounds, parts of speech, and how to diagram a sentence when she was in elementary school, probably could have used her skills to help me if there had been some understanding of what was needed.

When my parents were told about my dyslexia by the school, they were cautioned not to mention it to me. It was to be kept a secret probably because it was thought that it would damage my self-esteem if I was told I had a learning problem. How could I not know? I knew I couldn't read the way others did, but, and here was the crux of the issue, there was an unacknowledged belief by many school professionals at the time that the term dyslexia was simply a polite way of saying "not too bright." I am sure those of us with dyslexia back then taught at least a generation of teachers just how mistaken their understanding of dyslexia was.

Because no one really understood what dyslexia involved, my parents took me to an eye specialist who prescribed a gadget for me to look through. The gadget had a picture of a bird in front of one eye and a picture of a bird cage in front of the other. Each afternoon, as I looked through the gadget, I was to maneuver it back and forth until I saw the bird in the bird cage. My mother tried the gadget first. "I did it," she said. "Now, you do it, too." She handed the gadget to me.

I maneuvered the gadget madly but could not get the bird into the cage. "Really, Mom, it isn't," I said. Mother was distinctly unhappy with my response. That look was not hard to read. My father came home from work and was put to the same task.

"The bird is NOT in the cage," he said. "We are going back to that doctor and returning his useless gadget." All of us returned to the specialist only to learn what my father and I already knew, the gadget wasn't working. We never returned. The doctor's gadget might have been helpful for strabismus (cross eye or wall eye) or amblyopia (complete or partial loss of vision in one eye) problems, but it did nothing for dyslexia. Perhaps my mother had one of these visual disorders although she always appeared to see well.

I tromped home for lunch every day in my early school years even when the Chicago winds swept about me and snow filled my high, yellow rubber boots. At home, I would quickly shed my outerwear and then join my mother in the dining room for lunch or eat in the kitchen where Kazu Okata, my favorite maid, would serve me. I would sit at the counter on a shiny, high stool like the ones at the ice cream parlor, and eat soup and sandwiches with potato chips and coleslaw or potato salad. In winter, I had hot ham-and-cheese or fried egg sandwiches or leftovers. My favorite lunch, often made to please me, was a hot roast beef sandwich with mild horseradish sauce. Afterward, fortified and ready, I would race back to school.

I was, undeniably, a tomboy in those early years of my schooling, in part because I was my father's daughter, but also in part because even my favorite subject, arithmetic, created a need for subterfuge. If I wanted to do well in math on a day when my mother planned for me to wear a skirt without pockets, I would quickly don pants or my cousin's old knickers, call out a hasty goodbye, and slip out the door. Why? With pockets I could use my fingers to calculate. That time-honored tactile method was not allowed when I was in elementary school. I could excel in arithmetic only when I wore clothing with ample pockets to hide my busily counting fingers. Unfortunately, most little girls were expected to wear dresses or skirts and blouses in elementary school in the 1940s and 1950s, not pants or knickers. My mother let me know when she felt pants were not appropriate.

To be sure, I had plenty of pretty skirts and dresses. She and I made frequent trips to her dressmaker, Carol Morano. Mrs. Morano was a tiny, kindly woman with a twinkle in her eyes and a jagged row of pins between her teeth. She had a plaque on the wall that I always loved.

A friend is one who understands
What's in the heart of you,
Who stands for all your little faults
Because they're part of you.

As I turned around and around, she would patiently pin and then hem my clothing. Later, when I was in college, she would take my clothing in and out at the seams depending upon the time of year—slender going off to school, pudgy coming home.

Looking back, it seems to me that Mrs. Morano's plaque expressed the essence of my years at Braeside Elementary School. Braeside practiced the latest educational theories not all of which were as disastrous as the whole–word method of reading. Although it was a public school, it had all the features of a private school, including small classes. There were even a large number of audio-visual materials. True, they were a far cry from today's sophisticated materials, but they were novel for our time. The school also had a supply store right next to the principal's office. Students ran the store, which sold pencils, pens, and paper, among other things.

Our curriculum included art, music, chorus, band, woodworking, physical education, square dancing, ballroom dancing, and weekly all-school assemblies that enriched the school's strong academic core. As I progressed from first grade to second to third to fourth, real-life experiences were added to our studies. We were imbued with the spirit of Chicago through field trips to the big city. My classmates and I loved Chicago; I still do. To us, Chicago was the hub of the United States and represented everything that was American.

We were fascinated to hear about the city's humble beginnings. I can still remember learning in the early grades that Chicago had been just a portage between Lake Michigan and the Illinois River when Louis Joliet, a French fur trader and explorer, realized it could be a major transportation center. We were taught that his idea was to build canals that would link Chicago to major waterways throughout the country. He even envisioned the Great Lakes linked to the Mississippi River, and the Atlantic Ocean linked to the Gulf of Mexico through a system of lakes, rivers, and canals. Even though the system of canals Joliet envisioned was never built, railroads were, and we learned how they helped Chicago to become the Midwest's most vital city. Situated between New York and San Francisco, Indiana and Wisconsin, Chicago, we were told, connected the wheat fields and cattle ranches of the far west to the large cities of the east. We knew Chicago was, in Carl Sandburg's words:

Hog Butcher for the World,
Tool Maker, Stacker of Wheat,
Player with Railroads and the Nation's Freight Handler . . .
The city of Big Shoulders . . .

During my years at Braeside, my classmates and I visited almost everything that made our city great. We went to the Field Museum and to the Museum of Science and Industry. Both had many hands-on exhibits. We loved the beeps and other sounds that would emanate from the displays. We would huddle around them cheering our friends on as we waited our turn. One year, we went to the Board of Trade Building, which, at a height of 650 feet, was the tallest building in Chicago at the time. We were told to view its Art Deco design as a kind of artistic geometry. A statue of Ceres, goddess of grain, was placed at the top of the building. To this day I can remember being told the sculptor assumed no building would ever be tall enough for people to view the statue closely and therefore he never sculpted the goddess' face. Now, the building is surrounded by other tall buildings in the Loop, and people can easily see the goddess is faceless.

I also have never forgotten watching the Donnelley printing presses at the Time/Life Building. I still can see and hear in my mind the gargantuan presses rolling out newspapers and magazines. We were amazed by the size and speed of the presses and even more amazed when we learned that the ink dried on contact. Since then, I have never seen a *Life Magazine*, one of the most popular magazines of my day, without thinking of the

Donnelley presses churning them out with glorious photos and stories, page after page flashing by in seconds.

At the Tribune Tower, we visited a radio station with the call letters WGN, World's Greatest Newspaper. As we were children and, thus, quite literal minded, we thought these were strange call letters for a radio station. Once we learned how inventive the station had been since the *Chicago Tribune* (the "World's Greatest Newspaper") had assumed control of station WJAZ and turned it into WGN in 1924, we didn't care about the name. WGN—720 AM on the radio dial—was first to broadcast the World Series, the Indianapolis 500, and the Kentucky Derby. It had even placed microphones in the courtroom during the famous 1925 Scopes "monkey trial" in Tennessee.

At some point during these years, my classmates and I also visited the commodities market. We had a wonderful guide who kept us enthralled for the entire visit with the history of the market and explanations of the trades that were taking place. He explained to us how each farm had originally had its own grain elevator (storage facility for grain). As Chicago grew, these elevators were taking up valuable land needed for other kinds of buildings. It finally occurred to someone to build a few huge grain elevators to replace the individual ones. Farmers deposited their grain in the big elevators, separating the grain according to quality and kind. Slips of paper were used to record the quantity and kind of grain deposited, as well as the elevator in which the grain was held. These slips of paper were often then traded or sold. Soon, other crops, and even cattle, were handled the same way, which gave birth to the commodities market.

I remember we all were intrigued with the language of the traders, which was made up of hand and finger movements that we couldn't understand. Our guide isolated some of the motions and explained the meaning of each so we could understand what was going on. I recall watching a trader place a bid, another trader come in to take it, and still another top the first one to get the commodity. The whole transaction took only a few seconds!

As I neared the end of my years at Braeside, there was one trip that really jolted me—our trip to the Chicago stockyards. Chicago was the center of the meat industry. In fact, the first state-of-the-art refrigerated railroad cars were developed to ship beef from Chicago to the East Coast. An incredible production and distribution network then followed. At that time, I wasn't familiar with Upton Sinclair's 1906 muckraking book, *The Jungle*, about working conditions at the stockyards in the early 1900s. I didn't know what to expect, and I didn't know when I felt cold and was shivering if it was because of the refrigeration or because of the process I was witnessing. I couldn't even decide if I felt worse for the steer or for the blood-stained workers who had to split, cut, and carry the beef.

As I stood there, steers were clubbed on the head, passed under scalding water, lifted by their rear hooves, and attached to an overhead conveyor belt. One man, holding an enormous curved knife, slit the front of the cow, spilling its innards onto a conveyor belt moving just below the animal. Men standing alongside the conveyor belt sorted through the innards and removed the parts that could be used. The remainder was moved by conveyor belt to a grinding machine. After grinding, the meat was squeezed into a tube of skin and became a sausage or hotdog. According to our guide, the process was so smooth the side of beef we were looking at would soon be in New York, having traveled all the way on the same hook. I'm not sure we believed the guide, but the enormous refrigerator we were standing in left us too cold to discuss the issue. I must say it was a long time before I wanted a hotdog after I saw the stockyards.

Still, the shock of the stockyards was balanced by other Braeside events that year. It wasn't just Braeside's curriculum that made the school outstanding. The strong Braeside PTA, which my father and mother joined when I began school, made sure we had all the things we needed to grow into well-rounded young people. Our school had playgrounds, ball fields, and a large outdoor ice-skating rink—something that probably cannot be found at almost any other public school today. A one-room log cabin known as the "warming house" stood next to the rink and offered some protection from the brutal winter cold. We would sit on the benches close to the warmth of the Franklin stove to put on our skates. Once outside, the sounds of the waltzes played on the Victrola filled the air as we skimmed along on the ice.

My father taught me everything he knew about skating when I was quite young. In first grade, I raced the length of the rink at full speed and came to a dead stop wherever I pleased. As I grew a bit older, my friends and I played hockey and games such as Red Rover, Red Rover. For some, the excitement was in playing the games. For me, the thrill was always in winning. A few times, when the roads were icy, we actually skated to school. By that time, skating had become as easy as walking. As I entered my teens, I enjoyed carving figure eights and spinning figure threes. I loved the romantic quality of ballet-like movements on ice, and I was especially happy when a boy I liked would ask me to skate with him. I remember one snowy evening my father dragged our Christmas tree from the house, roped it into the trunk of the car, and then drove it to Braeside to place it next to the other trees already standing along the periphery of our rink. These trees, brought by caring PTA parents, helped to act as a windbreak as we sailed around and around the rink.

Many years later after I was married, I would go skating in winter on a pond at a farm owned by my father-in-law. At Braeside, the circle of ice had welcomed and challenged me, but the farm pond held little excitement. Perhaps it was because you can never recapture the excitement of your youth or because the skaters were not skilled enough to play the games I knew, and stared at me when I carved a figure eight or spun a three. They may have thought I was showing off. Certainly, I never meant to. In any case, the farm was sold before I got skates on my daughter, Kathy. Later, all four of my children took skating lessons, but I'm not sure they ever experienced the joy of whizzing and twirling around that my friends and I did at Braeside.

Once a year, the Braeside PTA would sponsor a field day, which was made up of a variety of track and field events—races, the shot put, the high jump, and the long jump. I won a ribbon in every girl's competition I entered. By the end of my Braeside school years, my ribbon collection covered several pages in my scrapbook which, along with my elementary, high-school, and college school papers and diplomas, ended up as casualties of one of my parents' moves after I had married.

As part of my extracurricular activities, I joined the Brownies and, at the appropriate time, "flew up" to become a Girl Scout. I was proud to wear my Brownie Girl Scout pin and uniform. I remember earning many patches, including one for learning about life on a prairie and another for magic tricks. Not surprisingly, one of my all-time favorite activities that I actually earned a patch for doing successfully was making chocolate/marshmallow s'mores on a campfire. As a Girl Scout, I sort of earned a patch in stargazing. Looking like a sea of pea green in the fading light, my fellow Girl Scouts and I stood outside one evening, and when darkness fell, were asked to "Point to the North Star and Big and Little Dipper." I didn't have a clue. The body language of the girl in front of me, however, suggested she had some idea of where to look, so I pointed in the same direction she pointed, diagonally to the right. Funny thing, a moment later, I realized she had pointed in exactly the same direction as the girl before her. All of us received the badge—I wonder how many real stargazers there were and how many piggy backers. About ten years after gaining my stargazing patch, I finally learned about the sky and could even recite the constellations.

Pretty pastel skirts, matching sweaters, and saddle shoes or penny loafers with copper pennies kept perennially shiny were de rigueur for the girls at Braeside when I was in school, but, then, pennies still bought something when I was young. Penny candy shops sold malted milk balls, wax lips, candy buttons, dots, Necco wafers, and more, all for a penny each. As we went through the elementary grades together, we became a close-knit group. Somewhat surprisingly, an eighth grade reunion forty-six years later refreshed and reawakened some of our long-ago friendships. We may no longer wear the outfits we wore when we were young, but many Braeside classmates are still good friends. We send e-mails, make phone calls, and send snapshots of the past or present from computer to computer.

It was at a class reunion that I discovered there had been other children in my first grade class who could not read. I didn't ask how they got through their school years. It seems we all struggled in our own ways. What we all did remember, however, was how difficult we'd made the lives of our substitute teachers. There was that unforgettable and massive spitball fight that occurred on one substitute teacher's watch, as well as a number of other things. We relished handing out torture to these unsuspecting teachers whose only sin was that of being there. One male class-mate remembered being held by the shoulders and shaken for what seemed to be two minutes after some particularly devious activity. Once the substitute had stopped shaking him, my class-mate had said to the whole class, "Now I know what a milkshake feels like." That announcement got him summarily shut in the cloakroom. The cloakroom was the narrow class clothes closet that ran almost the length of one side of the classroom and had no windows. Today, no teacher would be allowed to shut a child in a closet, and I am glad it never happened to me. Still, the boys who were shut in the closet didn't seem to mind. I suppose every generation has its own macho code. For us, it was the cloakroom closet.

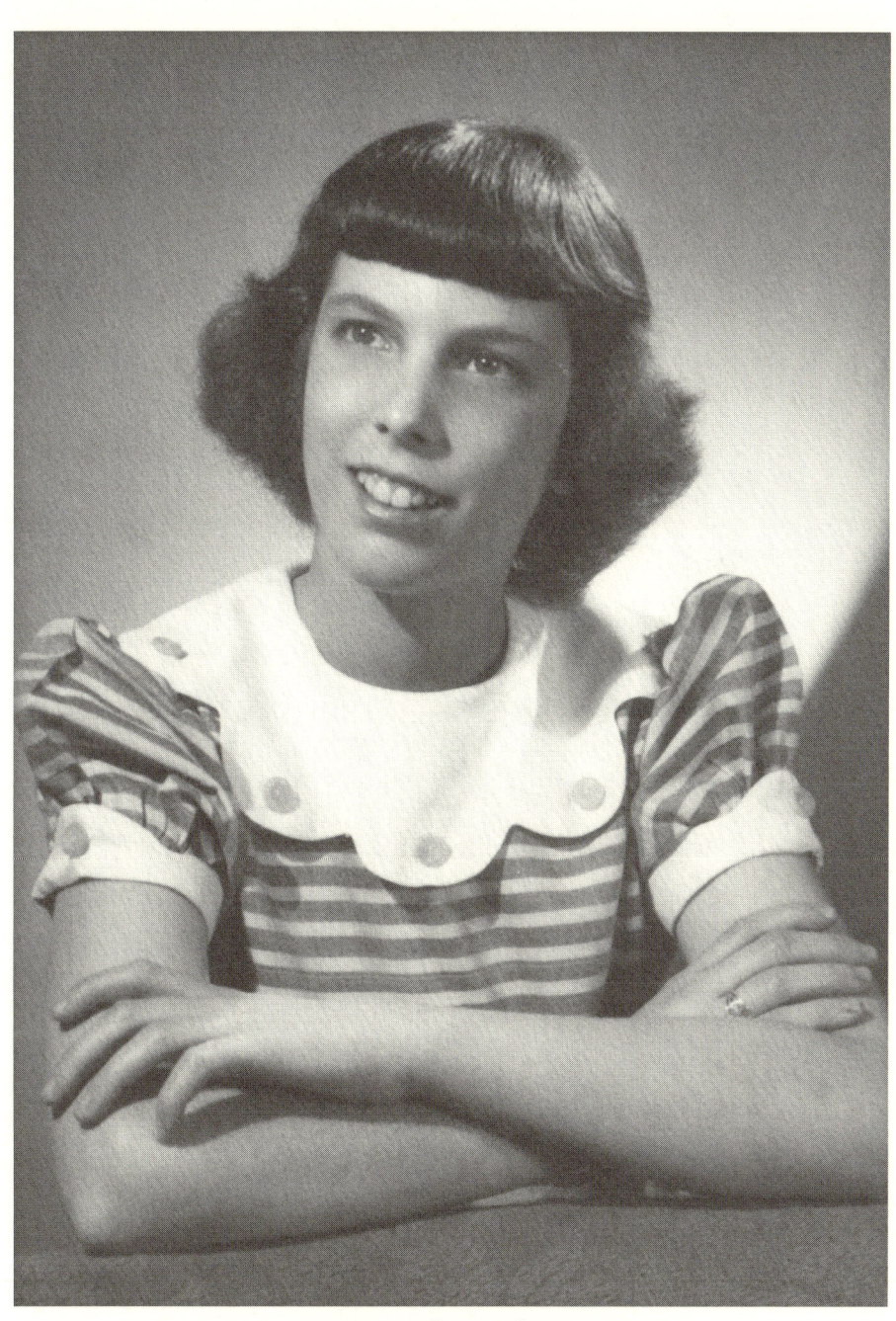

Nancy Ullman Lelewer
May 1947, age 12 years
Highland Park, Illinois

CHAPTER 10
Warm Weather Vacations: The Tradition Continues

The moment I saw what it took to deliver bananas to an awaiting boat, I knew I'd never look at that fruit in the same way. Men with dark, glistening skin, walking tall, carried the huge stalks on their heads up the gangplank, stalks facing forward. At the gunnel of the boat, each carrier turned sharply. Another man with a machete in hand slashed off the stalks, the cutting edge of the machete slashing just past the nose of the carrier. With one THWACK the bananas dropped into a net in the hold, and the stalks fell into the water.

I sat transfixed in a small, open boat in Jamaica with my mother and father and the boat captain. I was nine years old, and it was midnight, long past my bedtime. My parents had said I could stay up if I took an afternoon nap. I had agreed, so here I was awe-struck by the process and the beauty of the night. The sky was clear with a bright full moon making it easy to watch the loading process. When I looked up for a moment, there was a startlingly intimate view of stars filling the sky.

Year after year when I was young, winter brought me wonderful adventures. Following the tradition established by Grandpa SS, my father and mother would vacation in a warm climate for two to four weeks each year, and I often accompanied them. Thus, at some point during Chicago's brutal winters, I would be taken out of school and whisked away to some place warm much to the envy of some of my friends. Just because I was not in Braeside, however, did not mean that I was not in school. Following the tradition established by Grandpa SS, my parents made sure I spent out-of-school mornings in private schools or with tutors, but afternoons and evenings were different. They were filled with experiences that only travel can provide. Afternoons were for the beach, for taking dance lessons, or for going on educational excursions arranged by my father.

In second grade, I briefly deserted Miss Meyers and Braeside for Sarasota, Florida. I attended the Out-Of-Door Academy (founded in 1924), with another eight-year-old, a boy named Peter. I remember being told that Peter and his mother had come to Sarasota from London to escape the war. As an American second grader, World War II and the bombing of Britain meant little to me. What I did know was that Peter and I were friends and happily immersed in the life we were leading at that moment. I do recall thinking that the clipped way in which he and his mother spoke was funny. It was, after all, the first time I'd heard a British accent.

Each morning, Peter and I would take the bus to school together and join the other children around the flagpole to say the Pledge of Allegiance and the Lord's Prayer. That was followed with our individualized studies until our morning school program ended. On the bus ride home, we would work on our assignments and chatter about the upcoming afternoon fun at the beach with our families. Peter never said anything about the war, and I never asked him anything. To me, he was simply going to a different school for a while, just as I was.

Our winter trip to Jamaica when I was nine was memorable. Not only did I see the banana boats being loaded at the unheard of hour of midnight, I also helped my parents make new friends, and got to visit a local school in Montego Bay as they hunted for a place for me to attend school. As I recall, the Jamaican public school system was in its infancy when we were there that year. I remember a few of the children were nude, all were black, and we couldn't understand much of what the teacher was saying. There were only four desks in the classroom—two on the far right, one behind the other, and two on the far left in the same arrangement. A wide board was nailed to the seat of each of the two desks on the right side and spanned the distance between those seats and the seats of the two desks on the left side. Another wide board was secured to the slanted desktops in each row. The children sat on the flat board and used the slanted board to hold their slates while writing. No one used paper or pencils, and we saw few books.

For those reasons, I was provided with a private tutor who helped me with my academic work and also taught me to tap dance using Coke bottle tops held between my toes to make the tapping noise. Coke bottles had metal caps with crimped edges then, so they could make a good tapping noise. Remembering that particular bit of winter education always makes me smile. I like to think my feet could perform the dance even now, although, in reality, they probably can't.

It was while I was playing on the beach during this trip that I got to know Milt and Ilsa Doner who were from Michigan. I introduced them to my parents, and the four adults became good friends. Near the end of their trip, Ilsa became seriously ill. At the time, I didn't know what was wrong with her, but I knew she could hardly walk, and my father and Milt frequently made phone calls on her behalf. On the last day of their stay, my father and Milt carried Ilsa onto the plane. When my father got back to the hotel, I heard him tell my mother that he was going to take a shower and wash all his clothes. Years later I learned that Ilsa had malaria, and at that time, probably because there were few, if any, antimalarial drugs it was illegal to enter the United States with the illness. I don't know how they managed it. Once she was home, however, Ilsa got the appropriate treatment, and my parents and the Doners continued to see one another. Over the years, they got together in Illinois, Michigan, and eventually Longboat Key in Florida where they all spent their winters.

There are at least three other things that stand out in my memory of our trip to Jamaica that year. The first is a trip to a refinery that my father arranged so I could learn how rum was made and how sugar cane became sugar. I can recall the stench of the refinery to this day. It was terrible. The second is Jamaica's phosphorescent lake. If the scent of the refinery was awful, the glow of everything that moved in the lake was magical. Every movement of the fish created a blaze of light and color. The wake of our boat produced a huge brightness. When I put my hand in the water, it too lit up. I remember looking up at my parents and seeing the brightness of their smiles as they gazed down at me. The third is the soup I had for lunch at our hotel restaurant one day. As soon as I put my spoon in my cup, I noticed the bugs in the soup. I had been taught to use good manners and to eat everything placed before me, but bugs seemed excessive.

"Dad, there are bugs in my soup," I said.

"They won't eat much," he assured me.

"I don't like them."

"Then, eat around them," was the response, which is what I did.

In other winters, there were other trips. Several times we went to Miami Beach and visited with both sets of grandparents who liked to spend their winters there. And there was a fabulous trip to Cuba when I was a freshman in college. Of course, that was before Fidel Castro's time. Still, I'm not sure anything ever equaled our winter vacation in Hawaii when I turned fourteen.

We began our trip by traveling from Chicago to San Francisco. In San Francisco, we boarded the Matson Line's Lurline and sailed for Honolulu. It was the beginning of March, 1948 and I turned fourteen during the crossing. Our first evening on the ship, a man I'd never seen before came over to our table. My father introduced him to us as Chic.

"Would you and your wife like to meet us in the bar for a drink after all the children are put to bed?" he asked my father.

"Sure," my father replied.

My mother smiled as Chic and my father spoke, but I could tell she didn't know who Chic was any more than I did. After he left, she turned to my father and asked, "Who is he? Do you know him?"

"I met him when I was standing in line to get our room keys," my father answered. "He introduced himself by saying, 'Hi, I'm Chic, as in chicken,' so I said, 'Glad to meet you, Chic. I'm Joe, as in coat of many colors.' That was our whole conversation, dear."

That night, after I went to bed, my parents met Chic and his wife in the bar. Chic asked Mother to dance, and while they were dancing, she asked what he did for a living. When they returned to the table, she said to my father, "Chic's in the newspaper business."

Dad turned to him and said, "Chic, I sell hats but you don't look like the kind of guy who stands around selling newspapers. What do you really do?"

"I'm traveling incognito," Chic replied. "I write and draw the Blondie cartoon."

That was the start of a truly amazing trip.

Chic Young had begun drawing the famous, and some-times infamous, syndicated Blondie cartoons in 1930. After his death in 1973, his son, Dean Young, who was also on the trip, continued the strip. When Chic began the strip, Blondie was Blondie Boopadoop, a flapper with a bumbling but nice boyfriend named Dagwood Bumstead. Dagwood loved sandwiches that were as large as his head piled with endless fillings and downed with a frankfurter. In the comic strip, Dagwood's father owned all the property on the right side of the track, all the property on the wrong side of the track, and all 3,000 miles of the track itself! As the Great Depression wore on, Chic changed his story line to give it relevance to a weary, struggling audience. Blondie and Dagwood married, and Dagwood was disinherited. They lived in a rented house like everyone else, Dagwood took a bus to work, and they rarely went out for entertainment. Still, love conquered all—Baby Dumpling and Cookie were born to them. When I was young, everyone read and loved Blondie.

Chic was a jokester, and we had an inside peek at his wit while we were on that vacation. We were staying at the Royal Hawaiian Hotel, which was also known as Hawaii's Pink Palace of the Pacific. Chic, his wife, and their two children were at a condo a block away. One morning, we received a notice, seemingly signed by the management, that read, "Please don't hang your dirty laundry on the deck, the neighbors are complaining."

Chic the jokester, however, met his match in my father, who quickly guessed just who had sent the notice. When the two families got together at the beach later that day, nothing was said about the notice. The next morning, we received another notice from the "management": "Please cut your toenails. They are tearing our sheets to shreds."

After breakfast, my father had my mother and me cut our toenails and place the clippings in an envelope, which he then addressed to Mr. Chic Young. The envelope was delivered to the mailbox at their condo. Again, we spent the day together on the beach. Again, no mention was made of our notice from the "management." In fact, no mention was made of either the notices or the clippings until we met the Youngs in Los Angeles on our return from Hawaii. Chic and his wife had been kind enough to take our luggage home for us on the ship so we could stay in Hawaii for another few weeks and then fly back to Los Angeles. On our return, they met us at the LA airport and took us to their home where we retrieved our trunks.

"Joe," Chic said at that point, "We loved your joke. My children have even saved your toenails." At that point, we all exploded with laughter, but we didn't ask for proof.

As in previous years, I was tutored during vacation so I would not fall behind in my work. My tutor lived on the edge of Hickam Field, which is the U.S. Air Force base in Honolulu. Every morning I would take the bus to her house for lessons. After about an hour of work, I would get restless. My tutor would give me some juice or fresh pineapple and promise to tell me about the Japanese bombing of Hickam Field and Pearl Harbor after I had finished my work. I would go back to work for a while longer, and then she would point out where the Japanese planes had come zooming in and describe what it looked like when the bombs began to fall. World War II became real to me only after I saw Pearl Harbor and heard my tutor's stories of the attack. Prior to that, like many young people of my era, I thought primarily in terms of valiant allies overcoming all odds.

As my interest in Pearl Harbor and Hickam Field grew, my father decided we should take a tour of the naval base. What I saw at Pearl Harbor will always be with me—large craters in the earth where bombs had fallen, barbed wire along the beach, huge ships cut in two and lying at peculiar angles in the water. My father, looking uncharacteristically grim as he spoke, explained that the Japanese raid on December 7, 1941 was a defining moment in United States history. A single, carefully planned, surprise bombing of the U.S. Navy's fleet had thrust the country abruptly into the war with a severely weakened naval force. My father told me about President Roosevelt's impassioned radio speech about the day as " . . . a date that shall live in infamy." Later I heard this speech on a recording of great speeches my father owned.

I remember my father telling me that Grandpa SS had brought the Herbert Lelewer family to Chicago from Berlin just before Hitler slammed the door shut on Jews trying to leave Germany. Although I had heard that 6 million Jews had died in concentration camps, I was shocked when my father said that Roosevelt had known about the camps, but had done nothing to help the millions in them.

As we stared at the harbor, my father told me, "The war years were a time of great patriotism with signs and banners everywhere. People rallied around the cause. Young men wanted to defend their country and volunteered to go to war. Some women enlisted as well, and served as noncombatants in the Army

WAC's and Navy WAVES. Your Mom worked at the nearby USO twice a week."

"How come you didn't have to go fight?" I asked

"I was classified 1-A. Eventually I was called up. I asked for a six-month extension to get my business in order, and it was granted. During the six months, I had a birthday which put me over the age limit of men they were taking into the service who were married with a child."

Although my father and most Americans believed the attack on Pearl Harbor was a surprise, some historians claim there is evidence that Roosevelt knew an attack was imminent and let it happen. These historians argue that the attack allowed Franklin Delano Roosevelt to enter World War II with the support of the nation, which, until then, had been divided on the issue of involvement.

As part of our tour, my parents and I were taken to a building several stories high where sailors trained for the most dangerous scenario they might face in the navy, finding their way out of a damaged, submerged submarine. As I can recall, they were required to climb up a knotted rope, knot by knot, counting carefully before moving up a knot so as not to come up too quickly and get the bends. I could only imagine how difficult that would be in an emergency.

By the end of our tour, I was glad to return to the beauty of the Royal Hawaiian. I never ceased to be amazed by the flora and fauna surrounding the Royal Hawaiian. It was a tropical paradise of brilliant and luminous flowers I had never seen before. At least once a day, a fresh-cut pineapple tucked inside a whole pineapple was placed in each room. Whenever I lifted the top of the pineapple, I would find it filled with pieces of pineapple about the size of my middle finger. Their sweetness was a perpetual treat.

The hotel's outdoor luncheon was a buffet with intricate, exquisite ice sculptures on the tables. Every kind of salad, seafood, poultry, beef, fruit, and pastry was offered. I especially loved the avocados, which were the size of grapefruit, stuffed with chicken salad. I ate and ate and then got sick. I had forgotten the words, "Everything in moderation" told to me many times by my grandfather and father.

In the evenings, we would go to the Royal Hawaiian restaurant for dinner. The restaurant was multi-leveled. We would enter on the upper floor and descend several floors to our table. There was soft lighting on the stairs, and candles glimmered on each table. We could hear the surf rolling onto the beach from outside the open doors. The band would play softly from the left side of the room. Every evening, I would ask my father to dance with me the moment the music began. Every evening, he would smile and reply, "First, I dance with your mom, then you."

Each night, late in the evening, a male vocalist would sing part of "The Hawaiian Wedding Song" in a Hawaiian falsetto. Everyone who had been at the hotel for even a day or two would stop whatever they were doing to listen to the vocalist. As the newcomers quieted, I would hear the surf, the falsetto, and the orchestra blending softly together. To this day, I get a lump in my throat when I hear the song.

As part of our vacation, Mother and I took hula lessons twice a week in an air-conditioned dance studio. I was the only fourteen-year-old in a class of six, and it was a serious dance lesson unlike some of the burlesque versions of hula seen today. A beautiful young Hawaiian woman wearing a halter-top and a grass skirt was our instructor. Mother and the other women wore cotton skirts. I wore shorts.

Each hula dance, we learned, tells a story. The instructor would tell us the story and demonstrate the dance with the music playing in the background. Then she would break the dance into small parts, and we would learn the words and the appropriate hand and arm movements. After we had learned those, we would learn the hip and feet movements. We followed our instructor's every motion. Once we had learned each part, we would put the parts together to the music of "Lovely Hula Hands" or "Little Brown Gal in a Little Grass Shack."

Near the end of our stay, the band in the restaurant played "Little Brown Gal" one evening. A few women bravely got up. "Mom," I said, "Come on, let's join them." My father encouraged her, and she gave in. We all received a huge round of applause.

Before leaving Oahu, my father bought a halter-top and an authentic grass skirt for me. I remember I did the hula for my classmates when I returned to Braeside. The girls were impressed. The boys were a bit silly about the grass skirt. Amazingly, I still remember how to do the hula today, and sometimes it seems to me I can hear the music playing and smell the fresh pineapple I so loved.

1948, Sis, Nancy and Joe Lelewer on Waikiki Beach, Oahu

Top: 1948, Nancy and Joe Lelewer on Oahu
Bottom: 1948 Sis, Nancy and Joe Lelewer, lunch at the Royal Hawaiian Hotel

CHAPTER 11
Mixed Blessings

It sometimes seems to me that most things in life can best be described as mixed blessings. Take that piece of chocolate you were craving. It may have been incredibly yummy, but it also had those 1,000 extra calories you didn't really need. That parking ticket you received may have cost you an arm and a leg, but you weren't towed and you did make it into the store before it closed. My summer camp experience definitely fell into the mixed blessing bag.

The summer between third and fourth grades, I was sent to summer camp. The camp was to serve two purposes: I was to have fun, and I was to learn to swim. My cousin Dick, a year older, could swim like a fish by the time he was six. He and his friends were always in the deep end of the pool. I kept to the shallow end, never far from the edge, even at age eight. My parents knew how to swim, but my father was uncomfortable putting his head in water. Meanwhile, my mother, like most women of that time, did not want to destroy her hairdo. Given that, it was decided that a two-week YWCA camp in Michigan would be a good experience for me. Thus, it came about that, at age eight, I learned about the water and about myself.

I found myself in a cabin with a clique of five girls from Winnetka, Illinois. They were clearly long-time friends. When I tried to initiate conversations, they looked at me blankly and turned away. When an activity was called, they rushed to it together. I felt left out and began to feel invisible, so I trudged to the counselor with my tale of woe. She half listened and then said, "You'll see. You will all be one happy family in a short while." After that, she mumbled that she had just broken her nail and reached for her nail file. I left the cabin wondering if she had even noticed that I was gone. Cliques of schoolgirls are always difficult to handle, and it would have taken a far more mature and better-trained counselor than the one I had to have improved the situation. Still, some sign of awareness of the problem on her part would have made me feel better.

Sailing was one of my first activities even though I wasn't a swimmer. I was put in a boat with two older girls, but with no life preserver. The counselor pushed the boat away from the dock, the girls hoisted the sails, and we were off. I realized, as we sailed along and I looked down at the water, that, for the first time in my life, I could not grab the edge of the pool if I wanted to. Still, I didn't worry particularly because the sensation of sailing was pleasant. Near the middle of the lake, however, the wind picked up, blowing first one way then another. In short order, the wind grew ferocious and all three of us were pitched into the waves.

I came up from the darkness, grabbed the side of the boat, and held on for dear life, fingers like claws. I was too terrified to think in terms of swimming, which I couldn't do, or of donning a life preserver, which I didn't have. After what seemed like an eternity, a rowboat arrived. I was helped into the rowboat and then told to return to the boat I had been in.

"No!" I said and wouldn't budge. Fear and anger kept me glued to the seat in the rowboat, nails digging into the underside of the bench. I bit my lips as I was rowed back to shore. I couldn't, and wouldn't, speak.

After a shower that warmed me up and calmed me down, I went to tennis. All the terror of the morning came out in my game that day. I played a girl three years older than I and beat her soundly. Winning brought me some respect but did not guarantee friends. Still, I thought respect was a good start. I decided it was time to learn to swim. Within a week I was swimming the crawl, side, back, and breast strokes. It was at that point I realized I didn't need to feel the friendship of fellow cabin mates to succeed. I could forge my own path and create my own success.

I boarded the train to Chicago when camp ended. I couldn't wait to go home and see my parents again. When I arrived in Chicago, however, the station seemed huge and filled with people milling about. Conductors howled train and track numbers over loudspeakers. People screamed welcomes when they caught sight of their loved ones, "Charlie, Charlie, we're here!" My parents were nowhere to be seen. I scrunched into a chair for safety, shoved my luggage under my feet, and worked to keep my tears at bay. I thought I looked grown-up. In reality, I probably looked like what I was, a scared little girl. Finally, I caught a glimpse of two tall people coming through an outer door. I jumped up and yelled, "Dad, Mom!" They were a blur, running toward me. Hugs and apologies followed. "Nancy, they told us your train would be 45 minutes late. We went out for a bite to eat. We're so sorry." They talked almost in unison. I didn't care one bit why they were late, they were here now. Camp was over.

"I can swim now," I told them.

"Great," they said in unison.

"I won some tennis matches."

"Terrific."

"Let me tell you about sailing." I gave them every gory detail. They turned pale and looked at each other. In the years that followed, I went to camp in Wisconsin, Michigan, and Maine, but I never went back to that YWCA camp.

It seems that even dyslexia can be a mixed blessing. My sense of being an intelligent person, a bright kid as we used to say, was severely taxed at regular intervals because of my dyslexia. One day while in a car with some friends and one of their mothers, I pointed to a sign and read "anti-cues" for the word "antiques." I was horribly embarrassed when everyone laughed heartily. It was one of those mistakes I never repeated.

There was also that awful time a teacher had me read an article on government policy in front of the class. The article featured the word "political," which I read as "polly tickle." You can imagine the giggling and guffawing of the students whenever I read the word. When the ordeal was over, she asked me what the article was about. I had no idea. At that point, she told me the correct pronunciation of polly tickle. The hallways echoed with "polly tickle" for several days. I still shy away from politics.

At the same time, however, dyslexia taught me early in life to appreciate good teachers. Miss Ryan, my fifth-grade teacher, was one of those good teachers. In fact, she was one of my two favorite teachers, so when the *Chicago Tribune* held a contest on the topic of favorite teachers, I sat down and wrote a long story about her, which I then mailed to the *Tribune*.

For the next several weeks, I haunted the mailbox. Finally, a large brown envelope arrived with my name printed in important-looking letters at the top. It looked very official, and when I saw the return address, I knew it had come from the *Tribune*. My feet seemed rooted to the ground as I turned the letter over and over in my hands. It was on the second turn that I noticed a little bump in the middle of the envelope. That bump galvanized my body into action. "Dad, Dad!" I called, running to find him, holding the envelope in the air. "I think I won something from the *Chicago Tribune*. I hope it makes Miss Ryan famous. She deserves it."

My father was in the den. "Open it, honey," he said. I carefully tore across the top of the envelope and pulled out the letter tucked inside. In flattering and fancy words, it said I had tied for second place and had been made an honorary Quiz Kid. I was breathless. Me? A Quiz Kid?

"Congratulations," my father said, calling Mother into the room to share in my joy. My prize was a one-dollar bill, a lot of money in those days, and a gold Quiz Kid charm. The charm hangs on my golden bracelet today and is as shiny as the day I received it.

In sixth grade, Braeside students began ballroom dancing. By eighth grade, I was the third tallest girl in the class, taller than most of the boys, which made dancing lessons rather awkward. Ah yes, those mixed blessings again! Our teacher, Mrs. Spiel, said, "Be nice. Be kind to those boys. Many of them will be quite tall and you can't know which ones." She was right, but as one of my friends noted in an e-mail to me years later, it was "an odd way to throw boys and girls together—dress them up and make them clutch each other and move around together." She remembered that her dresses always "had wrinkles in the back where the boys hung on for dear life."

In case you think mixed blessings only occur when you are young, there was our remarkable seventh grade homeroom teacher, Mr. Crowell, who taught math in grades six through eight. He helped those who needed help and found interesting, challenging problems for math whizzes. As a result, he salvaged students who didn't understand math and kept the others fascinated with the subject. He became superintendent of schools in Highland Park, but I suspect he missed interacting regularly with students. You couldn't be that good if you didn't enjoy working with young people.

During eighth grade, Aunt Blanche, my grandmother's sister who was actually my great aunt, came to stay with me while my parents were on vacation in Trinidad. Like Grandma, she was warm and kind. Unlike Grandma, she was a great cook, not much of a talker, short, and a bit stocky. My parents had assured me that, while they were away, my life would be the same as it always was—school, piano lessons, and my favorite radio programs, *The Lone Ranger* and *The Shadow.* I figured I would miss my parents, but they would be back in a few weeks, and everything would be fine.

Knowing that, I sat down contentedly Sunday evening to listen to the Lone Ranger with his faithful, if terse, sidekick, Tonto, and his horse, Silver.

As soon as the words, "Return with us now to those thrilling days of yesteryear" were uttered, children across the country stopped what they were doing and waited breathlessly to hear the rest of the introduction, "A fiery horse with the speed of light, a cloud of dust, and a hearty, Hi-ho Silver away! The

Lone Ranger rides again!" I was no exception. I couldn't wait to hear the Lone Ranger say, "Hi-ho Silver, a-w-a-y—" and to hear Tonto call the Lone Ranger "Kemo Sabe," faithful friend. Each week, we all listened for the program's closing lines:

> *"Who was that masked man?"*
> *"Why, that was the Lone Ranger."*

As I listened to the Lone Ranger and Tonto ride off into the sunset that evening, I suddenly realized my Monday would have no such joyful distractions. Although my parents had left me the money for three piano lessons, I hadn't bothered to practice for my lesson. Not once. I would have to fake it this time.

My teacher led me into the music room on Monday and asked me to play. My playing was atrocious as my fingers skittered along the keys. Miss Jones snarled at me, "Is this the best you can do? Is this the way you position your hands? How dare you come in playing this way?"

I didn't know what to say. It was hard to look at her. She glared at me, then took my hand and banged it hard against the piano keys. My hand hurt, and my throat felt like sandpaper. I had to get out of there. Fast. I could never go back. I never wanted to see her again or the piano. I left abruptly.

Five days before my parents returned, I realized I'd have to explain why I hadn't had two of my lessons. I called Miss Jones and apologized in a quavering voice. A great deal was riding on her response. "I no longer have time to fit you into my schedule," she said, putting the phone down with a bang.

I suspected my parents, particularly my mother, were going to be less than pleased with the end of my piano lessons. In a slight panic, I called my friend, Beth, who played the violin.

She liked her teacher and was happy to arrange a lesson for me. I counted the money I had and discovered it would cover renting a violin and two lessons. Things were looking up. Beth introduced me to her teacher who taught at Braeside, and my lessons began.

My poor aunt must have suffered considerably in those last few days before my parents came home. I practiced incessantly and managed "Twinkle, Twinkle Little Star" with most of the notes intact. I played the piece for my parents on their return. "The violin is my instrument," I said with emphasis after their less-than-impassioned applause. "Twinkle, Twinkle Little Star" had actually been a duet, me on the violin and poor Mortimer howling with each painful note. Clearly his ears hurt. His may not have been the only ones. Having listened to both Mortimer and me, my father suggested I try out for *Inner Sanctum*, the radio program that preceded *The Shadow* (*"Who knows what evil lurks in the heart of man? The Shadow knows"*), my favorite program after *The Lone Ranger*. I didn't fully appreciate his comment until I discovered that the creaking door sound that introduced *Inner Sanctum* was made by a squeaking, squealing violin.

In eighth grade, I was elected president of the student council, a wonderful honor. At the same time, as president of the student council, I had to give a speech before the entire school. I asked my father for help. He recommended keeping the speech short and to the point. I did. I pointed out that I was only one person and needed suggestions from all of Braeside's students. Following my father's advice, I said that we all had to work together for the betterment of our school. It worked, and I discovered many of Braeside's students had great ideas.

One of my responsibilities that year was to meet dignitaries who visited our school. I felt honored to shake the hook of

Harold Russell, a star in the great 1949 World War II movie, *The Best Years of Our Lives*. Mr. Russell, who had never acted before, played the part of the wounded war veteran who had lost both his hands in the war. I remember that my picture was in the newspaper with him, shaking hook to hand. It was a proud moment for me.

The culmination of all our dance lessons took place on a balmy May evening in 1949 at the big eighth grade dance. There was a gentle breeze that night that cooled our faces and rustled our party dresses just enough to make them billow prettily. We couldn't hold back our smiles. We were "kings of the hill" and about to graduate. It must have been fun for the parents who were chaperoning. They had watched us grow from wide-eyed little ones holding our mother's hand on the way to school to self-assured eighth graders.

Every eighth grade girl had dreamed of a large, beautifully decorated room, and that's what we got. Braeside's Dance Studio had chosen the second floor of a building on Main Street in downtown Ravinia. It was sensational—a high-ceilinged, cavernous room with the feel of a movie set. I don't remember what I wore, but I know I spent a lot of time planning my clothes. We all did. And we all compared notes on the phone, in the hallways, and anywhere else we happened to gather.

Three years of dance lessons had given each of us an edge. We stood tall. I didn't fold over to hide my height and didn't even get silly when I realized the shorter boys' faces came to the middle of my chest. We just danced and had a good time gliding across the floor with not a care on our minds except how we looked and whether we'd get a chance to dance with the boys we liked best.

The evening was designed to prevent anyone from being a

"wallflower." The chaperones planned for "Boy's choice," "Girl's choice," and "Mixers." No one was allowed to stand against the wall for any length of time. Everyone danced the whole evening.

I had just begun a fox trot with Jim Barton when we heard voices from the doorway. Two firemen had entered the room, looked about for a moment, and then approached Jim's parents. "Come quickly," they said. "The Ravinia Opera House is burning. We have to spray your home with water, since it's close to it. We're going to try to protect your house from burning and keep the fire from spreading."

I remember going outside with the Bartons. From a few miles away, we couldn't see what is now known as the Ravinia Pavilion, but was then called the Ravinia Opera House, but we could see the sky was red with flames leaping into the air. As we got closer to the park in which the Opera House was located, more and more wailing fire engines and police cars arrived on the scene. The area was cordoned off for at least a block in each direction around the park. The heat was indescribable and terrifying. Even from a block away, it felt as if your skin were burning. The heat, the red flames shooting into the sky, the sky itself a ball of fire, the hoses, the sirens, the barricades—all left a deep impression on me.

Firefighters worked through the night but, despite their efforts, the fire was still smoldering in the morning. In my mind's eye, I still can see the trees that faced the fire, charred and blackened, with sap running down their trunks like sticky tears. It was unbearably sad. Our Ravinia Opera House was world famous and had attracted great musical artists. Now there was nothing left but ash and blackened ruin. I grew up a little that evening.

Eighth grade culminated in a beautiful graduation

ceremony. We marched down the aisle, the boys in suits and the girls in white dresses and white shoes, feeling as though we owned the world. It was wonderful to graduate from Braeside, and yet, in true mixed blessings fashion, there was one large cloud on my horizon—I had to go to summer school in Chicago. I was to go to typing classes in the early morning and then attend modeling school until 1:00 P.M. Monday through Friday. Touch-typing was to help me in high school and college; modeling techniques were to make me graceful. I disliked the idea of both classes, but my parents felt strongly that these were important and I would appreciate them eventually.

My typing class was held in a huge room filled with typewriters, all with blank keys. There were sixty of us in the class, all of my classmates were older than I. There were no computers and no air-conditioners. Each of us was given a book and taught which finger to use for each key. The sweat would roll down our cheeks as we stared at a large chart of the keyboard showing the keys with their numbers and letters and let our fingers pound on the blank keys. We were given a test a week. I hated every

Braeside 8th Grade Elementary Graduation–Class of 1949
Nancy Lelewer is in the front row, fifth from the left.

moment in that class, but in college all my papers had to be typed, so, in time, I came to appreciate having the skill. My parents were right about that.

After typing classes, I walked over to the studio building, climbed several flights of stairs, and braced myself for what felt like unmitigated torture. Five days a week, twenty-one of us struggled to learn how to be ladylike. Our time was divided into segments. "Imagine a string attached to the center of your head being pulled up." I imagined and imagined, but my chin became preposterously tilted. In time, I discovered I did not need to tip my head and look up, but rather to think of a marionette with a string holding its head upright and steady.

"Walk up and down the stairs without letting the books you are balancing on your heads fall," said a voice that carried up and down the staircases. The good news was that the books kept my head in proper alignment.

We were instructed, "Never cross your legs." That, we discovered, was a rule, indeed a cardinal rule. Still, once we got that far, we were allowed to go outside and practice getting in and out of a car the "proper way." What a sight we must have been! Back in the room, Sophia, an acquaintance of mine, sat with her arm resting across the top of the sofa as we talked. "No arms on the backs of sofas!" our teacher called out loudly. Sophia leaped and moved her arm to its proper position.

From car entry and arm placement, we turned our attention to runway walking: "Walk down, turn your eyes, your head, turn your body—come back. Let me see, were your feet right on that turn? Do it again."

I got through all of that, but proper makeup was the final straw. There is no appropriate word for how I looked after that lesson. My brows were blackened, my cheeks rouged, my eyes circled in black like actresses of old, and my lips were colored a deep maroon. Before stepping outdoors, I raced to the bathroom and scrubbed it all off. I decided right then and there that my role model would be my mother, who, with her sense of how to look beautiful without much makeup, was more stylish and attractive than any of my teachers.

After class, I would race down the stairs to meet my father for a late lunch without giving a single thought about the position of my head. No matter how dramatic and continuous my complaints at the start of lunch, I would be cheerful by its finish. My father could always make me laugh, even at myself. If the White Sox were playing a home game and my father could get away from work, we would go over to Comiskey Park, where he could always get good seats. We'd munch away on foods not recommended for models, and I would sit any way I wanted and call out the names of my favorite players. I looked very little like the lady I was training to be. On days when there were no games, my father would deliver me to the train station, and I'd head home delighted to have had a happy lunch.

Eighth grade taught me many things, including typing, posture, and the violin, but, most of all, it taught me about mixed blessings. The Ravinia Opera House burned down, and I learned that things can happen fast and unexpectedly, that I had to be ready for anything. I also learned that hard work and determination can bring about amazing results. Six weeks later, the Ravinia festival opened on schedule, housed under the shelter of a thirty-three ton canvas cover originally designed as a hangar for a B-29 bomber. After that season, a new pavilion was built with double the audience capacity and acoustics as fine as its predecessor.

CHAPTER 12
High-School Years

Braeside Elementary academics had presented me with a number of challenges, but they were nothing compared to the academic challenges of Highland Park High School. My father had not been given homework at the University of Chicago's Lab School. My mother's homework had been done in study halls with the aid of helpers. In contrast, I worked and worked, studied and studied. Still, Highland Park High School offered some wonderful opportunities to its students. Like many high schools of its day, the school had a full orchestra, and my desperate switch from the piano to the violin in eighth grade gave me a chance to join the orchestra. I played third chair in the first violin section. The two violinists in front of me were far better musicians than I, but I played better than the first violins behind me and the entire second violin section. My parents attended all the concerts and always had kind things to say.

My parents also never missed a parents' night. They knew all my teachers and invited several of them to dinner while I was in high school. In fact, Harold McMullen, "Mac," my biology teacher, and my father became such good friends that my father and I stopped to visit Mac and his wife at Cross Village in Michigan on our way to join my mother and grandmother one summer.

My father recalled that Mac's summer house was on the shore of Lake Michigan. "The second floor was held up by a totem pole Mac had carved," my father said, "and if anyone had pulled the totem pole out, the whole house would have come down. In addition, there was no running water. You had a bar of soap and went into the lake if you wanted to have a bath. If you wanted to go to the bathroom, you went to the outhouse behind Mac's home."

"The village was populated only by Indians except for Mac, his wife, Mil, and daughter, Melinda. One of the most memorable things Mac arranged for us was for the Indians to have a pow-wow and present us with a 'key to the city.' The Chief was in full regalia with plumes, headdress, war paint and all the stuff in which they adorn themselves for special occasions."

Mr. McMullen was more than just an interesting person, more than just the fellow who helped my father build a tool shed against the side of our home. He may have changed the course of my life. "I just burned Nancy's biology exam," he told my father on the phone one evening. "I'll tell the administration I lost the exam. She'll get a B as her final grade."

My father was speechless. Mac knew how hard I had worked. He knew I had done every assignment, turned in all the extra credit work, and had a B average going into the final exam. By the end of the year, however, I couldn't remember half of what I'd memorized. "She's very bright, and the B may help her get into a good college, which is where she belongs," Mac said. At Mac's bidding, I never took another science course.

If it seems surprising that my parents would know my teachers well enough to invite them to dinner, it shouldn't. Even though my parents led busy lives, they always were involved in my education. My father's schedule was incredible: Six days a week he awoke early, did chores around the house (turned on the sprinklers in summer, shoveled snow in the winter, fed the dog), then showered, put on a suit, ate breakfast, and dashed to the 8:00 A.M. train. He got home each night at 6:00 P.M. After dinner, he played baseball, bowled in a league, or took classes on the nights he and my mother didn't have social engagements. His energy never lagged.

Mother, too, was busy. During my freshman, sophomore, and junior years in high school, she did whatever she could to ease Bodo's adjustment to a new life and to keep our family life on an even keel. The task was not an easy one, and she frequently consulted with Bertha Korman at the Jewish Children's Bureau.

It was Ms. Korman who encouraged Mother to find a career outside our home. Shortly after that discussion, my father had lunch with his cousin, Stanley Goodfriend, who had just bought a real estate firm on Chicago's North Shore. At some point during the lunch, my father must have mentioned Ms. Korman's advice because when my parents returned from a trip to Mexico celebrating their twentieth anniversary, there was a letter from Stanley congratulating them and offering my mother a job. Mother accepted the job and then went to talk to Justine Kahn whom Stanley had hired to run his office. Justine said, "You know I don't like you, but I have no choice since it's Stanley's business and he has hired you."

"Why don't you like me?" my mother asked.

"At Stanley's wedding, when I met you for the first time, you said to me, 'Oh, you're the pretty Kahn girl's sister-in-law.'"

While it was not an auspicious beginning, by the end of the first year, Mother and Justine were good friends. In time, Justine bought the business from Stanley and became the most successful broker on Chicago's North Shore. She took her husband into the business, saying "I always wanted to be married to a millionaire, so I married Herb and made him one." Eventually, she sold the firm to Coldwell Banker.

Compared to today's prices, real estate was cheap when my mother was selling it. As I recall, Mother once sold a beautiful home on riparian property (In Highland Park that meant land next to Lake Michigan with access to the beach.) for $80,000. In the late 1990s, a home comparable to that sold for $1,300,000. Through her contacts with the Jewish Children's Bureau, Mother received the names of three caseworkers who wanted to live on the North Shore. Since social work did not then, and does not today, pay well, she showed them the simple but nice houses that were being built on Burton and Pleasant avenues. The houses were selling for $16,500. Thirty years later, these houses sold for $49,500. Twenty years after that, they sold for $90,000 to $100,000.

Mother sold real estate for twenty years. She finally retired because of her hearing loss and some difficulty she was having with her left leg. The day she left, she handed Justine a list of her customers and the brokers in the office to whom she'd assigned each. "Justine," she said, "we are leaving on a trip and I'm not returning to work after it." Before my parents left the next morning, a florist arrived with a beautiful orchid corsage and a note thanking Mother for all she had given to J.H. Kahn Reality.

There seems to have been an independent streak in the women born in Peoria, Illinois, in the early 1900s. My mother became a real estate agent. One of her Peoria acquaintances became a writer. Bettye Naomi Goldstein was ten years younger than my mother, but Peoria was a small town and both attended Anshai Emeth Temple, and thus they and their parents knew one another. Bettye dropped the *e* from her name, graduated from Smith College, married Carl Friedan, and in time, wrote a book about the roles of women in industrial societies. Her book, *The Feminine Mystique*, which came out in 1963, is known for starting the "Women's Liberation Movement."

My parents' social life was equally active. Their friends included members of the Pot Luck Club, relatives, and a wide range of other friends many of whom were charismatic and successful businessmen, such as Irving Harris and Edward Gudeman.

As a family, we often got together with the Gudemans and their children. Ed Gudeman became President Kennedy's Under-Secretary of Commerce in 1961.

Irving Harris and his brother Neison sold Toni Home Permanent to Gillette in 1948. Later, Irving donated money to the University of Chicago to found a school which, in 1990, the university named the school the Irving B. Harris Graduate School of Public Policy. With his second wife, Joan, Irving financed the Joan W. and Irving B. Harris Theater for Music and Dance in Chicago's Millennium Park. Irving was also a benefactor of the lab at Boston's Children's Hospital in which I worked.

I still can remember the party Neison Harris had at his home on the shore of Lake Michigan in Highland Park. My parents had been invited, and I went along to sit outside with several other kids to listen to Louis Armstrong's entire band which was there with Ella Fitzgerald. It was a beautiful night and, although we couldn't see them very well, we could hear them perfectly.

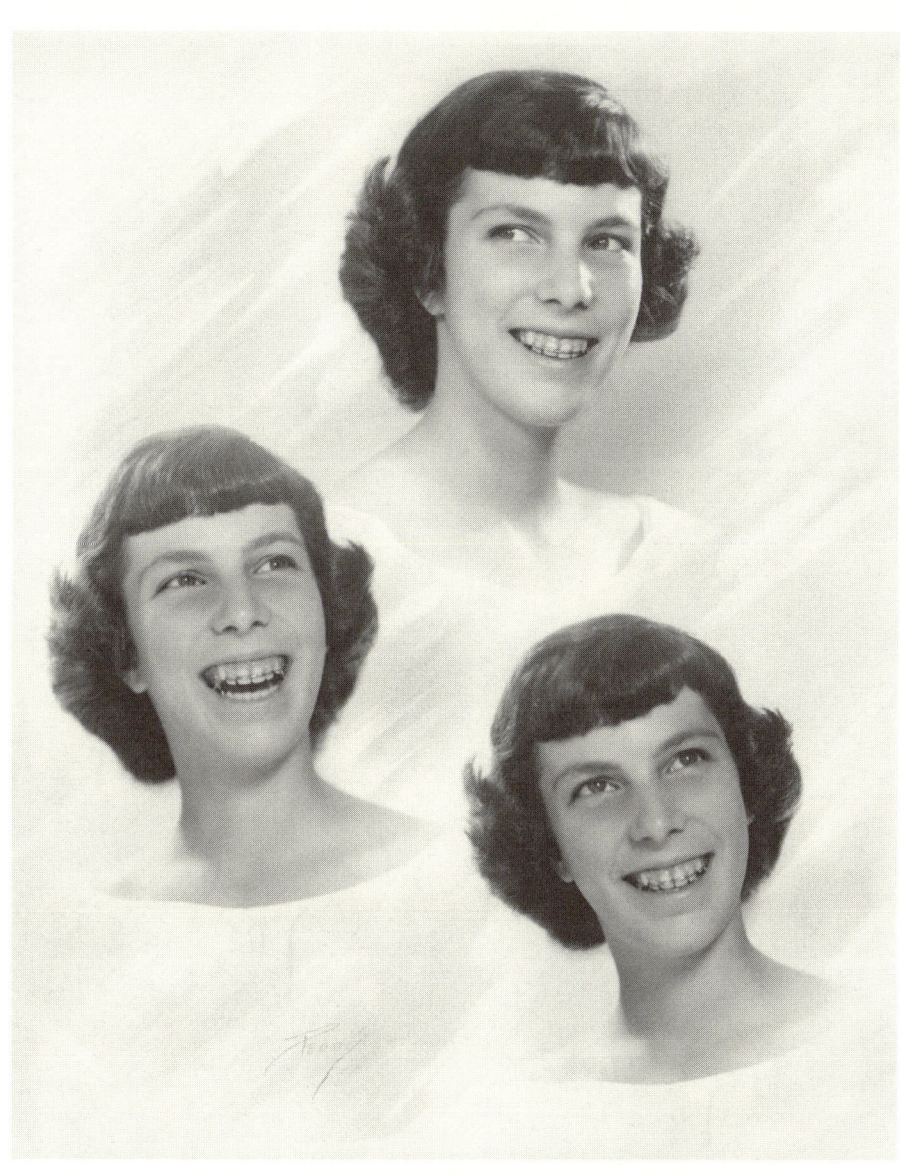

Nancy Ullman Lelewer
High School
Highland Park, Illinois

Irving Brooks Harris

The Winter brothers, from Milwaukee, came through our home frequently. Jack was a pant manufacturer with whom Dad did business. His brother, Elmer, started Manpower with Aaron Scheinfeld, who lived a couple blocks down our street and whose family we saw socially. Ruth Scheinfeld was six years ahead of me at Sarah Lawrence and Irving's daughter, Roxie Harris, started Sarah Lawrence the year before I did. Later, when Stephen Sonnabend and I got married, Irving and Rosetta had a magnificent dinner party at Lake Shore Country Club for our wedding party and out of town guests, and Fran and Eddie Gudeman gave a luncheon at their home for the same group.

The poster for the Highland Park High School Talent Show went up one day at school. I kept my fingers crossed that Mom and Dad would participate in it as ballroom dancers. I waited until dinner to ask. Dad looked especially handsome in his dark jacket, Mom particularly pretty in her elegant blue crepe dress. I felt a bit breathless. Would they say "yes?" I saw an opening in the conversation and blurted out, politely but a little louder than usual, "Dad, Mom—would you be willing to be a feature at our Talent Show?"

It was asking a great deal, I knew. They would have to choose music, find their own records or tapes of the music, and find time to practice. What worried me most, however, was the possibility that they had prior commitments. I needn't have worried. I didn't have to cajole. They simply smiled and said "yes." They loved my school, loved making me happy, loved to dance, and were good sports.

I was excited from the moment they said "yes" through the night of the talent show. On stage that night, they looked like dancers in movies from the 1940s, slick and smooth, anticipating each other's movements over the roughened wood floor. My father wore black; my mother, a red and black full skirt, a red peasant off-the-shoulder blouse, high heels, and her incredible, flashing smile. Nothing fazed them. They danced the waltz, fox-trot, cha-cha, jitterbug, all with passion and poise. I wasn't the least bit surprised. Over the years, I had witnessed my father and mother's artistry as dancers on our winter vacations. All eyes would be on them as they spun around the dance floor with the big bands of the day providing live, "surround-sound" music. My mother—slender and tall, with a lovely carriage—was the ideal partner for my father. She slipped gracefully into his arms and could follow his moves with the ease born from years of practice.

I don't recall precisely what my friends and I said to one another as we watched them that night. Probably, whatever was the slang of the day—"hip," "neat," "groovy." All of those words would have fit my parents' performance. In the name of fairness, we applauded every act with the same intensity, but, I knew my parents had reached the audience in a special way. I could tell by the way my friends high-signed me with thumbs-up. One friend even used an unusual word for my generation. Leaning over to me, she whispered, "Spectacular." I beamed, but was not surprised.

It wasn't by accident that my father danced like a professional. He had studied with his era's best known teacher of ballroom dancing—Arthur Murray—when he was still in elementary school. Grandpa SS and the family were in Florida for a winter vacation one year, and it seems that Arthur Murray was also there offering classes. Although Grandpa SS had read Murray's ads and believed his comments on the correlation between athletic skill and good dancing, it was probably Grandma who had the final word. She was a firm believer in the social graces for her sons. Like most small boys, my father had been reluctant to take dance classes, even ballroom dance classes, and, in fact, had sat in the corner and cried during his first session, but my grandparents had insisted. As a result, for the rest of his life, my father danced as if he were gliding with a layer of air under his feet, the Arthur Murray way.

When I was young, like lots of other little girls, I learned to dance by standing on my father's shoes as he glided over the floor in our front hall in a slow dance. I had even bounced on his feet in the fast dances, and from childhood on, I was aware of how beautifully he danced.

Maybe because they themselves loved to dance and socialize with their friends, my parents were more than willing for me to have high school parties at our home. Our finished basement was the perfect place for them. Indeed, my father had designed the main room for parties. It was large, paneled, and possessed a shiny linoleum floor. All in all, it was just the place for slow dancing, talking, or playing ping-pong. One section of the floor even had a shuffleboard court designed into it. The cues for the game hung on a nearby wall.

I would buy the party food—potato chips, two dozen doughnuts, and bottles of Coca-Cola—with my own money. As many as 100 kids might have shown up at one time or another during the evening. The food usually ran out early, but no one seemed to mind. Everyone wore what was the high school uniform of the day; for girls, skirts, sweaters, bobbie socks, navy and white saddle shoes or loafers; for boys, sports shirts, cord pants, and white "ducks" (suede shoes). We would stack records on the record player (the equivalent of today's CD player) and start to dance. Almost always, my friends brought their favorite records. We would listen to the music, slow dance, or occasionally jitterbug until the party ended. We all knew my parents were at home upstairs. Most of my guests knew and respected my parents. They also knew, because I told them, that my father would be down in a second should a problem arise. No problem ever arose, although my parents missed coming down the time we played Spin-the-Bottle, but that's only because I didn't tell. After the party, a few girlfriends would stay to help clean up. We enjoyed talking and gossiping about who was "going steady" and who was "pinned." When we were done, there were no signs that there had been a party in the room. "Clean as a whistle," we would say.

When I wasn't hosting a party, I was going out with one of the boys from high school. I distinctly remember introducing the center on the school basketball team to my parents one evening. As I brought him into the room, there was my six-foot tall father standing on a dining room chair. "Hi, I'm Nancy's father," he said, holding out his hand to shake. "Good evening, sir," answered the young man, who didn't quite know what to make of it. When we got into the car, he said, "Your father is really a character."

My father seemed to know instinctively how to guide my choices without my being aware of it. When I was little, he spent a number of years patiently listening to me chatter about saving money to buy my very own horse. When I finally told him that I thought I had saved enough money for the horse, he had asked gently, "Can you house and feed the horse?" I had never even thought about that, as my father had suspected would happen. By that time, however, a horse seemed more of a liability than a treat. I was growing up and knew I could go riding with my father on Sundays, as we had always done, using the horses at the stable.

When I turned sixteen, I wanted wheels. Clearly, my father had known this would happen, because he made a deal with me on the spot. "Would you like to have the use of my car all day while I'm at work?" he asked. "You'll have to take me to the train early in the morning and pick me up at 6 P.M." What an incentive for me to pass my driving test!

I suppose one could say I wasn't a complete novice when my father began my lessons officially. Steering lessons had begun when I was five. Once we reached our driveway on our way home from some outing, I'd climb over from the back seat and plop myself down on my father's lap. He would work the pedals, and I'd steer the car into our garage. My official driving lessons began on a dead-end street with no buildings or traffic in the way. Steering was not a problem, as I'd already learned the art of turning the wheel just so. Parking, however, required a lot of muscle for pulling on the wheel, as there was no power steering then. I still can remember having to learn hand signals as part of my driving lessons. Cars didn't have built-in turn signals, so, I had to learn arm out straight, left turn; arm up at a right angle, right turn; arm out and down, stop. Bicyclists still use those signals today.

My father taught everything in increments, with great patience, lots of encouragement, and always long before I needed to know it well. My father was interested in the process part of my learning, my mother preferred the product, and my grandparents loved everything I did. I was, therefore, surrounded by cheerleaders almost all the time.

My father had put together our car deal at least in part to save my mother from her role as chauffeur. She was so foggy in the morning, she never had time to dress before taking my father to the train, and she worried she'd break down somewhere with only her nightgown under her coat. As I had to go to school, I was at least up when it was time for my father to catch the train.

Under the terms of our deal, I would sit beside my father as he drove to the station to catch the 8 A.M. Northwestern train. On days when we got off to a late start, we could see the train pulling out of the Braeside station as we arrived. My father would floor the accelerator, and we would race to Glencoe, the next stop en route to Chicago. That's when I wished I had something to hold onto. The train only had to speed along a straight track. My father had to negotiate a winding road, traffic lights, and stop signs along the 1.25 miles to the Glencoe station.

Northwestern trains are laid out in a manner similar to the English system. Trains go into Chicago on the left track and come out of the city on the right track. There was a stop light at the Glencoe station. If the light was red, my father would jump out of the car, cross the street, and run in front of the train, which would have, by this time, begun to move. On those days, it was impossible for me to see if he had boarded the train. I would shift over to the driver's seat and head to school, wondering if he had made it safely. If the light was green, he would make a left turn, cross the tracks, jump out, and dash for the train. There were no gates across the street where the trains passed. Often, the train already would have begun to pull out, so he would have to grab hold of the train's vertical handrail and swing himself onto the steps. Sometimes, when we were particularly late, the steps of the first car, and even the second, would have been pulled up. At that point, my father's only chance to catch the train was to grab the vertical rail on the last car before the steps were pulled up. I always worried that he would fall as he ran alongside the train or that he would lose his grip on the rail as the train picked up speed.

No matter how hard we tried to get away from the house on time in the mornings, there would be days when we would run late. Neither of us ever said a word to my mother about my father's hair-raising race, as she would have worried herself sick. Since she did not know, she always had a smile for us on our return a little after 6 P.M. each evening. Sometime later, my father gave me his old car and bought himself a new one, so I no longer had to take him to the train station. At that point, I began a car pool. I would pick up a few of my friends and drive them to and from school. Since gas for the car was my responsibility, I'd get everyone to chip in a nickel, and we'd purchase a couple gallons of gas for a quarter. Those were the days of very cheap gas.

The spring of my senior year brought the event that my friends and I had been waiting for since at least ninth grade—the senior prom. I went with the first love of my life, Bron. Bron fell into what could be best described as the "hubba-hubba" category. He was tall, over 6 feet to my 5 feet 8 inches, with short blond hair, sky-blue eyes, and a melting tenor voice. He was a junior, and I was a senior, but when he had asked me to go steady at one of the parties at my house, I had said, "Yes," without a moment's hesitation. It didn't hurt that he was also an Eagle Scout. Clearly, he had passed the test on stars, including those in my eyes.

Half an hour before Bron arrived to take me to the prom, I slipped into my sophisticated long dress of shimmery blue-black fabric. Mother and I had begun our quest for this dress three weeks earlier at the mammoth Marshall Field's in the city. Marshall Field's was known for its thirty-one miles of carpeting and seventy-six elevators. How my mother negotiated the store in high heels, I will never know. As we entered the store, I had ogled the magnificent dome of the South Rotunda as I always did, but this time the one million plus pieces of colored Tiffany glass seemed to wink at me. This was no ordinary shopping trip.

We saw dress after dress, gown after gown. If there was one that my mother liked, I could tell by her expression. To her everlasting credit, however, she said nothing and waited for my okay. It never came.

We broke for lunch—one of the famous Marshall Field's open-faced sandwiches for me and something else for Mother. Marshall Field's sandwiches were not quite Dagwood sandwiches, but still very satisfying. They featured a large slice of bread, lettuce, gobs of thinly sliced turkey, tomato, several pieces of bacon, and Russian dressing, along with potato chips and dill pickle. As my mother was there, I didn't wolf it down, but I remember I wanted to.

We decided to spend the afternoon visiting small boutiques along Michigan Avenue. At these stores, we would sit in the fitting room while the sales people brought out their gowns, one by one, usually with some commentary about why each was perfect for me. Since the saleswomen worked on commission, it was their job to make the dresses sound wonderful. I tried to look comfortable, but by mid-afternoon, my anxiety was growing.

In the third boutique, a young saleswoman made the usual promise, "I have the perfect dress for you." By then I was weary of those words. I looked down, certain of disappointment. When I looked up, I felt my cheeks flush with excitement. She was right. It was perfect, everything I had hoped for. I quickly put the dress on, looked in the mirror, and nodded, yes. In my mind, I looked at least twenty years old in this fashionable creation.

Although this shopping spree marked the end of my childhood and of my living at home, all I thought about at that moment was that I loved the way I looked in the dress and my mother's smile of approval. If my mother's smile was bittersweet in recognition of the loss of her little girl, I didn't know it. That very day, my mother had arranged for my hair to be washed and set at a beauty parlor, and I had had my first manicure. Now, before Bron arrived, I again looked into a full-length mirror. The image in the mirror was perfect.

My father came in and broke my reverie. "Let's talk," he said. "Come to the den." I remember gliding down the two half flights of stairs and standing as he talked to me. I didn't want to wrinkle my dress by sitting on it. "I know," he said, "this is a special moment in your life and I want you to hold on to it and really savor it. You have a date with your first love, you are in a new dress, you look beautiful, you have no responsibilities, and you will be with good friends at a fun dance tonight. Nancy, it doesn't get any better. Later in life, you will have responsibilities and not be carefree like tonight. I hope life will be good and I'm sure you will have much happiness to look forward to. Sometimes we don't appreciate what we have until it's over. I want you to know what you have now."

The doorbell rang then. I felt both light as air and completely grown up as Bron and I left the house. On that night, I had a good sense of where I fit into the world and a feeling that I was headed toward joy. That evening, we jitterbugged and twirled and wiggled the rumba and held on to each other in those wonderful slow dances of my era, especially when they played our song, Richard Rogers' and Lorenzo Hart's 1934 classic, "Blue Moon."

After the dance, a group of us changed clothes, drove to the beach, built a fire, chatted, and snuggled together into the wee hours of the night. We were young and believed that we would be together forever.

CHAPTER 13
Sarah Lawrence

In June, having been inducted into the National Honor Society, I graduated from high school, along with my best friends, Margerie and Sheila. During my high school years, I had played a variety of sports, had been involved in a number of other extracurricular activities, and had studied almost nonstop. I had received mostly As, a few Bs, and, thanks to Mr. McMullen, only 1 C. The one C I had received was in second year Latin, not biology. I had found translations difficult, and, on my final exam, I had married a woman to a tree. During the summer that followed graduation, that C didn't seem to matter any more. The days were warm and bright with sunshine, and my summer was free and filled with friends.

In the fall, I left my parents and boyfriend in Chicago and sat up all night on the train to New York, scared and crying. In New York, I transferred from Penn Station to Grand Central, got the train to Bronxville, deposited my luggage and myself into a taxi, and arrived at Sarah Lawrence College. The taxi dropped me off at the administration office, next to the tennis courts. I checked in and promptly learned I would be in off-campus housing a block away.

As I began to lug my suitcase and footlocker down the path to the street, I thought I heard someone call out, "Nancy." I paid no attention. There were surely other girls named Nancy at Sarah Lawrence. "Nancy Lelewer," the voice now said. I whirled around and saw a handsome man, probably in his thirties, wearing tennis whites and holding a tennis racket.

"Hi," he said. "I'm Harold Taylor. You're a tennis player, right?"

"Yes," I said with some bewilderment.

"Do you have your racket and tennis clothes in that luggage?"

"Yes."

"Well, hurry up. We need a fourth and we'll wait for you."

And that was the start of my college years. I suspect there are not many college students who can say the first person they met at college was the school's president, because that is who Harold Taylor was. At the same time, Harold Taylor was not the usual college president.

He had been inaugurated president of Sarah Lawrence in 1945, at the age of thirty, and as such, was the youngest president in the college's history.

Prior to his inauguration, he had spent six years on the faculty of the University of Wisconsin. During his fourteen years at Sarah Lawrence, he became the spokesman for progressive education at the college level. To those of us in school, however, his ability to remember the name of every student was even more important than his academic credentials. Throughout his tenure, students and faculty alike would go out of their way to get a cheery personal greeting from him.

My new home-away-from-home was Kober House, which just recently had been acquired by the school. Nestled in woods and surrounded by lawn, it was a magnificent, huge house with commanding bay windows. I gasped in disbelief when I first saw it. My room was on the second floor. It was a triple, large and bright, with windows on two sides, comfortable beds, and sizable desks. There was even a bathroom attached to the room, so I didn't need to march down the hall shedding towels and toothpaste. I was in the process of changing into my tennis outfit when a girl my age came into the room. "Hi," I said and smiled at her.

"I'm Jane. Which one are you?" she asked.

"Nancy."

"Where are you from?"

"Chicago."

"Oh, you're the good one. My father checked. You come from a good family."

It certainly was not the best way to start an acquaintanceship, but fortunately, her words did not register with me.

"See you later," I said and rushed back to the campus for the game. Frankly, I have no recollection of the game, my partner, or the score. I was too scared and too flustered to take any of it in.

I met my other roommate, Carol, later that day. Carol had graduated from high school early and badly missed her friends who were still in high school. During our freshman year, she seemed perpetually sad, her down-turned mouth like the one found on a tragedy mask. Jane, on the other hand, was anything but sad. She often danced around the room in the middle of the night to music she played on her record player. While her dancing could last for hours, there were at least moments of silence between songs when she had to change records. The lights were always on in our room. I learned to sleep though light, noise, everything, which was, I suppose, good training for motherhood.

Even before classes officially began, the assignments for them were posted in the library. When I saw how much reading was required for just my first class, I gulped. As I wrote down the requirements for all my classes and realized I'd have three more assignments once conferences began, I thought about the train schedule back to Chicago. Suddenly, I could hear my father's voice in my head, "One step at a time", "Just keep plugging away", "Give it your best and you'll succeed." I started to read, read, read. I would pull myself out of bed to begin studying at 5 A.M. It was a work pattern that continued throughout my college years. Even so, Sarah Lawrence soon began to feel perfect for me.

Perhaps it was perfect for me because we met individually with our professors once a week to discuss our conference work. Perhaps it was because we took no more than three classes each semester, and there were no more than six students in each highly interactive and ungraded class. Everyone came to class prepared, so discussions were lively and thought provoking. Perhaps it was because there were many papers but no exams. Whatever the reason, I found Sarah Lawrence a challenging but satisfying intellectual experience. No matter how hard I worked, I never quite got to the end of the material. Yet, I began to "get into the groove" because of stimulating classes and one-on-one weekly conferences with nationally and internationally known faculty. I had never been just a number in elementary school or high school; I wasn't one at Sarah Lawrence.

Top: President Harold Taylor
Bottom: President Harold Taylor playing the clarinet with Rex Stewart
Both pictures courtesy of the Sarah Lawrence College Archives

Nancy Lelewer, Sarah Lawrence College

At the end of my freshman year, the Dean of Students told me she was worried about Jane, who was not keeping up with her studies, and asked me to room with her again during our sophomore year. "If you agree to it, you'll have that choice triple room again in Kober, and you can choose the third roommate," she offered. I'd like to say bribery doesn't work, but it can. Jane and I were roommates once more.

Yoko Ono, later the wife of John Lennon of the Beatles, lived in the room next to us. She kept to herself and I really didn't know her, but I would see her at dorm meetings. Both of us spent a lot of time in the library, studying.

After spring break that year, Jane told me she had eloped and was living with her husband in a secret room off the kitchen of Kober House. Their tiny new living space was like one of those secret rooms that appear only when you touch a hidden button somewhere on a mirror or a paneled wall.

Perhaps I should not have been surprised by Jane's announcement. After all, my sophomore year had begun with a bang. I had been elected head of all social activities on campus at the end of my freshman year. During the summer, my committee and I had decided to fill the first fall weekend with a dance and a concert. The dance was to be held Saturday night and was to be followed by a jazz concert Sunday afternoon.

I had returned to school early to make sure everything was in order, only to discover that Harold Taylor had canceled the jazz concert. I was furious! I had already hired the musicians, sent out the notices, and made posters. Seething with anger, I marched right into his office. He asked me to take a seat. I sat down but fidgeted.

"What can I do for you?" he asked quietly, looking straight at me.

"How could you cancel the jazz concert I planned without consulting me?" I fumed.

"Nancy, I'm head of the school!"

"Yes, and I'm head of all social activities on campus, so you could have at least had a conversation with me."

"Frankly, I didn't think anyone would come."

"If there's no concert, they certainly won't come. We need to do something to bring students together on this campus."

"You really believe the students would have come back early just for a concert?"

"Yes!" I answered. I could feel my face flushing in anger. "That's why we planned the concert in the first place. But now, even if you say the concert is on, I doubt I can get the musicians I hired to come back for the show."

He sat back slowly and rubbed his chin against his hand. "You know I'm a bit of a jazz musician myself," he said, with a wry smile.

"Yes, I've heard that."

"If I put a group together and play with them, will students come?"

I smiled, "Yes, definitely."

"OK, I'll do that," he said and then continued, "I've just finished writing this press release. Would you read it and tell me what it says in your own words?"

It was the McCarthy era, a time when many college presidents were busy writing press releases in support of their faculties and schools. People from all walks of life faced accusations of being soft on communism and the possibility of blacklisting. Nearly a dozen professors at Sarah Lawrence were targeted by Joseph McCarthy, the senator from Wisconsin. Even though these professors were not called before McCarthy's senate subcommittee, the accusations could have tarnished their reputations and careers. Throughout their ordeals, however, Harold Taylor and the college's board of trustees stood by them. Taylor and the board's clear-eyed courage are considered by historians to be a rare exception to the hysteria of the period. To those of us who attended Sarah Lawrence, this courage was not surprising. Sarah Lawrence was proud of its commitment to individualism.

I read the press release carefully and told President Taylor what I thought it said, pointing to one part that wasn't clear to me. He asked me to come back after my last class to read his re-write, which I did. From that day on, he always called me to his office to read what he'd written and tell him what I understood it to say before he released it to the national press. I was honored to be asked and even more honored when he invited my parents and me to his home for dinner.

We met at the beautiful, Tudor-styled house that was allotted to a president of Sarah Lawrence during his or her tenure. The house had five large, stone chimneys, beautiful stained glass windows, and wood and stucco walls. The glow of the stained glass moved throughout the rooms of the house—a splash of yellow here, a fragment of rose there, a piece of blue for just a moment—as the sun moved across the sky. This was a house that seemed to hug its occupants.

Although Harold Taylor was known to be a casual dresser around campus, on this occasion both he and my father wore coats and ties. I remember I wore my favorite red dress with gold earrings and a golden buckle at my waist. My mother wore a lavender-colored dress, the same color as the orchids that made up the corsage Harold Taylor had given her. In those days, corsages were for special occasions, special people, and my mother was delighted.

Cocktails were served in the living room where a fire crackled in the great stone fireplace all evening. I sat on the floor, near the fire, petting the sheep dog, a huge and cuddly animal. When it was time for dinner, we went into the dining room.

There was a welcoming, personal feel to the settings—a pretty tablecloth, fresh flowers, sterling silver. I can't recall any shiny goblets or glorious chandelier. The house seemed to reflect its occupant—a handsome, down-to-earth educator, jazz musician, entrepreneur, and salesperson who used his charm and knowledge to collect a great faculty. Although their teaching burdens at Sarah Lawrence were heavy, educators came because of Harold Taylor and the school's philosophy.

The day at Sarah Lawrence and the dinner gave my parents the opportunity to see my new college for themselves and spend time with the charming man at its helm. The conversation flowed easily. My father and President Taylor took to each other at that first meeting and continued to keep in touch by letter and phone. In time, I came to realize that one of their common interests was their affection for me, a heady feeling for a sophomore college student.

Looking back now, I am amazed at how fortunate I was during my college years. I was, for example, often invited to dinners at the home of my advisor Adda Bozeman.

Adda, as she asked us to call her, was a brilliant woman, who was head of the International Relations Department and a consultant to governments. She was stunningly beautiful—tall and slender, with a long neck and beautiful posture. She usually wore her hair swept into a regal bun. She had been born into a Baltic German family in Geistershof, Latvia. After graduation from l'Ecole Libre des Sciences Politique in Paris, she had studied law in England and had become a lawyer at the Middle Temple

Inn of Court in London. In the 1930s, she moved to the United States. She was the author of numerous influential books on diplomacy, world politics, and global conflicts, as well as a recognized expert on the Middle East, Russia, and Southeast Asia.

Dinners at Adda's were leisurely affairs. We would have a simple meal, perhaps a chicken pasta casserole, salad, and dessert and then talk for hours about our families. I would leave when the candles had burned all the way down. I was always reluctant to go. Adda's heart was as warm as the candles' flame. Indeed, in many ways, the candles were merely a reflection of Adda's own warmth. She was a constant through my years at Sarah Lawrence. I always turned to her if I needed something, and, even after I left the school, she was there for me when I needed advice.

Advisors weren't the only ones who welcomed students into their lives. Caring, great teachers were the rule at Sarah Lawrence. It wasn't unusual for a student to be invited to a professor's home for a meal. One evening, dressed in a party dress and carrying wine and flowers, I left campus to visit my Spanish teacher, Justa Lopez Rey, at her home in New York City. When I knocked on her door, I heard, "Hello. Um, who is it?" This didn't sound like the Justa I knew. The door opened slightly, and she peeked out as I peered in through the crack. Her lovely face was covered with paint patches the color of sage, her nose was green. I could see a paintbrush in her hand. I couldn't think of anything to say, and neither, it seemed, could she. Finally, the silence was broken.

"We were expecting you tomorrow," she said with a gasp.

"I'm sorry," I said, my head down in embarrassment. "I always confuse Jueves [Thursday] for Viernes [Friday]. I'll come back tomorrow."

Before I could flee, Justa reached out with her one clean hand and led me into the apartment. "Thank you," she said, gently taking the wine and the flowers. "Green paint on the bottle never hurt the taste of wine. We'll really enjoy these later on tonight."

"At least the flower stems are already green," I thought to myself as Justa hunted for some old clothes for me so I could join the painting party. Justa, her husband, and I painted and laughed and laughed and painted until the room was finished. I have no idea how long it took, but when it was done, I too was partially green. We stood in the middle of the room and turned from wall to wall, admiring our work. The room had changed from some nondescript color to a soft green. Dinner followed. I don't recall the food, only the laughter of the evening, and the good feeling I had that, through an error, I had helped make a room come alive.

The kindness and caring Sarah Lawrence offered its students did not end with graduation. Almost twenty years after I graduated, I found myself turning once again to Adda Bozeman for advice. In the 1970s, I was struggling to write an instructor's guide for the 1, 2, 3 Instructional Program I had developed. In desperation, I turned once again to Adda who urged me to call Rudolph Arnheim, a former Sarah Lawrence professor of psychology and a pioneer in the study of the psychology of art for help. At the time, Dr. Arnheim was head of the Carpenter Center at Harvard University. "Use my name when you call him," Adda said calmly.

After I said goodbye to Adda, I took a deep breath, and picked up the phone again to call Dr. Arnheim, a living legend, while I still had the courage.

"My name is Nancy Lelewer Sonnabend. You don't know me, but—"

Adda Bozeman
Courtesy of the Sarah Lawrence College Archives

Justa Lopez-Rey
Courtesy of the Sarah Lawrence College Archives

"Sure I know you, Nancy. You were Maria Perez's roommate. What can I do for you?"

I hesitantly explained I had created some learning games but was having trouble with the instructor's guide for them and that Adda had suggested that I call him. I was sure he was too busy to see me.

"Where do you live," he said, "and when should I come over?"

I was so surprised, I couldn't say anything. After what seemed like several minutes of silence, I finally managed to say, "No, I'll come to you, and please say hello to Mrs. Arnheim for me." (Mrs. Arnheim had been the librarian at Sarah Lawrence.)

I will never forget Dr. Arnheim's kindness. I spent several hours with him and his wife one evening at their home in Cambridge near Harvard Square. We set up the materials on a large coffee table, and he listened carefully to my explanation before asking questions. He and his wife then played the games, and we all ate the pretzels that were the rewards for playing. Mrs. Arnheim topped the evening with tea and cookies. Before I left, Dr. Arnheim gave me his latest book, *Visual Thinking*, and wrote on the flyleaf, "For Nancy Lelewer Sonnabend who thinks with her eyes inevitably. Rudolf Arnheim Oct. 1970." What thrilled me even more than the book, however, was his parting comment, "Thanks for coming. I've learned much from you tonight."

His carefully considered critique of my instructor's guide arrived at my home a week later. Since I was still not sure how to write the instructor's guide, I called Dr. Gary Marple, a brilliant and close friend. Gary took my 100-page instructor's guide and Dr. Arnheim's critique and condensed it into 5 succinct pages. Gary asked only for the first copy of the 1, 2, 3 program when it was published. A few years later he received it.

Top: Dr. Gary Marple
Bottom: Rudolf Arnheim (Credit: John Gay, Photographer)
Courtesy of the Sarah Lawrence College Archives

While I was a student at Sarah Lawrence, I studied many weekends, but also found time to visit boys from other colleges, go skiing, and take Saturday theater trips to New York. Brown University in Providence, Rhode Island was one of my favorite weekend destinations, because it was close to Sarah Lawrence and close to my childhood friend Margie Ellman, who was at Pembroke College. I met several young men from Boston at Brown, including Don Saunders. Don was a roommate of Joel Davis, a friend of mine from Highland Park, whose parents had moved to New York City a few years earlier. I had carte blanche to stay at his parents' apartment any time I wanted.

I spent one weekend at Princeton. A friend fixed me up with a date there. My date got drunk Saturday night, stood on a table, danced, sang loudly, and then proceeded to fall off the table into the crowd. I didn't see him again that night or the following day, and he never called to apologize. This experience left me an unfavorable opinion of Princeton men.

A handsome West Point cadet sat next to me on a flight from New York to Chicago. He invited me to a spring weekend at the academy. The weekend featured a gala Saturday night dance. I accepted the invitation. The cadet, striking in his spotless uniform and well-shined shoes, gave me a tour of the campus in the afternoon. My favorite building was the granite Cadet's Chapel, which has a medieval fortress appearance and stained glass windows, one of which is inscribed Duty, Honor, Country. The dance that evening looked like something out of a movie and felt almost surreal. All the cadets were in their dress uniforms and wore white gloves. We were not allowed to dance cheek to cheek, but for one designated song we were allowed to get a little closer to one another when the lights went down. After the dance, the cadets escorted their dates to a hotel pickup area. The next day, however, my date and I went to Kissing Rock, and he did kiss me. He was charming, good looking, and well mannered, but I lost track of him during my junior year abroad.

For a brief while, Dartmouth filled several weekends. I loved spring and autumn weekends there, but the winter cold was piercing. I remember walking close to my date in the frigid air as we studied the intricacies of the Dartmouth ice sculptures at the Winter Carnival. The sculptures were spectacular and almost worth the cold, especially when a visit to them was followed by a big cup of hot chocolate. Although my date didn't drink, most of the members of his fraternity did, and I was not comfortable visiting his fraternity house. In time, I lost interest in visiting.

Later, I dated a drummer from Yale and spent a few weekends in New Haven with him. Unfortunately, I soon discovered he loved his drums far more than me. I got tired of sitting around while he practiced and played, so I decided it was better to get my homework done than to play second fiddle to a drum. Still, he was quite a performer on the high hats, not, of course, in the same league as my favorite drummer, Gene Krupa, but good.

Occasionally, we received permission to take the Sarah Lawrence van on ski trips to Killington and Stowe, Vermont. The trips took six hours each way, and our lodgings were the cheapest bed-and-breakfast possible, usually several miles from the ski slope. We would ski all day Saturday, half a day on Sunday, and then drive back to school Sunday night. More frequently, a friend and I would pair up and go into New York City. For $1.80, we could stand behind the wall of the orchestra and watch a Broadway play. Before intermission, we would scan the theatre for empty seats to sit in for the second half. After an inexpensive dinner, we would buy tickets to a second play for that evening. I wish I could remember the names of the all the plays I saw.

I do know I saw every musical on Broadway that was playing while I was at Sarah Lawrence.

It was during my sophomore year that I decided I wanted a change in schools, at least for my junior year. I sent off applications to three schools: Smith College, Stanford University, and University of Michigan. My first choice, the one I had my heart set on, was Smith College. Smith offered a year abroad in Spain, which I desperately wanted, but was afraid I might not get because my Spanish language skills were not that strong. My second choice was Stanford University, which offered a warm climate, strong academics, a coed campus, and a good sports program. The University of Michigan was my third choice. It would be cold in winter, but it too offered a coed campus, as well as a midwestern congeniality and an active sports program.

Once the applications were mailed, I waited and waited and waited some more for a response. The wait was beginning to seem interminable when, on Thursday, May 19, 1955, I received a telegram from Jean Bratton, the director of the Smith Junior Year Abroad Program in Madrid. She asked if I could meet her the following day, Friday, at 3 P.M. at the Biltmore Hotel in New York, and said I should confirm the appointment by calling her at Smith's Spanish House.

Reaching her seemed to take forever, but at last she answered, described what she looked like, what she'd be wearing the next day, and told me she would wait for me under the famous clock at the Biltmore Hotel. I thanked her, hung up, and went to work choosing my wardrobe for the following day.

As I walked through Grand Central Terminal, New York's Beaux Arts landmark, on the way over to the hotel the next day, I could feel my heart pounding with a mixture of excitement and nervousness. I arrived a couple of minutes before 3 P.M. and saw a woman standing in front of perhaps forty to fifty suitcases—the heavy, old-fashioned kind—lined up next to each other in a long row. Suddenly, the woman teetered backward and fell onto the suitcases. As everyone stared, the suitcases tumbled over like dominoes. The woman was wearing a navy blue dress with a white collar and a red scarf, which was exactly what Jean Bratton had said she would be wearing. I offered her my hand, helped her up, and introduced myself. The suitcase incident didn't seem to faze her. She thanked me and dusted herself off. Her carefree manner put me at ease, at least until I thought about having to answer questions in Spanish.

While chatting easily in English, we took the elevator together, chatting easily in English, to a junior suite. I couldn't help wondering how many young women she had seen before me, and how many more were to come. A yellow pad waited her scribbling about my suitability for the odyssey to Spain. I was to discover as we talked that she took notes speedily. "¿Habla español?" she finally asked.

"Si, pero cuando alguien me habla no comprendo nada [Yes, but when someone speaks to me I don't understand anything]," I answered. My father had always told me to tell the truth. There was a silence. I wasn't sure what her expression was—bemusement or shock? Had I heard a gasp? Although her demeanor remained the same, gracious, with that wonderful take-charge edge of an academic, she didn't ask many more questions after that. I left hoping that I had said the right thing and praying that my application had made it clear just how much I craved total immersion in the language and culture of Spain, its art, architecture, history, philosophy, and literature. A week later, a letter arrived from Smith. I held my breath as I tore it open. I had made it. Stanford University and University of Michigan were forgotten immediately in my joy. It was only on the second reading that I noticed the date at the top of the letter—May 13, 1955, one week before I met with Jean Bratton. The interview had been a formality.

Jean Bratton, 1955

CHAPTER 14
Spain!

The summer before I left for Spain was a busy one. I filled out the required paperwork for Smith, applied for Smith's group health insurance, renewed my passport, took a course in international relations at Northwestern University, organized my clothes for the trip and saw the doctor who gave me the shots I needed for a year abroad. At the going away party my parents gave for me at the end of the summer, I even met my future husband. Of course, I didn't know it then, but still, it is a good indication of just how full my summer was.

It was the summer of 1955. The cost of Smith's year abroad program was $1,800 and included room, board, and tuition from August 1955 to June 1956. My round trip ticket on the SS Independence cost my father $500. The average wage in the United States was $3,851 per year. The minimum wage was $1.00 per hour. A new house cost about $11,000, and apartments rented for under $80 a month. Gas was 23 cents a gallon, new cars about $1,900. The Salk polio vaccine had just become available, and a year earlier, in 1954, the Supreme Court in Brown v. The Board of Education of Topeka had declared the doctrine of separate but equal unconstitutional, thus paving the way for the civil rights movement.

My excitement over going to Spain spilled out over my friends and family. My world was open. I was thrilled, anxious to get going, and yet as I packed my suitcases, I thought about a year without my family and friends and shivered a bit. After all, I didn't know the person I would be living with, and I could only call home in an emergency. I wouldn't see my parents again until spring vacation when we would travel together through Portugal, Spain, and North Africa. How badly would I miss them? Would I be lonely? I straightened my shoulders, faced my fears, and finished packing. What would be would be. Fifty years later, when the eleven living members out of the fourteen of us who had been in the program gathered for a reunion, we agreed the program had been all that we had hoped for and more. Our year in Spain left us with friends, experiences, and memories that never faded.

My mother, father, and roommate from Sarah Lawrence, María Perez, traveled with me to New York and saw me off on the SS Independence. They waved goodbye as the ship slowly pulled out of the harbor. Once I no longer could see them, I headed to the cabin that I was sharing with three other members of the Smith program. Nothing better exemplifies how time had changed for the Lelewer family than my trip to Europe.

My great-grandfather had crossed the ocean squeezed into the lowest portion of an old, creaky ship with countless others. His living quarters in steerage were dank and dark; his future, unknown. I shared a third-class room with three others, but the room was clean, and our hearts were free of cares. I was funded

Nancy Lelewer, 1955 just before leaving for the
Smith College junior year abroad program in Madrid

by my parents, could get more money if I needed it, and was, if necessary, only a phone call away from parental guidance.

I quickly discovered that my three roommates, particularly Vicki MacFarlane, and I had a lot in common. Like me, Vicki was from the Midwest, but she had gone to Mills College in California, which meant that she, too, had never before attended Smith. Our conversation was easy, and I had the feeling we would become good friends.

That evening, Vicki and I decided to venture into one of the bars on board the ship. There, we soon met two attractive men. Of the two, I was more intrigued by John Chalfant. John was twenty-eight years old, over six feet tall, thin but strong and well built, with dark brown hair. He had gone through college and graduate school on a mix of athletic and academic scholarships and was now en route to Istanbul to teach at Robert College.

We danced and then stayed up talking until 4 A.M. In fact, we spent the entire crossing together, swimming, eating, walking, dancing, and mostly talking. It seemed that we would never run out of conversation as we watched the many moods of the ocean. The weather was beautiful during the days, and at night we would dance the evening away. Occasionally we would sneak into the first-class section at midnight to graze on the late night buffet that was only offered in that part of the ship. The mischief made the food all the tastier.

Everyone in the Smith group disembarked at Gibraltar. It was while we were there that I came to realize Jean Bratton was a travel wonder. She could find every interesting thing for us to do wherever we were. As part of our stay, we saw the island's highest point (1,396 feet above the strait) and were given

Top: My parents Sis (age 44) and Joe Lelewer (age 49) seeing me off on the deck of the S. S. Independence
Bottom: John Chalfant (age 28) and Nancy Lelewer (age 20) on the deck of the Independence

a tour through the installations inside the rock, which were well fortified with munitions.

It was a fascinating time to be in Gibraltar. Under the dictatorship of Francisco Franco, Spain had renewed its claim to sovereignty over the island, at least in part because Queen Elizabeth II had come to celebrate the 250th anniversary of Gibraltar's capture. I found myself comparing Gibraltar to the Maginot line between France and Germany.

While Jean could ease our entry into Spain and Spanish customs, she could not ease our introduction to European bathrooms. From Gibraltar on, when there were toilets, the toilet paper was like sandpaper. Unfortunately, there were frequently no toilets to begin with. It would take time for us to get use to that.

After we toured Gibraltar, we flew to Madrid on board an unpressurized DC3. The plane flew at 2,000 feet or less. The view was spectacular, even if the flight was nerve wracking.

We were taken from the airport to the Instituto Internacional, where our classes would be held once we were proficient in Spanish. We were given lunch there and then boarded a train to Santander which is located on Spain's northern coast. It was a long and uncomfortable journey.

In Santander, we attended a special program designed by Jean Bratton for the fourteen of us. The three week program was demanding. It was designed to boost our knowledge of the Spanish language and introduce us to early religious Roman and Spanish architecture, Spanish art, and the country's geography. Formal instruction in Spanish filled our mornings. We were an incredibly lucky group. We studied under the right professors at the right time. Sra. De Menendez Pidal, whom we would meet again in Madrid, was well known in literary circles. She based her Spanish course on her Ph.D. thesis, which dealt in part with the errors Americans made in pronunciation, including placing the wrong accent on spoken syllables. In order to be sure we could be understood and did not have telltale mispronunciations and accents, we were drilled over and over on the correct pronunciation of often-used words. Lectures in castizo or local Spanish helped to reinforce pronunciation and vocabulary lessons. We were awash in proper, beautiful Spanish. As a result, the correct accents and intonation permeated our beings.

Our afternoon language study was less formal, but still effective. Jean Bratton asked us to talk with the handsome young male students from other programs who were at the beach every afternoon. We did not complain. We donned our Catalina or Jantzen one-piece bathing suits, the haute couture of the day, and trotted off to the beach where the young men, who were soon to head to Madrid for further study, greeted us ecstatically.

While we were in Santander, we visited the prehistoric caves of Altamiras with flashlights in hand. Nothing protected the drawings back then. We were allowed to climb inside and touch the walls. The ceiling was spectacular with detailed drawings of bison, red deer, horses, and boar. The uneven surfaces of the cave created the illusion of movement. As we stared at the paintings, even the fur of the animals and the heavy manes of the horses in their monochromatic shades of ochre, black, and red seemed to come to life. Today, because of the CO_2 breathed out by the many visitors over the years, only 160 visitors a year can visit these spectacular caves.

After we completed the program, we traveled through the north of Spain and down through the Meseta. Although I loved the caves, the art history and geography courses we took did not capture my attention in the same way. Antonio Floriano, the professor who taught art and architecture, had written two important books on the subject of Guadalupe and Extremadora, but I was a Jewish kid from the Midwest who was not yet fluent in Spanish, was unfamiliar with the tenets of the Catholic religion, and had little or no knowledge of church architecture. Consequently, I was often bored as he guided us along Spain's northern coast and down through the heart of the country.

Although we were granted permission to visit remote architectural gems that were not usually seen by outsiders, one church looked like another to me. I couldn't tell Roman from Romanesque from Gothic, one fresco from another, or even determine the country that had inspired the work. I did know the buildings were imposing, that some were beautiful, and that a few were amazingly high. I also knew that some were dark and others glowed with stained glass windows.

While my observations were valid, they did not serve me in good stead on my mid-term exam. Still, I loved the countryside, the women in my group, and even our uncomfortable bus rides on bumpy and sometimes terrifying dirt roads through the mountains. The most fun was swimming nude in the Cantabric Sea with its vast, empty beaches. We felt unencumbered, free, and full of joy.

At various intervals during our trip, we all came down with the equivalent of Montezuma's revenge—diarrhea and vomiting at the same time. In the best of situations, Montezuma's revenge is unpleasant. Unfortunately, the sanitary facilities in Spain's monasteries at the time were not the best of amenities.

During one particular siege, we were staying in a monastery with only a communal outdoor toilet. When nature called, we would stand on two blocks, one foot on each block, next to someone else standing on two blocks, who was next to someone else, and so on. A trough ran under the blocks to carry away the waste. The smell was terrible. There was a bar above the trough that you could hang on to for balance. While we agreed it was primitive, it seemed to us an effective way to handle both our problems simultaneously. We were young and resilient, fortunately.

Once, Vicki and I were late returning to the monastery and found the door locked. As we ran through a wooded area along the side of the building to find an open window, we saw a priest and nun having sex. We raced past them, climbed through the window, and told no one, but the image remained in my mind. I wondered if the nun was there by choice and what would happen to her if she became pregnant. It may have been 1955, but in some ways Spain and its fascist dictatorship were still in the sixteenth century.

I would spend my year trying to understand the soul of this country I was beginning to love. I knew its people had suffered through a painful civil war and had few material things, but they seemed warm and wonderful with an unerring sense of right and wrong. Later in the year, I would watch my date, Estevan, give our streetcar fare to a beggar we passed on the street. Estevan said the beggar needed it more than we did. His gift left us without a centavo between us and with a long walk home, but he was right.

September 29, tightly clutching a piece of paper with the name Cristina Lana written on it, I arrived at my Spanish home-to-be via a taxi in Madrid. Vicki was on her way to her Spanish home, so I was alone and scared when I knocked on the door. I was greeted by a slightly pudgy, beautifully attired, petite woman with a radiant smile. To this day, I can remember the warmth of Cristina's smile as she greeted me that day. She made me feel comfortable from the moment I met her.

"Traiga las maletas de Nancy aquí. [Bring Nancy's suitcases here]," she said to Juanita, the maid, as she took me by the hand and led me into my bedroom. I felt at home as soon as I entered the room. There was a double bed with a pink bedspread, two night tables with lamps, a comfortable stuffed chair, a brasero to keep me warm, a large mirror in a simple, brown, wooden frame, a chest of drawers, an enormous wardrobe, a soft green, white, and pink carpet on the hard wood floor, two big windows, and pink and white draw curtains. The walls were a light gray color. After my travels through northern Spain, the room seemed large and beautiful with a cozy feeling to it.

Cristina then led me to the bathroom, where an old-fashioned tub with iron legs was filled with hot water and awaiting me. "Aquí están tus toallas. [Here are your towels]." She handed me the towels and smiled as she left. I know I harbored the hope that this deeply satisfying bath would be a daily or weekly treat. It wasn't to be. The owner of the apartment building controlled hot water, and we were allowed only a few minutes a day, usually when I was at school. Juanita must have boiled many pots of water on the wood-burning stove to fill that tub before I arrived. My next bath was over three weeks later and not at all warm. In fact, sponge baths in frigid water were the norm. On that first night, however, Cristina knew how to make her young guest feel at home and made sure I had everything I needed.

My year with Cristina was not a year in the lap of luxury. To press clothes, hot coals had to be inserted into the iron. There was no refrigerator. Juanita had to go to the market twice a day for our food. There was no vacuum cleaner. Carpets were hung out the window daily and beaten. We rarely ate meat, which I really didn't mind, as I could never tell if the meat we did eat was lamb, beef, or pork. Central heating was only a dream. One night

Cristina Lana
Madrid, Spain 1955

when it was brutally cold, I didn't put the brasero's coals out before I went to sleep. Cristina discovered me in bed, sleeping soundly, comfortable and warm.

I can still remember how angry she was when she woke me. I could have burned down the building if a spark had flown, she said, and then let me know it was never to happen again.

Yet, if Cristina was quick to scold me when I had done something wrong, she also had patience, endless patience. With her help, I learned Spanish. "Vamos a dar la vuelta [Let's go around]," she would say again and again. She would describe things in simple terms and in different ways when I didn't know a key word. We ate all three meals together, every day, and we spoke in Spanish during them about her school, my boyfriends, my family, her family, the various men who had wanted to marry her, the situation in Spain, places we wanted to travel to, and more. We went to the theatre together, ate out together, and attended family weddings and parties together. When I began dreaming in Spanish, I knew I had finally become fluent.

During my time in Spain, I came to learn much about Cristina's life, loves, and dedication to education, but I don't think I ever considered the possibility that she would build an educational empire. When I lived with her, her school, Colegio Santa Cristina, was small. I didn't know that her dream was a school of 1,500 students, buses, and a farm to which her students could go. In the years that followed, when I visited her, Cristina would share with me her business and real estate dealings. I would sit with her when she met with bankers, lawyers, business and real estate men. I admired the way she controlled the show, got what she wanted, and always left them laughing. In the 1950s and '60s, Spanish women inherited money; they didn't accrue it through business dealings. Few were top educators, and none were Cristina's equal in business or real estate. Cristina defied the rules. She refused to stay in her place, refused to be defined by the mores of her time.

Looking back, my arrival on Cristina's doorstep was akin to winning the lottery. Cristina always smiled. She was nurturing, patient, loving, and held her hand and heart out to me. She was close in age to my mother, had no children of her own, and wanted—no, needed—companionship. In no time at all, she became my second mother. Even before I had command of the language, we were honest and open with each other. While my relationship with my mother was always rather formal, in Cristina I found a mother who bubbled with enthusiasm at my accomplishments, made me know she was there for me at all times, and never used silence to express disappointment. Like my father, Cristina could soothe my terrors and bring me peace if I was tense. She knew how to make me laugh, even at myself, the kind of laughter that cleanses the soul and gives you the courage to conquer demons. Over the years, Cristina would have many students, all of whom she cared for deeply, but I was her only "child."

Cristina taught me many things, but the most important thing she ever taught me was to appreciate what I had. One day I went on a tirade about how hard my life was. "There's never any hot water or heat, except from the brasero. The subway wasn't running this morning, and I had to walk to school in the rain," I said angrily. I ranted on about how I had been wet, soggy, and cold in school all day because the rain had gone through my raincoat. My hands had been so cold I could barely take notes. I complained bitterly over how I had to go to the public library last week to study the card catalogue for a paper, and how the cards had been illegible with their pale pencil markings. I grumbled that I had to wait a full hour for someone to fetch the book for me as only library employees were allowed into the stacks, and that the book had proved to be useless, so I had to repeat the process again and again over next several days. "Then," I said, my face flushing with anger, "I went back today, and there was a sign explaining that the library was closed for a Saint's Day. Closed!"

Cristina just stood there watching me as I went on and on. She said nothing when I finally stopped talking. A moment passed, and then she drew me to the window. She pulled the shade down and let it snap up. "That's freedom," she said quietly. "To be able to pull a shade down and let it go up any time you want, to go out of doors whenever you want and to come back to your own apartment when you want, to be able to complain that the subway wasn't running or that you were cold and wet at school, that's freedom," she said again, lowering her head and closing her eyes. It was then that she told me of her months-long confinement in a cave with more than one hundred women during the Spanish Civil War. "We were not allowed out to see the light of day, and we had no toilet facilities. I can't describe the foulness of the cave. Food was thrown to us like animals. We had to grab any piece that came our way. When we were finally released from the cave, we were blind. It took days for our eyes to acclimate to light. Through it all, although we had been treated like animals, we didn't turn into animals. We lived through the horror."

She stopped speaking. The silence between us was profound. I stood with my mouth open, and then slowly shook my head in disbelief. Tears welled in my eyes. I wanted to say, "I'm sorry, I'm sorry," over and over, but I didn't. What I did do was stop complaining. I didn't fuss over closed libraries or wet shoes. I wore an extra sweater under my raincoat. Nowadays, they call it not sweating the small stuff, but it was much more than that. It was an understanding and appreciation of the freedom that allowed me to complain.

After her nightmarish cave experience, Cristina had walked back to the pueblo in Cataluna where she and her sister had lived. There she found that most of the houses had been destroyed. Italian soldiers occupied her home. There were no jobs available. She became friendly with a soldier who gave her money for a one-way train ticket to Madrid and room rent for a month. As soon as Cristina arrived in Madrid, she let it be known that she was available to tutor children. Her reputation as an educator grew quickly. Soon she rented a second room and tutored there, as well as in her own room. In time, she bought a small building and began a coed preschool.

Several years after I left Spain, Cristina bought a larger building and planned to increase the size of her preschool. Because she didn't have enough money for the purchase, she used the coming year's tuitions, borrowed money from the bank, and put up her current school and her apartment as collateral. It was a major gamble, particularly as the building was zoned residential, and the neighbors didn't want a school. Cristina asked her lawyer to obtain a zoning variance and went to work eighteen-hour days, seven days a week creating her new school. She even slept on the mud floor of the building. Exhaustion and pernicious anemia finally slowed her. To restore her health, she took one bigger gamble and with her last pesetas bought a cruise ticket.

"Qué será, será. [What will be, will be]," she said. The gamble paid off. The rest and sea air on that trip restored her health, and she returned to find her lawyer had obtained the needed zoning variance. Until her debts were paid, Cristina ran her new school as a preschool. Once she was out of debt, she began adding one elementary grade each year. Some years later, she bought a bankrupt American school and moved her students to that property. Here again, her lawyer, whose children she had educated, played a pivotal role. For the purchase of the American school, Cristina had pledged and borrowed everything she could, but she was short a quarter of a million dollars. Her lawyer signed a personal note to cover the discrepancy. Within a few years, she had paid off her lawyer's note and all her other debts. The school was hers.

The school had a large concrete area where the children played kick ball, basketball, and other sports. Because she believed children should have fresh air, as well as a chance to play soccer on a grass field, swim in a pool, plant crops, learn about agriculture, and be around animals, Cristina went searching for a farm. In time, she found El Sotillo, just twenty minutes from Madrid. It had a lovely house, beautiful swimming pool, and lots of land for growing crops, grazing animals, and playing sports. Under her direction, a soccer field and basketball courts were added, many crops were planted, and the place became a mini Noah's Ark. Finally, she bought buses and had the children transported from her school to El Sotillo for part of one day each week. Before her death, she created a self-perpetuating trust so that any school could take its students to play and learn at El Sotillo.

Perhaps because of her experiences during Spain's civil war, Cristina always kept an apartment in Madrid and a small home in Alpadreti which is where my daughter, Kathy, once spent a month. When she was in her seventies, however, Cristina acquired a magnificent palace next to her school in Madrid and connected the two buildings. To purchase the palace and have money for the renovation and connection to her school, she used her school, the farm, and everything else she had as collateral. Again, she paid off all these debts and owned everything free and clear. Before her death, Cristina turned Colegio Santa Cristina over to the state and received a gold medal of honor.

Cristina never turned her back on her family as her educational empire grew. She educated her sister's two daughters and their daughters for free, paid for her nieces' weddings, and employed one of her niece's husbands. Unfortunately, as time went on and Cristina became more and more successful, her family became jealous of her, so she enjoyed their company less and less. In fact, she couldn't find other women like herself in Spain. Those who had money and were available to do the things she could afford were widows of wealthy men, well educated but not educators, and not involved in the high stake world of business and real estate that Cristina had mastered. Thus, I was Cristina's best friend. With me, she could discuss all the things dear to her heart. For thirty-one years, until her death in February 1986, we bounced ideas, heavy and light, off each other. "One needs to live sixty-five years in order to have a perspective on life," I remember her saying. "Cynicism is too easy to come by. Don't become cynical."

During the year I lived with Cristina, she insisted that I should be included in all family occasions and any social events she attended. Thus, in October of that year, Cristina and I went to the wedding of her cousin in Don Benito, a pueblo in southwestern Spain. I was to be a member of the wedding party, and I had been excused from classes for the event. The train trip from Madrid to the pueblo took seven hours. I remember explaining during the rehearsal that I didn't want to kneel and cross myself, as everyone else was doing because I was Jewish. After I made that statement, the whole town came out to see "the Jew." There I was, half a head taller than everyone in the room, feeling like a sky-scraper on a prairie. For the wedding, I knelt and crossed myself.

On the ride back to Madrid, we traveled on a single track in pouring rain. About halfway through the trip, we came to an abrupt stop on the side of a steep hill. The message passed to us was "Accident ahead. Track's torn up. Train will come from Madrid." There was nothing to do but wait in the freezing cold train. Several hours later, we disembarked and carried our suitcases, skirting around the overturned cattle cars and piles of dead animals thrown from them. As it was a single track, the new train had to slowly back its way to Madrid. It stopped once, for just a couple of minutes, so we could open our windows and purchase sandwiches and water from local vendors. Had any of this happened almost anywhere else, I would have complained bitterly for several months, but this was Spain. I was with Cristina and I was happy.

It was my midterm art history exam that threw at least a gallon of cold water on my enjoyment of the year. I was close to frantic when I received a 34 on the exam. I wanted to return to Sarah Lawrence in the fall and take the courses that interested me rather than having to fill up on courses for a stated major at Smith. To do that, however, Sarah Lawrence said I needed a B or better in every course I took in Spain. That meant I would need an A on my art history final. In essence, I would have to learn the material for the whole year in one semester. It seemed hopeless, particularly since my professor's southern accent made learning the material difficult even in small doses. I talked to Cristina. As usual, she came up with a solution: She would hire a tutor, and she and the tutor would begin to help me learn the material in January when I returned from vacation.

Over the Christmas and New Year's break, I traveled to

Nancy Lelewer and Sheila Blumenthal at the foot of the Matterhorn

Switzerland to meet my friend Sheila Blumenthal who was at-tending the University of Geneva. Sheila, four of her classmates, and I rented a chalet in Zermatt at the foot of the Matterhorn for the holidays. We were in luck. We each paid one dollar a day for the spacious chalet which was situated next to a Swiss bakery offering hot bread and strawberry preserve, and only a short dis-tance from the ski lift.

Sheila and her friends had skied weekends and knew many members of the Swiss ski patrol. We were deluged with handsome skiers, all of whom spoke French, as did Sheila and her friends. I decided I had to learn the language, particularly as I planned to travel with Sheila and her friends during the sum-mer.

Upon my return to Madrid, I found a Parisian woman who taught French to elementary school children. She wanted to learn English; I wanted to learn French. Until I left Madrid, we met twice a week in a small tasca (bar) where we spoke one hour of English and one hour of French with Spanish as our com-mon language. It was a great arrangement, as it didn't cost either of us one peseta. The more we drank the better we spoke and, of course, we feasted on calamares fritos (fried squid), gambas a la plancha (grilled shrimp), almejas (small clams marinated in salt and garlic), queso (cheese) and aceitunas (olives). I learned enough French to get along over my summer vacation, and as a senior at Sarah Lawrence, I was able to take second-year French. Of course, I was tutored for my conference work and one of my roommates that year was French and helped me.

When my spring break arrived, as we had planned even before I left for Spain, my parents flew to Portugal and met me in Lisbon, which we toured for a few days. From there, we traveled to Granada in an Iberia DC3 airplane. The unpressurized DC3 skimmed over the landscape. We were coming in for a landing when I noticed Dad's nose pressed on the window and his brows furrowed. "Is there a runway here?" he asked. "I don't see anything but cows."

I looked out. There was a runway of sorts: a patch of hard-packed turf with a fence on each side to keep the cows away. After landing, we lugged our things over to a shack near some dilapidated taxis. We climbed into one of the taxis, our luggage was tied to the roof, the cab door was tied shut, and we began our drive to the Alhambra Palace Hotel in Granada. As we rode, we alternated between looking out the windows and watching the ground go by through the holes in the cab floor.

In time, we arrived at the hotel, which was surrounded by white-tipped mountains. All the rooms had terracotta floors, oriental rugs, and ceilings of wood. Our room, named after a poet—I don't remember if it was Lorca, Olvidos, or Falla—was on the tower floor and had a stunning, high, Mudejar ceiling.

When we reached our rooms, my mother headed straight for the bathroom and my father and I began to sort out the luggage. Suddenly we heard loud, rattling noises. My father, thinking my mother had accidentally locked herself in the bathroom, rushed to rescue her. The noise grew louder. I raced out to the hall where I saw the chandeliers in motion, their crystals smacking into each other as they swung from one side of the ceiling to the other.

Only one thing could cause this type of action, I thought—an earthquake. I returned to our main room, where my father and mother stood pale and silent. Although the rattling had stopped, my insides were shaking like the chandeliers and would continue to do so for some time. "Welcome to Spain," I said. My parents looked at each other, then at me, and then began to laugh. My father walked to the window, where my mother and I joined him. We gasped as we looked out. We'd been lucky. This had been neither the time nor place to be on the top floor of the Alhambra Palace Hotel. It was fortunate the earthquake's center wasn't closer.

The next day, we visited the Alhambra, "the pearl set in emeralds," as it is sometimes called. Its majestic Moorish architecture and columns can take your breath away. I was awestruck by the mathematical imagination displayed in the endless variety of patterns embedded in the architecture. From the Alhambra, we went to the Generalife, the beautiful gardens made by the Moors in the early fourteenth century. My favorite part of the tour was the bath with three faucets: one for cold water, one for hot water, and one for perfume. The king found peace in these gardens away from the hurly-burly of court life. How lovely to have a place of great beauty and solitude when you wish to be alone.

After Generalife, we headed west to Seville and joined some friends of my parents for dinner in a glittering Spanish restaurant. I had not met the couple before, and they struck me as the type of American traveler who gave a bad name to our country. I had spent most of the year feeling that I was representing my country and trying to make a good impression. This couple spoke too loudly and acted superior to the Spanish people they met.

After dinner, I took my father aside and told him of my feelings. "Ugly Americans" was the term I used to describe such crude travelers. My parents did not behave in this way, so I was surprised that they tolerated it in others. My father listened to me courteously and somehow managed to convince the couple to continue on their travels without us, while we went on to take a brief tour of North Africa.

There we saw people dressed in potato sacks, living in caves, huddled together for warmth. The contrast between what we saw there, what we had seen in Seville, and life in our home in Highland Park was almost overwhelming.

By the time we had completed our tour of North Africa, my spring break was almost over, and I returned to Madrid with my parents. Once we were there, Cristina invited my parents to a sumptuous luncheon, the highlight of which was raw seafood of all varieties. "I'm not eating that," my father said in English, staring at his plate, his eyes open wide "I just saw it move."

I translated, loosely, "Christina, Dad says it's delicious." While everyone was staring at an intricate candle placed in the middle of the table especially for their visit, my mother managed to remove any suspect creatures from Dad's plate. I remember wondering how she managed to handle two helpings of wiggly, live seafood. Somehow she managed a glowing smile between gulps. It was a truly remarkable acting job.

At the end of my spring break, my parents continued their trip visiting France and England before returning home. For me, it was back to classes, many hours of studying, and the unrelenting efforts of the tutor and Cristina to teach me everything I needed to know for the art history final. I suppose if a miracle is going to happen, Spain is as good a location for it as any. I got an A on the final exam. It was hard to tell whether the tutor, Cristina, or I was more excited about it, but we all went out to dinner, on me, to celebrate.

CHAPTER 15
The Busy Years and Alan Trustman

Although my year abroad officially ended with my art history final, I did not return home immediately. Instead, I spent part of the summer of 1956 traveling throughout Europe. Earlier, during Christmas vacation, in fact, I had made plans to do so with Sheila Blumenthal, and now much to my delight, John Chalfont had reappeared in my life. We spent two weeks in Italy, then went our separate ways, met again in Paris, and made plans to travel together to what was then known as West Germany. About the same time we were firming up our plans, my father called.

Back then, even on good days, transatlantic phone calls were full of static, and you were often disconnected mid-sentence. I listened to a lot of static before making out the words, "So, now you know why I've called." It seemed unlikely that the connection was going to improve, so I didn't say, "I'm sorry. I couldn't hear you." Instead, I said "Yes." At that point, we were disconnected.

"John," I said, looking at my twenty-nine-year-old travel companion, "I know Dad called me for only one reason: He doesn't want me to go to West Germany with you."

John's expression darkened in a flash. The deep furrows in his brow and his tone of voice made his reaction clear, "Well, are you going to listen to your old man for the rest of your life, or are you going to do what you want to do?"

The harshness of his words stopped me in my tracks. I found myself wondering what kind of relationship John had with his parents and what kind of a father he'd make. I had thought he was everything I ever wanted when we were traveling in Italy. Now, I wasn't sure I felt quite the same way about him. Even so, I decided to go to West Germany with him. Unfortunately when we boarded the train in Paris, we got on a troop train to Kaiserslautern by mistake. When he realized I was the only woman on board the train, even John was worried.

I suppose because it was a troop train, it did not stop at the border between France and West Germany, so our passports were not stamped. After John left to return to the United States, I took a train to Austria to meet Sheila. At the Austrian border, the West German border guards eyed me with suspicion. "Why isn't your passport stamped leaving France and entering West Germany?" I was asked. I didn't dare tell them about the troop train, so I spoke Spanish, which they didn't understand, and pretended not to understand their English. I was beginning to be worried by their questions when they finally stamped my passport and let me go, saying, "OK, stupid American."

That summer was the last time I was to see John. We had made plans for him to visit me at Sarah Lawrence in the fall, but in the late summer, he sent me a letter telling me that on his arrival home, he had learned he'd fathered a child. He had married the mother and was now living in a basement apartment. I never answered his letter. Nearly fifty years later when I was interviewing candidates for headmaster at a boarding school where I was chairwoman of the board of trustees, I met a candidate who had been the headmaster of Robert College in Istanbul. I asked him if he knew John Chalfant. He said John had been the headmaster before him, had worked for wealthy Saudis, and had made lots of money. He added that John and his beautiful wife did not live together and rarely saw one another.

At the time I received John's letter it upset me, but I soon came to realize I'd had a lovely romance and I moved on with my life. Looking back, I have no regrets. I had no interest in becoming involved with a married man and John's response to my father's phone call had made me study the man I thought I loved, and made me think about the kind of man he was. In thinking about my father's phone call and what I believed it was about, I have come to the conclusion that it is important to tell children what you think. They may not always do what you think is the best thing to do, but possibly your comments will have meaning to them later.

In any case, after traveling with Sheila and her friends, I went home to Highland Park just in time for Bodo's crisis and then returned to Sarah Lawrence for my senior year.

That year, I lived in the annex of Harold Taylor's home with my roommates, Marie from France, and María from Columbia. I spent much of the year going to and from Boston, as I was dating Stephen Sonnabend.

Stephen and I had met very briefly at my going away party the year before. Evidently that brief meeting had been enough. Stephen had added my name to his little black book, and when I returned from Spain, he had contacted me.

Stephen and my parents attended my graduation in the spring. The commencement speaker for that year was Eleanor Roosevelt. I remember her saying toward the end of her speech, "Great minds discuss ideas; average minds discuss events; small minds discuss people." As I can recall, she finished with "You have been fortunate to have spent four years in an environment which stresses the creative process and sharing of ideas. I hope you will continue this process and dialog and bring your ideas to fruition." I listened carefully to her words, planted them firmly in my memory, and went home to marry Stephen.

I was twenty-two when I married Stephen and moved to Boston. By the time I was twenty-eight, I had four children. I have described my eighteen years of child rearing in *SOMETHING'S NOT RIGHT* so I'll refrain from going into detail about that here. I have come to think of these years as my "busy years," but not just because of my children. During these years, many things happened, and many people entered my life. One person in particular brightened my days and enriched my life back then: Alan Trustman. I had known Alan for some time when he made an unusual announcement. It was 1966, and Stephen and I were at a dinner dance at Belmont Country Club with Rene and Alan Trustman and a few other couples. Alan had asked me to dance, and as soon as we began to fox trot he said, "I'm going to write five movies."

I was used to the unexpected from Alan, so I did not stop dancing. "Everyone says you write as good a legal brief as any attorney in the city, and I know you well enough to know that no one has a better fantasy life. I think you're well suited to write movies."

"Do you want to hear the story line of my five movies?" he asked.

"Just tell me the first."

Twenty minutes later, I told Alan that I thought he had a winner. I was fascinated. "Have you written it yet?" I asked.

"No, but if I write it will you read it?"

"Of course," I replied and promptly forgot about it.

Several months later, Alan arrived at my doorstep early one morning and shoved a manuscript into my hands, saying, "Here."

"What's this?"

"My movie. You promised you'd read it."

With that, he left, and I went back to my usual morning routine. Several times during the day, he called to see how I was enjoying the script. At the time, I was a slow, dyslexic reader with four young children, a large house, and a dysfunctional marriage, so I suspect my response was a bit tart after the second call. Finally, I explained that I could not possibly start reading until the children were in bed. However, I did promise to stay up all night, if necessary, to finish it. I also told him the title, "Blood in the Snow," would never do for a movie.

"Well," he said, "if you know so much, come up with a better title."

Once the children were in bed, I went to work. I read until 3 A.M. I was totally engrossed. I loved the whole thing, except for the ending. The next morning I called Alan and told him that he should make a few minor corrections.

Women, I pointed out, wear sleeveless, not armless, dresses. I also told him that the ending should be different. I had no idea what it should be, but I did know it should be different.

Alan made the minor changes and sent the manuscript off to Alfred Hitchcock, who returned it without reading it. Crushed but persistent—a lawyerly trait if there ever was one—Alan

Top: Gertrude "Peanut" Petersen (who helped me raise the children)
Bottom: Samoset Hotel, Rockland, Maine
Left to Right: Patti, Eric, Kathy, Wendy Sonnabend

kept trying. Eventually he turned to the William Morris Agency and connected with John Flaxman. John suggested that Alan have his hero, who had robbed the bank at the beginning of the movie, rob the bank again at the end. Alan called to tell me of John's suggestion.

"That's great, Alan, if you can think of a different way for Crown to rob the bank," I replied.

Alan laughed. "Nancy," he said, "I worked in a bank one summer and was so bored that much of the time I just thought of different ways one could rob it. Nothing's easier."

"That's terrible!"

"No, it isn't. It's only bad if you do it!"

Alan wrote the new ending and not too much later called me to say, "John Flaxman just turned down an offer for my movie. I hope he knows what he's doing." The next time Alan called, he told me that Flaxman was working on a deal that would include Norman Jewison, Steve McQueen, and Faye Dunaway.

Alan had decided that he wanted me to meet John and Judy Flaxman, so Stephen and I flew to New York and had dinner with Alan, Rene, and the Flaxmans. During the evening, John Flaxman said to me, "I have the two hottest properties on the market today, your friend and a fellow from Yale who wrote a love story."

I think I congratulated him on his good fortune, but didn't think much more about it. In fact, even after I saw the movie *Love Story*, I didn't make the connection to John's dinner conversation. It was only sometime later when one of my children was reading Erich Segal's *Love Story* that I picked up the book and discovered it was dedicated to John Flaxman.

Before the filming of Alan's script began, he and I selected some of the sights we thought would work well for a few scenes in the movie. When the filming actually began in Boston, I was on location for several days and was an extra in an outdoor scene at Pier Four Restaurant. I remember being tremendously excited about being an extra and meeting Steve McQueen and Faye Dunaway. Unfortunately, my big scene was cut in the video and CD version of the film. When the filming was completed, I flew to New York to see the rushes (an early viewing of the film). Alan was too nervous to go which may have been just as well. His name was spelled wrong in the credits and had to be corrected. By this time the movie had gone through a couple of name changes and was now known as *The Thomas Crown Affair*.

Before the movie opened in theatres, and much to my surprise, Alan told me that he had heard Michel Legrand would win an Academy Award for "Windmills of Your Mind," the song Legrand had composed for the movie. Since the movie hadn't even opened yet, so no one had heard the song, it seemed highly unlikely to me. To this day, I don't know if Alan made this up or simply made a lucky guess, but whatever the case, Michel Legrand did win an Academy Award that year for the best original music for a screenplay.

Some time before the movie opened, Stephen and I spent the weekend in New York City at the Plaza Hotel, which was then owned by my father-in-law's company, Sonesta International Hotels. Noel Harrison, who had sung "Windmills of Your Mind" for the movie, was the featured performer at the hotel's nightclub at the time. I loved the song, so I asked the hotel manager to send a note to him, saying I would be in the audience Saturday night and would appreciate his singing "Windmills of Your Mind." That evening, he sang a few songs and then dug out the manager's note and said, "I'm sorry, Mrs. Sonnabend, I've never heard of the song, 'Windmills of Your Mind,' so I can't sing it."

Alan R. Trustman

"The Windmills of your Mind" from The Thomas Crown Affair *(1968) won an Oscar for Best Music, Original Song: Michel Legrand (music), Alan and Marilyn Bergman (lyrics).*

I was flabbergasted. After the show, I got the room number to his suite and rang his doorbell. He opened the door. "Hi," I said. "I'm Nancy Sonnabend, the one who requested you sing 'Windmills of Your Mind.' You recorded this song for the movie, *The Thomas Crown Affair*. I don't understand how you can say you've never heard it."

"Can you sing a few bars for me?"

I sang the opening lines.

"Oh, now I remember. My agent arranged for me to record the song in a studio, but I'd forgotten about it. What's the movie about?"

Our conversation took place in the doorway to his suite. Behind him, I could see people sitting on cushions on the floor, smoking. Of course, in 1968, the only possible question was, "Smoking what?" Probably it is just as well that it did not occur to me to ask that question.

The Thomas Crown Affair opened in Boston on June 19, 1968. That night, after the movie ended, Stephen and I had a big party for Alan, his friends and ours, some of the dignitaries, and all of our children. It was a memorable evening.

Thirty years later, in 1999, a new version of *The Thomas Crown Affair*, starring Pierce Brosnan and Rene Russo, was released. The story is the same, but it takes place in New York City instead of Boston and the robbery is art from the Metropolitan Museum rather than money from a bank. The ending was also changed. I find the new version to be too slick. Of course, I'm slightly prejudiced, but the first version, which I have seen many times, is like an old house. As you peel one layer of paint off, you find another layer and each new layer brings some new discovery. It seems to me the later version lacks the depth of the original script.

True to his words to me, Alan wrote a number of other screenplays in the 1960s, and I read them, but none of them made it to the big screen. One that I didn't care for, but remember quite clearly, was about a man with a brain tumor who climbed a tower and began to systematically shoot people he felt should be eliminated to make society a better place. Two weeks after I finished reading the script, Charles Joseph Whitman got onto the observation deck of an administrative building at the University of Texas at Austin and began shooting people. Whitman's killing spree made headlines all over the country. Like Alan's character, Whitman had a brain tumor.

Alan did have a second successful movie: *Bullitt*. This time, Alan's screenplay was an adaptation of a mystery entitled *Mute Witness* by Robert L. Fish. The hero of Fish's mystery was a sixty-five-year-old Jewish detective in New York City. For the movie, which, like *The Thomas Crown Affair*, came out in 1968, Alan turned Fish's hero into Frank Bullitt, a San Francisco detective, and added a girl, a Mustang, an airport chase, and a car chase. To this day, Steve McQueen's drive through the hills of San Francisco in the movie is probably one of the greatest car chase scenes ever filmed.

Alan began working on the movie while he and his family were visiting Stephen, our children and me in Rockland, Maine. I remember sitting outside with Alan, discussing various possibilities for the movie. We talked about whether the detective should be black, Irish, or Jewish, who would be the best actor to play the role, and how Alan would lay out the scenes.

Several years later, I found myself sitting next to Alan on board a plane to New York. Alan had arranged for me to demonstrate the 1, 2, 3 games I had invented for my son to executives from Parker Brothers and General Mills who were in New York

City for the annual toy fair. During the flight, I watched Alan flip through the pages of a paperback book. Finally, my curiosity got the better of me. "What are you doing?" I asked.

"Reading."

I simply could not believe that anyone could read that fast, so I grabbed the book from him. "Okay, tell me what you have just read." He repeated the page to me almost verbatim. I was stunned.

Once in the city, we each went our own way. My appointment with the toy executives was not until 6 P.M., so when the time came to go to the toy fair, Alan picked me up at the Plaza Hotel in a limo. At rush hour a taxi would have been almost impossible to find, so this was a practical solution to the transportation problem and great fun. Neither of us had ever ridden in a limo, and in some ways, we behaved like kids. We pushed the many buttons that operated the limo's accessories and peered out the limo's windows at the passing pedestrians.

Before I even began to demonstrate my games, I was handed a number of legal looking papers to sign. I looked desperately at Alan and whispered to him that it would take me a long time to read them. He flipped through them, handed them back to me, and said, "They're okay to sign."

Since the best way to understand the games was to play them, I invited the executives to sit on the floor with me and play the 1, 2, 3 games. They seemed fairly enthusiastic, perhaps because a pretzel was the reward for winning a game, and the gentlemen were all very hungry as they hadn't had lunch and it was now after 6 P.M. Parker Brothers decided to try out the 1, 2, 3 games with children and gave me positive feedback as a result, but the company never manufactured the games.

In exchange for some consulting work that I did for Pressman Toy Company, they manufactured 100 copies of the 1, 2, 3 games, which a hospital supply company, J. A. Preston Corporation, hoping to get into the special education market, then sold. Although the games sold out quickly, I couldn't find anyone to finance the production of more and didn't want to sink my own money into production costs, thus no more were produced.

In time, Alan and Rene divorced. Alan remarried, and then divorced again. At some point, he left Boston, so even with occasional calls to wish him a happy birthday, there have been long periods of time when I have not seen or heard from him. Thus, when the phone rang one day in 2003 and a voice said, "Hi Nancy. This is Alan," I found myself frantically trying to determine which Alan it might be.

"Hi," I said.

"You don't recognize my voice, do you?"

"Well, I'm trying to."

"Alan Trustman."

"Alan! To what do I owe this unexpected pleasure?"

"Michelle and I are having a party and would like you to come."

Michelle? I racked my brains for a moment and then remembered that after his second divorce, Alan had married Michelle Urry, the cartoon editor of Playboy magazine. "That's very nice, Alan. When and at which of your homes is the party or will it be held somewhere else? Is this a special occasion?"

"The party is a week from Tuesday, in the evening, at our home in Soho. Can you come?"

"Perhaps, can I get back to you on that? What is the dress code?"

"Just the usual,"

"That's helpful, Alan. How can I reach you? You don't

answer your e-mails or your phone. And if I am to come, I'll need directions."

"Okay, just leave all that information on Michelle's answering machine."

I went to the party. When I got to the door, there was a Chinese man, dressed in white, who let me in and escorted me down a long hall to an elevator. At that point, I was turned over to another Chinese man, again dressed in white, who opened the elevator door for me and pushed the button to Alan and Michelle's loft. When I exited the elevator, yet another Chinese man dressed in white escorted me down a hall where I encountered Alan, who greeted me warmly and introduced me to some of the guests, most of whom seemed to be prominent lawyers, authors, and artists, as well as people from Playboy magazine. What seemed to distinguish me from the other guests was the simple fact that I'd known Alan longer than anyone at the party, including his wife.

It was a beautiful party. There was an orchestra, an enormous bar, and more Chinese men in white, preparing drinks and serving hot hors d'oeuvres. The loft was large, nicely renovated, and filled with priceless works of art. I had some quality time with Alan. During it we filled each other in on our children, grandchildren, and what we'd been doing since the last time we had talked. All the people I met were interesting, and I had a wonderful time.

Michelle passed away in 2006, and I rarely hear from Alan these days. Rarely, however, isn't the same as never. On October 25, 2008, I received the following e-mail from Alan which he edited again in December 2009:

"Flew Miami/Aspen early March 2008. Plane held on tarmac at Dallas 4 hr 15 min for rain. Spent [the time] fighting attendants for cart. Got it for 1 hour, six Bloody Mary's. Did not know heavy salt content bad for you. Did not know salt in Bloody Mary's. March 7th best day skiing, four, five mile runs, no shortness of breath, no fatigue. Came home, collapsed, awoke at 3 am with congestive heart failure. Fought John [son] about hospital. Did not want to die in some jerkwater hospital in Aspen. Finally went to hospital, terrific place, gave me oxygen. Loved oxygen. Oxygen is marvelous. Oxygen is to opium as opium is to pot. Four hours of oxygen, and I was happy, really happy. I told John I had just had a near death experience, what did I want out of life I had never had? Decided I wanted to marry woman I'd just met. What woman? I told John I had only met her two weeks and three days previously so I hadn't told him about her. Tried to call her, no cell phone coverage in hospital. Sent John outside to propose. He objected but finally did, and much to his shock she accepted. Bliss. Gave her spectacular sapphire in Miami two days later. Widow, 62, three children, seven small granddaughters. Crazy about her. Went to Cleveland Clinic in Cleveland for open heart surgery March 28th. Chest cracked, mitral valve repair and unexpected hole in heart (latter probably explains lots, certainly poetic) repaired. Returned to Miami for 60 days R & R, over June 1, but atrial fibrillation and fast pulse had to be fixed with second procedure, planned ablation. Outpatient but serious.

Had third procedure to correct lingering afib. Planned to marry in fall when survival clear. Finished teaching at UM May 1. Tried unsuccessfully to raise $50 M for five $10 M movies, considered it a 500:1 shot. Love 500:1 shots. Did marry lady September 1. 15 months later am 79 years old, health excellent, no more heart problems, don't take a single pill and have sex every day. Consider self luckiest man on the planet. Have two novels with agents and publishers, no reply as yet. Otherwise nothing new."

I treasure the time Alan and I have had together. He is one of the most brilliant and impossible people I've ever had the great good fortune to know. There is no other person who so consistently challenges my mind and makes me think and see things from new perspectives.

CHAPTER 16
Grandparents on the Go

During my busy years, those years of child rearing and marriage, my parents spent their summers in Illinois—first in Highland Park, then in Winnetka, and then, after another move, in Highland Park again. Spring, fall, or winter was spent wherever their fancy took them. Over the years, their fancy took them to Cuba, Mexico, Jamaica, Russia, Africa, Greece, Japan, and Belize, as well as Nassau and Eleuthera in the Bahamas. In the summer, they attended the Ravinia Opera frequently, were invited to parties, played bridge, and went out to dinner. In the winter, they would spend a few weeks in Palm Beach and, in time, six months in Sarasota, Florida, where they had lots of friends, who, like them, had gone south for the winter.

For years, they celebrated the New Year with an annual New Year's Day party at their Longboat Key home. If New Year's celebrations belonged to Florida, during my busy years, the Christmas holidays belonged to Boston. Each year, my parents would travel to Boston to join Stephen, the children, and me for the holidays. It was during these years that my parents became close friends with my in-laws, Sonny and Esther Sonnabend.

Circa 1970, Longboat Key, FL
Joe Lelewer taking a walk on the beach before all the tall condos were built

1976, Longboat Key, FL, Nancy Sonnabend and Joe Lelewer on his 70th birthday

My father-in-law, A.M. Sonnabend, known to his friends as Sonny, was an entrepreneur who purchased profitable companies, paid for them out of their own excess working capital and future earnings, and then merged them into a company with net operating losses (NOLs). Then he would phase out some of the unprofitable divisions of the company losing money and use the NOLs to shelter the profits of the companies making money. These tax credits were also carried forward into future years.

Sonny fine-tuned this technique, which became known as the Botany formula, with his purchase of Botany Mills. Over the years, he purchased other companies, including Consolidated Retail Stores and the Seagrave Corporation.

In 1943, Sonny became involved in hotels as a real estate investment. As a result of this involvement, the Sonnabend Operated Hotels came into being, other hotels were acquired, and in time, most of them were merged into the Hotel Corporation of America, now known as Sonesta International Hotels Corporation. Real estate investments seem to have many consequences. Because Sonny invested in hotels, Stephen was sent to Chicago to work at the Edgewater Beach Hotel in 1955, and we met just before I went abroad.

By the late 1950s, Sonny's business acumen was so well known and so well regarded that business schools invited him to speak to their classes. I remember driving him to Harvard Business School once when he had been invited to give a lecture there.

When we got to the parking lot, there were no spaces, and we had to hunt for a spot down the street. As we worked our way through the crowd, Sonny said to me, "I wonder what's going on?" Neither of us realized that everyone was there to hear him speak.

I watched the audience as he spoke that day. He mesmerized them. They couldn't get enough of him.

I was very fond of Sonny. During the fall and spring of my senior year in college before Stephen and I were married, I had spent many hours with Sonny while Stephen was at work. I would spend the mornings of my Boston visits reading and writing papers as Sonny talked on the phone at his small, wooden desk. The drawers of the desk held paperback westerns and toys for his grandchildren. He didn't need to file anything—his memory and his briefcase were his file cabinets. At lunch we would grab a bite to eat and then go for a walk. As we walked, he would explain his latest business deal to me. When Stephen and I became engaged, Sonny gave me a lovely gold watch, which I treasure to this day. Later I acquired the gold charm of the Plaza Hotel, which Sonny received the day he fulfilled his dream of becoming president of the hotel.

Sonny and my father got along particularly well. Their friendship had developed as they had gotten to know each other during summer visits to Rockland, Maine. For a few weeks each summer, my parents, Stephen, the children, and I would join my in-laws in Rockland, Maine for our vacation. When all of us gathered at the Samoset Hotel for tennis, we would sometimes have three generations on the same court. Other times, my father and I would play Stephen and his father. My father once said, "Sonny was an exciting man, a raconteur, A-number-one, and the best company in which I've ever been."

Occasionally, Sonny would present my father with a business opportunity, and my father always made money on it. One of the most interesting involved the Hathaway Shirt Company. When Sonny decided to purchase the Hathaway Shirt Company, he showed my father the company's balance sheet for the preceding five years. For four of those years, the company had broken even but had not made a profit. In the last year, it had lost a sizable amount of money, because it had taken a large loss on inventory, and was considering going out of business. At the time, the stock was selling for about $11.00 per share, mostly because of the Hathaway name. Sonny said he was planning to buy the company because he felt he could sell it for a profit.

After looking at the balance sheet, my father asked, "How much are you going to pay for it?"

"Twenty-two dollars a share."

"I thought you would buy it at a discount."

"No, you can't buy it at a discount. The name is the number one name in the shirt industry, and you have to pay a premium to get it. Would you like to come in on the deal?"

"I don't know. It doesn't sound great to me, but I'll talk it over with Sis."

My parents talked it over that night. They knew that whatever Sonny did usually succeeded, so they decided to take a little gamble. The next morning, my father told Sonny they had decided to buy 1,000 shares, which meant they had to put up $22,000. My father asked Sonny if he should give him the money right away.

Sonny said, "No don't give me the money now. I'll put you down for 1,000 shares, and that's all that's needed for the time being."

Two weeks later, before my parents returned to Chicago, my father said to Sonny, "What about the deal?"

"Oh, it's coming along fine."

"Well, should I pay you now?"

"No, don't pay me now. I'll let you know when you get home."

Around Christmas time, my father called Sonny and said he hadn't heard from him on the Hathaway deal. Should he send him some money?

"Oh, no, don't send me any money; we sold the company."

"I didn't know we had bought it yet."

"Yeah, we bought it, and we've already sold it."

"What did you sell it for?"

"We sold it for $33.00 per share, and you have an $11,000 profit, but you can't get the money yet because we have to wait six months, for tax reasons, before we can complete the sale."

In the late spring, my father received a check for $11,000. I can remember him telling me about the deal later, smiling as he shook his head and said, "What percentage return on investment is that?"

Not only did Stephen, the children, and I visit my parents in Illinois and Florida regularly, each child, from the age of five on, paid a solo visit to my parents in Illinois at some point during the year. For the flight from Logan Airport to O'Hare International, the traveling child would wear a string with a tag attached to it around his or her neck. Written on the tag was the child's name, address, phone number, my name, and the name, address, and phone number of my parents in Highland Park. I must say that my youngest daughter's first trip to visit her grandparents made me very glad that I tended to label everything in sight when the children were young. Even though my father always liked to say, "All's well that ends well," I suspect Patti's first flight aged them considerably.

Patti's plane took off on time. When the plane left, I called my parents and told them Patti was in the air, just as I had on prior occasions when each of my other children had flown to Chicago. My parents went to O'Hare ahead of time in case she

A.M. "Sonny" Sonnabend 12/8/1896–2/11/1964

Summer 1958, A.M. "Sonny" Sonnabend on the deck of his cottage Flume at the Samoset Hotel, Rockland, Maine

arrived early. While they were waiting for her, her airline suddenly announced that the flight had been sent to Midway because of storms over O'Hare. As my parents debated whether one of them should stay at O'Hare and the other drive to Midway, there was a second announcement: There were now storms over Midway, and because the plane was running low on fuel, it had been diverted to Milwaukee. My father pushed his way through to a clerk at a counter. "We have a five-year-old granddaughter, traveling alone, on the flight that was just diverted to Milwaukee."

"Don't worry," he was told. "It will refuel in Milwaukee, wait for the storms to clear here, and then return to O'Hare."

My parents sat down to wait and worry. An hour later, Patti arrived, all smiles and holding the hand of a good-looking man in his early forties. He introduced himself to my parents and then said, "You have a remarkable granddaughter. She told me all about the musical Oliver and said that I must take my children to see it. I know all about you, her sisters, her brother, and your daughter. When we arrived in Milwaukee, there were horrendous winds, so I carried Patti to the airport terminal and, later, back to the plane. She would have been blown away otherwise. The flight attendants paid no attention."

Patti stood by nodding seriously. My father shook her protector's hand, thanked him profusely, and said, "She was in good hands. We were lucky." With that, my parents and Patti waved goodbye. Patti got down to the business of visiting her grandparents, and my parents got down to the business of recovering from their worry.

When they weren't hosting their grandchildren or visiting us in Boston and Maine or entertaining friends in Florida, my parents traveled the world. Every few years they would pick a country to visit and set off to see as much of it as they could. I still remember the postcard my father, who knew perhaps four words of Spanish, sent me from Mexico one year: "Dear Baby, Today I ordered my entire breakfast in Spanish: 'UN NÚMERO UNO, POR FAVOR.' Love, Dad."

Their favorite trip, they always said, was their trip to Africa. Initially, my mother had not wanted to go, but my father had always wanted to see the animals in their natural habitat. At a cocktail party one evening, he said to a group of women, "I'd love to go to Africa, but Sis doesn't want to go. Are there any takers?" Five women said yes immediately, and my mother decided the trip sounded like fun.

Once in Africa, my parents took a bus tour from Nairobi to Tanzania and then to Uganda. During the tour, the group stopped at various schools. I remember my father was impressed by the students' good manners. He noticed that whenever the group entered a classroom, the children stood up immediately and remained standing until the teacher said, "You may sit down."

There were twenty-five people on the tour. However, in order to travel by Land Rover into the bush to see the animals during the safari portion of the trip, the guide broke the group into smaller groups of five. On the second day of the safari, a man knocked on my parents' door and asked, "Would you like to join us for the rest of the trip, and we'll pick a lady for the fifth person?" My parents promptly said yes. Their new friend was a surgeon at John Hopkins Hospital with a charming wife. He was trying to capture the sounds the animals made, and my father was taking movies of the animals, so they complemented each other and had terrific fun together.

While they were on safari, the group stayed at the Treetops Hotel in Aberdares National Park in Kenya. The hotel is built in the branches of trees. You enter the hotel by a stairway that is then pulled up after you've climbed it. Every night, the twenty-five members of the tour would gather to have drinks and hors d'oeuvres on the hotel's big observation deck.

One evening while on the deck, my father tried to get a picture of a gorilla with a baby in tow. Because his camera had a long distance lens, he had to back up to get a good picture. He kept backing up and backing up until he finally he bumped into somebody. He automatically said, "Excuse me" and then turned to apologize again. At that point, he discovered he had just apologized to a gorilla, who seemed rather unimpressed. I don't think my father or the other members of the tour ever got over his apology.

When he was telling me about their trip, my father said, quite seriously, "At Treetops, we had to lock our doors and windows whenever we went out because the gorillas would come in and steal everything they could find." Of course, he couldn't resist adding that their entire stay at Treetops had involved a lot of monkey business.

One year when my parents couldn't figure out where to vacation, my father decided to spin the globe in his study. He put his finger on the globe as it spun and wherever his finger was when the globe stopped spinning would be where they would go. His finger was on Belize, British Honduras, when the globe stopped. They didn't know anything about Belize, but that's where they went that year. When they arrived, the temperature was 110 degrees in the shade, and their hotel had no air conditioning, just slowly rotating ceiling fans like the ones in Casablanca. Sleep was impossible that night. By morning, they had tossed and turned so much, their sheets were tangled in a heap on the floor. "Let's go for a sail," my father said. "Out on the water, it will be cooler."

They wandered down to the dock and hired a 30-foot sail-boat. The boat's captain agreed that he and his first mate would take them out for an hour and a half after lunch. Everything was fine when they began their sail. There was a slight breeze, the sky was clear, and the temperature was comfortable.

Once they had cleared the harbor, the captain said, "You see that lighthouse on that island ahead of us? It would be nice to sail out there. It won't take too long." Unfortunately, it took longer than the captain had planned because the boat became becalmed about two-thirds of the way there.

As the boat bobbed aimlessly on the water, my father, having heard the expression "whistle up the wind," began to whistle. He must have overdone it. All of a sudden they were hit by a breeze that took them to the island in no time, but when they stepped ashore and my father turned around to look back at Belize, he discovered that it was no longer visible. Dark clouds seemed to have covered it completely. "Skipper, do you think that is a hurricane or a tornado or whatever you have down here?" he asked.

"No. It couldn't be because we don't have them this time of year. They only hit in the summer," the captain responded.

"Well, it looks very ominous to me. I think we'd better get back as fast as we can."

They left immediately, but about one-third of the way back, they were hit by a terrible hurricane. Rain poured down in torrents. It was pitch black, and the winds tore at the boat, first from one angle and then from another. When the storm first began, my parents heard the captain say what sounded like, "Herman! Herman!" to the first mate, so they assumed that Herman was the man's name. When they realized the captain was actually saying, "Hurry man! Hurry man!" my father began to envision the newspaper headline for the next day: Chicago Merchant and Wife Drown.

As the storm worsened, my father leaned over the side of the boat with his feet locked under the seat on the other side. When the wind shifted direction, he would shift and do the reverse. My mother stayed on the floor of the boat, repeating the same prayer over and over. The boat turned and twisted about. There were no running lights, no life preservers, and the captain kept telling the first mate to take down the sail. As the first mate was trying to take down the jib in the howling wind and rough seas, my father could see the fins of sharks following the boat.

The hour and a half sail ended up taking ten hours. They reached shore at eleven at night, drenched and freezing. When they got to their room, my father said, "I sure don't ever want to see water again." My mother agreed heartily and then filled the bathtub with hot water and climbed into it to get warm. The next day, they called me. Stephen and I were in Palm Beach, and my parents flew over to spend the rest of their vacation with us.

Unlike Belize, the winter months spent in Palm Beach or Sarasota, Florida, every year were never disappointing. Over time, my mother's deafness worsened, her health slipped, my father had a mild heart attack and eventually major surgery, but they never stopped going to Sarasota in the winter. In fact, they continued to go for several months each winter through 2003.

When my children were young, Stephen and I often would visit my parents with the children for at least a part of their Florida stay. One year, Stephen and I left Kathy, age two and a half, and Wendy, age one, with them while we traveled to South America. That year, my parents were staying in Palm Beach at the Sun and Surf Club which had a house right on the beach.

On the first night after Stephen and I left, my parents put the girls to bed and returned to check on them a little later. Much to their horror, they couldn't find Kathy. She was not in her bed. They looked down the hallway and in the bathroom, searched the entire house, and then began looking up and down the beach. Frantic and trying to decide whether to call the Coast Guard or the police, or both, they went back to the girls' room for one final check. All of a sudden, my mother spotted Kathy sound asleep in a large overstuffed chair, surrounded by many dolls. She was so snuggled in they hadn't been able to distinguish her from the dolls.

A few years later, when my parents were in Sarasota for the winter, they invited us to come for a visit. We accepted and talked a few of our friends into joining us there. Shortly before we left for Florida, Stephen called my father and said he thought the children might enjoy seeing the Sailor Circus while we were there. The Sailor Circus is a four-ring youth circus production put on by students from fourth grade through high school who live in Sarasota and the surrounding counties. The students do all the circus acts including the high-wire and trapeze acts. They are trained by retired circus performers. (Sarasota is the former home of the Ringling Brothers Barnum and Bailey Circus.)

"Fine, I'll buy tickets," my father said. "How many should I get?"

Stephen replied, "Buy twenty-three tickets. A few of our friends are coming down with their children."

My father later said that he almost collapsed when he heard that. During the evening performance, all of the children, with the exception of Stephen Trustman, who was three years old, fell asleep. My father just smiled and said, "I guess we all had a great time."

CHAPTER 17
Good Friends, High Adventure

My marriage to Stephen was difficult from the start and adding four children to the mix made it more complicated. By the summer of 1977, Stephen and I had been separated for four years. Most of my weekends were spent with David, who later became my second husband, at his summer home at the water's edge on Chappaquiddick. For those who don't know, Chappaquiddick lies off the eastern end of Martha's Vineyard, right across from Edgartown Harbor. If the time I spent with David did not lead to the traditional happily-ever-after ending, it did lead to wonderful friendships with Claire and Rex Kaiser and Andi and Mike Dubroff.

David's house on the island had a wide porch where I could sit and read or look out over the water. I spent a good part of the summer of 1977 on that porch, looking up from my book to observe a family of seven who lived on the Yacht Claire, a sailboat that was moored near David's dock. From what I could observe, there was a husband who appeared on weekends, five children (or so it seemed—they moved constantly, which made counting difficult), and a mother who organized the children, got them to and from sailing and swimming classes before going off to play tennis, and did everything that needed to be done—from the laundry by hand to the cooking to the airing out of sleeping bags. I remember thinking to myself, "This lady is either crazy or a really neat person. I'm going to go meet her."

As I recall, David was off somewhere when I decided it was time to meet the lady on the boat. Although I had never driven a Boston Whaler, or any other boat, I had seen others, including children, do so, which led me to think it couldn't be too difficult. I turned the key, pulled the rope, and David's Boston Whaler started right up. I untied it and headed out to the Yacht Claire. I circled the boat, afraid to get too close, and called out, "Anyone home?" A voice answered, "Yes," and a pretty woman appeared.

"Hi, I'm Nancy and I'm visiting my friend, David," I said, pointing to the house. "We'd like to invite you all for dinner tomorrow night."

"I'm Claire, and nobody invites us for dinner. There are too many of us."

"I know there are seven of you. I have some children too. So does David."

"Do you have chairs for everyone?"

"No, it will be very casual. The children can sit on the floor or the steps. We'll dig clams, which we can have as hors d'oeuvres before dinner. David will catch a couple of blue fish, I'll make a big salad, and we'll have watermelon, ice cream, and cookies. Come at six."

"Sounds great, we'll be there."

They came, and it was the first of many great times with

them. Rex and Claire Kaiser are two of the most down-to-earth, fun-loving people I have ever met. Furthermore, they are one of the few couples who are equally fun to be with together or individually. Over the years, as we have met and talked in their home and mine, watched sunsets from the Yacht Claire, walked together at Winterthur[8], attended one of our many children's weddings or parties, and eaten out, we have become fast friends.

When I first knew Claire and Rex, they spent their summers on the Kaiser Gale Force Yacht Claire, and the rest of the year in Delaware, first in Centerville and later in Wilmington.

Every year, whether in Centerville or Wilmington, the Kaisers have invited over 120 guests to their home to celebrate that most Irish of holidays, St. Patrick's Day. For years, the start of the festivities were marked by a St. Patrick's Day party given by the Kaisers' friends Norman and Muriel Borish the night before the Kaiser's St. Patrick's Day party.

Shortly after I met Claire and Rex, they invited me to their party. Since I knew that they did all the cooking for their guests, I offered to arrive a couple of days ahead of time to help. My early arrival soon became a tradition that neither snow, nor sleet or dark of night could disrupt. So set is this tradition that one year, when the forecast called for a large snowstorm to move up the coast from the south a couple of days before St. Patrick's Day, I immediately packed, went to the airport, and got on the first plane out of Logan for Philadelphia. I tried to call Claire at their Centerville home before leaving, but only the answering machine picked up the phone.

It seemed to me there was zero visibility as the plane landed in Philadelphia, and after we touched down, the pilot

---

[8] Winterthur, an American country estate, is the former home of Henry Francis du Pont (1880–1969), an avid antiques collector and horticulturist. In the early 20th century, H. F. du Pont and his father, Henry Algernon du Pont, designed Winterthur in the spirit of 18th and 19th century European country houses. It is a museum and also has 60 acres of naturalistic gardens.

Top: Rex and Claire Kaiser on the Yacht Claire
Bottom: Andi and Mike Dubroff

announced, "The good news is we have just arrived at Philadelphia International Airport. The bad news is the airport is now closed. We were the last plane to land."

It was bedlam inside the airport. All flights had been canceled, and absolutely no form of transportation seemed to be leaving the airport. I was beginning to be discouraged when I spotted a van that had "Wilmington" written on the side of it. Wilmington, I remembered, was where Rex's father's home was. The van's driver was about to start the trip back to Wilmington with the passengers he'd just brought to the airport. He had one empty seat and, after some pleading, agreed to take me along. I tried calling Claire again, and again got the answering machine.

It took two hours to drive through the snow and deliver all the passengers to their destinations. Unfortunately, I did not have the address or phone number of Rex's father's home in Wilmington, so I gave the driver the Kaiser's Centerville number and the number of a friend of theirs. With any luck at all, I thought, there would be someone home at one of the houses who could give us an address.

As I huddled in the van, the driver stood with the snow swirling around him at an outdoor phone booth trying both phone numbers. The driver, too, got the answering machine in Centerville, but he was able to obtain the Wilmington phone number and address from their friend. Because he got a busy signal when he called the number, he decided to take me to that address. We arrived at the door, covered in snow and looking like Eskimos.

Looking through the peephole of the front door, Rex could only see a figure enveloped in a fur parka with a hood that covered most of the face standing next to a man whom he'd never seen before, holding a suitcase. "Who is it?" he asked.

"Nancy. Here to cook. Let me in, please." The door opened.

That year, Claire, Rex, and I moved the party to Rex's father's home in Wilmington, and we called all the guests to tell them of the change in location. We also retrieved all the food from Centerville and pulled it up the driveway on sleds. The blender wasn't working, so I whipped two quarts of whipping cream with an eggbeater. It took forever, I remember, but it was needed because, in spite of the snow, there was a great turnout.

Over the years, there are certain chores which have become mine and I always do them for the Saint Patrick's Day party. These include folding the forks into the napkins, whipping the cream, and organizing the cookies on platters. Even if I am not scheduled to arrive at the Kaisers' until the middle of the afternoon on the day of the party, Claire leaves these things for me. I have to admit I could not show that kind of restraint myself. I would probably become so nervous waiting that I would start folding the forks into the napkins with one hand and whipping the cream with the other.

In fact, one of the things that I have always loved about Claire is her ability to take things in stride. She is the most laid-back person I know. Even when I was a bit short with her brother while I was visiting them in Wilmington, she did not get angry with me.

Rex and Claire had gone out for a few minutes and left me to answer the phone, which I did. A voice on the other end of the line said that his name was Charlie Brown and that he was Claire's brother. I had no memory of Claire saying she had a brother or ever introducing me to a brother, and I certainly would have remembered the name Charlie Brown. Thus, when Claire returned, I laughed and said, "Some character called, claimed his name is Charlie Brown, and that he's your brother."

"I do have a brother named Charlie Brown."

It seems that Claire's sister-in-law had been ill for a long time, so her brother, Charlie Brown, had not always been present when the family got together.

On another occasion, after telling Rex and Claire all about *The Professor and the Madman*, a book about the creation of the *New Oxford English Dictionary*, Rex had said, "Remind me to show you something when we get back to the house." I had finished the book on the flight from Boston and had found it so fascinating that I had spent most of our dinner time on the topic. Back at the house, Rex showed Claire and me a leather-bound, gold-tooled edition of the *New Oxford Dictionary* on the shelf in their library.

"Where did you get that?" I asked.

"I never knew we had it," Claire said in amazement and left the room to answer the phone.

Rex handed me the first volume of the multivolume set, which had an inscription printed on the first page.

"Who gave it to whom?"

"My uncle, John J. Raskob, gave it to my Dad."

"Who was John J. Raskob?" I asked. After all, the *Oxford English Dictionary* is no small gift. Rex said something about the Empire State Building, which I didn't get, then Claire came back and the conversation changed. I forgot all about John J. Raskob until the following summer when I was on the Yacht Claire. At that point, I suddenly remembered our previous conversation and said to Rex, "Now, who was your uncle and what did he have to do with the Empire State Building? Was he a builder or an architect?"

"It was his idea and he financed it himself. He hired the architectural firm Shreve, Lamb, and Harmon to design the building and it has been said that he asked Lamb, "How tall can you make it before it falls down?" He hired Starrett Brothers and Eken, who were very inventive for their time, to be the general contractors. From ground breaking to completion took one year and forty-five days, and only twenty-seven months elapsed from the time my uncle first met with Lamb to the building's opening on May 1, 1931."

"How did your uncle make his money?"

"Wall Street. They say he spent nearly $41 million to finance the building. He was also a director of General Motors and Dupont."

"I've known you all these years and you've never said a word about your family's connection to the Empire State Building. Do your friends in Wilmington know?"

"Some. I don't talk about it. After all, I didn't have anything to do with it."

One year, the neighbor's dog ate all the corn beef for the St. Patrick's Day party while it was outside cooling. Claire simply went back to the market, bought more corn beef, and began cooking all over again. I would have been out of my mind; Claire just shrugged and laughed.

Another time, I arrived three days before the party, and neither the shopping nor the cooking were finished. Instead, in the front hall, was an enormous bolt of cloth resting on two wooden sawhorses.

"What are you going to do with that material?" I asked

"Make draperies for the living room and entrance hall."

"When, after the party?"

"No, now before the party."

"Do you know how to make them?"

"I have a video that will show us how."

"Do you have a sewing machine?"

"No. We'll cut them, drape them over the rods that are already up, and stuff the bottoms."

We watched the video, and Claire went to work. She would pull off some material, measure it with her arms, and we would cut. As the roll got smaller, I worried that we would run out before we finished all the windows because she had told me there was no more material available. Claire wasn't worried. As it turned out, we did run out of material, and, to this day, there is one window in the living room that has draperies on only one side. No one seems to notice.

There is a lot to be said for entering into the Kaisers' philosophy that things will work out as they should in the end if you are sensible.

Toward the end of one summer, I was on the Yacht Claire with Claire and Rex taking it from Edgartown Harbor to Mattapoisett. We were pulling a whaler full of supplies. We had gotten as far as Hadley's Harbor on Naushon Island, part of the Elizabeth Island chain, when the fog rolled in and visibility rolled out. There was no fuss. Instead, we anchored, Claire brought out cheese, crackers, and wine, Rex pulled out the keyboard that was built into the center table, and we sang. Eventually, we ate dinner and went to bed. The next morning, the fog cleared and we pulled out of the charming harbor. It was a lovely experience. A subsequent sailing experience with the Dubroffs was more exciting than lovely.

I first met Andi Dubroff in almost as casual a way as I got to know Claire and Rex. Both Andi and I love tennis, thus I met her on a tennis court on the Vineyard. As we chatted after a game, we discovered that we were both raising a bunch of children and loved sports. Back then, Andi was small and thin with thick, reddish hair and rapid-fire speech. Mike, her husband, was over six feet tall, balding and quiet. They both liked to be active. Our friendship grew over time until, at last, we were keeping in touch and getting together even when the Dubroffs were in Newburgh, New York and I was in Boston.

In October, 1983, a number of years after I had gotten to know the Kaisers and the Dubroffs, Andi and Mike Dubroff invited me to sail from Martha's Vineyard to Norfolk, Virginia on their forty-foot Fuji. Andi told me there would be five of us on the trip. Mike, she said, had hired a man called Rory to help with the sail, and they had invited their Newburgh neighbor Rita to join them. It seemed to me the timing was perfect. There were five months before the Kaisers' St. Patrick's Day party, so I wasn't worried about missing it, and David, who was now my husband, was headed to Italy to deliver a paper at a conference. I accepted their invitation and made plans for a short, relatively easy, five-day sail.

The Wednesday I was to leave for the Vineyard, I awoke with a dull pain in my tooth. I decided to ignore it, as there were many things that needed to be done before I left: shopping, baking cookies, making a casserole for one night's dinner on board, calling my children and parents to notify them of where I would be for the next five days, and packing. I included a bottle of Bufferin and a half dozen codeine tablets in my duffel bag. Once packed, I caught the mid-afternoon bus to Woods Hole, which connected with the Vineyard ferry. Andi was on the dock to meet me when we pulled into Vineyard Haven.

That evening, the five of us gathered at the Dubroff's Edgartown home. I had never met either Rita or Rory before. Rita was forty-five years old with long, brown hair and bangs. She had two sons and appeared to have a relaxed disposition.

Rory was thirty-two years old, six feet tall, with small eyes and a dark beard and mustache. Mike Dubroff and Rory were seasoned sailors which gave me a sense of comfort and safety. Andi also had a fair amount of sailing experience. Rita and I knew sailing terminology and what to do when given directions.

We organized our gear, food, and drinks, loaded the boat for the trip, and ate dinner. Before we went to bed, Mike checked the weekend weather forecast with the Coast Guard. I slept soundly that night. When the alarm went off before sunrise Thursday morning, I groped to shut it off and, as I did so, immediately became aware that my tooth had not stopped aching. Once again, I decided to ignore it. Before we left, Mike checked the weekend weather forecast with the Coast Guard one more time. The report was the same as the previous night's: Unseasonably cold weather on Friday with sun and some overcast skies throughout the weekend. Depending on the winds, Mike estimated we'd make Norfolk sometime late Sunday or early Monday.

My spirits were high as we left Edgartown Harbor and were treated to a magnificent sunrise send-off. The Atlantic had small swells, the sky was clear, the temperature was in the 50's and there was a nice breeze for sailing. Mike charted our course along the eastern coastline, and the five of us agreed we would each take a four-hour shift at the wheel. In just a few hours, the Vineyard shrank to a tiny dot and then disappeared from view. I found being out of sight of land beautiful, but a bit intimidating. As we sailed from one marker to the next using the LORAN (LOng Range Aid to Navigation) as backup, the pain in my tooth became intense. With each change of shift, I downed two more Bufferin.

That evening, I'd been at the wheel for nearly two hours

when Rory came out to check on me. The small swells had become enormous mountains, and I was exhausted from trying to hold a steady course. I said, "I'm tired and worried about the size of the swells."

"This is nothing," Rory said reassuringly. "I'll do the rest of your shift and then my own. Go take it easy for a while."

I happily turned the wheel over to him and headed to the cabin. As I entered it, Mike popped a pill in his mouth and took a swallow of water. "What are you taking?" I asked.

"Something like Dramamine. I frequently feel queasy in this type of sea. With only two men on board, I want to be sure my stomach stays settled."

I felt slightly nauseous myself and took one of Mike's pills and a codeine tablet. By 10 P.M., I was snuggled into my sleeping bag and beginning to drift off to sleep. When I awoke, it was pitch dark, the sea seemed very rough, everyone was inside the cabin, and we were under motor power. "What time is it?" I asked groggily.

"9 A.M."

"How come it's so dark out?"

"A bad storm is approaching. A couple hours after you went to sleep, the Coast Guard told us we were heading into a storm. We decided not to run for shore because we don't have sufficient power to get to land before the storm hits. We'll be safer in deep water."

The mainsail had already been dropped, but the jib had jammed and had to be left up. We were headed south into the wind, and the waves, which were coming from the shore, were pushing us farther out into the Atlantic. Even worse, the LORAN was not working. Mike had read it two hours previously, but couldn't get coordinates now. Although the Coast Guard knew our position somewhere within a 200-mile radius, with the storm raging they couldn't send a plane or boat for us until we had established our precise location.

Over the next hour, the storm became increasingly violent. The waves rose to thirty feet. We felt as if we were on a giant roller coaster as the boat rode up and down them. Each time we came down, the bow crashed into the sea, causing the boat to vibrate with such intensity that we couldn't help wondering if the next vibration would tear the boat apart. After each crash, there would be a momentary silence as we submarined beneath the water, which put maximum stress on the automatic bailer. We were taking on water and, consequently, we were always wet. The mood in the cabin was somber, yet no one ever spoke of being scared.

For two and a half days, we braced our feet against the cabin's walls or the bottom of the opposite bunk and gripped the bunk we were on tightly. I was in good condition, but my muscles became sore in short order. Had I not been concentrating so hard on holding onto the bunk and bracing my feet against the wall, I probably would have thought of my parents' trip to Belize.

Getting to and from the head became almost impossible since, as soon as you tried to stand, you felt nauseous. Initially, we would crawl to the door, open it, and then close it. As time went on, no one bothered to shut the door. No one ate or slept—with the exception of Rory, who took one nap. Our infrequent conversations always dealt with problems at hand—the LORAN, calling the Coast Guard, wearing life jackets, or having the life raft quickly available.

Mike Dubroff spent the two and a half days in the chair at the controls. We were on autopilot, so he held on with one hand

and tried to work on the LORAN with his free hand. At the start of our ordeal, the Coast Guard had tried to establish our position by taking soundings. When that had failed, they had us try another instrument that was on board. Unfortunately, it required stability to get a reading, which was simply impossible. When that failed, they asked for our names, addresses, phone numbers, ages, next of kin and our present state of health. I suddenly understood why the "Chicago Merchant and Wife Drown" headline had passed before my father's eyes.

After we gave the Coast Guard the information they had requested, they told us to report to them every half hour. I made it my responsibility to be timekeeper and each half hour reminded Mike to make the call. It gave me something to think about, which helped to ward off panic. In between calls, Mike continued to work on the LORAN until, at last, the coordinates giving our position appeared on the screen. Mike radioed them to the Coast Guard.

"Roger that. Sending a rescue boat. Due to storm and distance, estimated time to reach you will be about eight hours."

Throughout the storm, everyone experienced strange, flu-like symptoms, including extreme heat and profuse sweating, followed by severe chills. One minute we would be so hot that we would want to take off our sweaters or jackets, the next minute we would be shivering. Because it was difficult to get the life jackets off and on—and certainly not safe—we wore them for the entire two and a half days.

Given our symptoms, it was fortunate that Andi had purchased five new sleeping bags for the trip. The zipper on each bag ran down the length of one side and across the bottom, which allowed the bag to open completely. When we had chills, we used the opened sleeping bags as large blankets.

Each of us also kept a flashlight and water within reach. I attached my flashlight to my belt and put a $100 bill in my pant pocket. For whatever reason, this gave me the feeling that I was going to be able to bail myself out of some future problem. Although I was fearful my life might end at any moment, I don't think I really believed I was going to die, thus being able to bail myself out was important to me.

About four hours after the Coast Guard had radioed that they were sending a cutter, we were hit squarely on the starboard side by a massive wave. The force of the wave flipped the boat upside down and tore the shelves and their contents from the starboard side, sending them flying against the port wall. At the same time, the main cabin table, housing all the liquor and silverware, ripped out of the floor and also landed on the port side of the boat. No one was injured, but for the first time, Andi, Rita, and I panicked. We yelled at Mike, "Call the Coast Guard! Call May Day!"

"May Day means your boat is breaking up and sinking. Our boat's in good condition," he replied as the boat righted, and we returned to our roller coaster ride. He went on to explain in somewhat the same tone I used with my children when I wanted to calm them, "The Coast Guard is en route to us. If they think we are sinking, they might stop trying to reach us and rescue a boat they have a better chance of saving."

As we had the radio on, we knew that other boats, including a ninety-foot trawler, were in trouble. In fact, we were probably the last to see the lights of the trawler before it went down with no survivors. It passed close to us as we were riding up a wave in the middle of the storm.

We each took occasional sips of water and held on for the

next four hours. I remember thinking briefly about how my children would fare if I drowned. It was a fleeting thought. My toothache seemed to have disappeared. In fact, my system seemed to shut down so that it could cope with only what was required at a particular moment.

Finally, the Coast Guard radioed that they had a cutter nearby and a helicopter overhead. Because of the storm, we never heard or saw the helicopter. We were notified that there was no way to take us off our boat and were told to put one person, with lifelines, on the bow's deck. Rory donned the only survival suit we had, opened the hatch, and climbed onto the deck. During the few seconds the hatch was open, gallons of water showered down on us. The waves were thirty feet high, and the wind was blowing forty-five miles per hour with gusts up to ninety miles per hour. It was not safe for the cutter to get close to us, or we might crash into one another. Suddenly, I realized that the Coast Guard's attempt to save us could also be dangerous.

The men on the cutter tried to get a line to Rory but could not. Eventually, they radioed for Rory to lie down on the deck, so they could shoot a line over the bow. I wondered if the bullet would hit Rory or the boat. Mike opened the hatch to yell instructions to Rory, and more water poured in on us. The sound of the wind was so loud that Rory had difficulty hearing Mike's words, and Mike had to repeat the instructions. When Rory was flat on the deck, which was under water much of the time, the cutter shot the line and Rory grabbed it. A few minutes later, the Coast Guard radioed to have Rory give the line some slack, but, before the instructions could be passed along, the line broke. One of the men on the cutter radioed, "We only have one ballistic left. We'll shoot it with all the line we have on board. If you don't get the line this time, there is nothing more we can do for you."

Once again, we waited for the bullet to carry the line over Rory. This time Rory was able to grab the line, recover the large line attached to it, and fix it to the bow of the boat. By the time Rory stumbled down the steps into the cabin, two hours had passed. He'd taken in a lot of salt water, his skin was stark white, and he was spent. We stripped off the survival suit, dressed him in dry clothes, and covered him with a dry, open sleeping bag.

While the Coast Guard cutter, a boat the same size as ours, but with powerful dual engines, was towing us, we were so badly banged around that Mike had to radio them to slow down. After a couple hours under tow, I asked Mike, "How much longer before we'll reach shore?" He made some calculations and said, "At our current speed, we should reach Ocean City, Maryland in about six hours."

I remember saying, "That soon? How wonderful." In retrospect, it is clear that I'd lost all sense of time.

After a few more hours, the storm subsided, and by the time we got our first glimpse of land, the sun was out. As we neared Ocean City, my toothache returned with a vengeance. I took a codeine tablet, but the pain did not ease. A half hour later, as we docked, I swallowed a second codeine tablet and climbed off our boat. I felt like I was still at sea as I tried to walk down the dock. The codeine had no effect. I was exhausted and in excruciating pain. The only evidence of our time at sea were the miles of Coast Guard line covering the deck and the Kleenex size remains of the jib hanging from the mast.

I found a phone and called my parents in Winnetka, Illinois. My mother, who was profoundly hard of hearing by then, answered. It took a while for her to understand who was calling. The conversation ended with my learning my father was playing tennis and Mother was happy I was safely ashore after a wonderful sail. It was hardly what I had told her, but it was what she had understood.

Mike rented rooms for us in a local hotel so we could bathe and get into dry clothes. Rita and I shared a room. Rita wanted a hot bath before anything else, so she disappeared into the bathroom. I undressed in the bedroom and couldn't believe what I saw when I passed the full-length mirror. My body was totally bruised. One bruise ran right into the next, up and down my arms, legs, breasts—every part of me. I looked like I'd been in the ring with Cassius Clay (Mohamed Ali). I knocked on the bathroom door and said, "Rita, I don't know you very well, but I want to come in and show you my body."

She laughed. "Come in."

I walked into the room, and as we stared at each other, we began to laugh. Rita's body was just as bruised as mine. I'm sure some of it was driven by relief, but we went on laughing until tears ran down our cheeks.

Cleaned up and dressed, the five of us gathered for lunch at a local restaurant. I had a drink, the only one I've ever had with a noon meal, and took another codeine tablet. Because of the pain, I was unable to eat anything. Mike then hired a large taxi to drive four of us—Rory stayed with the boat—to a nearby airport. I boarded a small commuter plane for Washington D.C., and Mike, Andi, and Rita left by car for Newburgh, New York. Although I ran the entire length of the airport with all my gear when the plane landed at National, I just missed my connecting flight to Boston. With an hour to kill before the next flight, I called my husband, David, who was back from his conference, told him briefly about being lost at sea, my tooth, and my arrival time at Logan.

Top: October, 1983, Lunch in Ocean City, Maryland after "Lost at Sea" weekend
Left to Right: Rory, Nancy Lelewer Sonnabend, Mike Dubroff, Rita Forester, and
Andi Dubroff

Bottom: July, 1987, Martha's Vineyard
Left to Right: Andi Dubroff, Nancy Sonnabend, Claire Kaiser

It was late Sunday afternoon when David met me at the airport and took me directly to his periodontal office. After an examination, he told me which tooth he thought had abscessed and said he wanted to open it. Although I'd always trusted his judgment on dental issues before, this time it seemed to me that the tooth he wanted to open was not the one causing me pain. We finally agreed that he'd give me a shot to relieve the pain. When we got home, I immediately went to bed. At 1 A.M., I was in so much pain, we returned to his office and he opened the tooth he had wanted to open originally. It was badly abscessed.

The following morning, David left for work before I awoke. That night, when he returned at 7 P.M., I was dressed and lying on the bed. "What did you do today?" he asked.

"Nothing."

"What do you mean nothing? Did you talk on the phone, eat, read, go out?"

"No, I just lay on the bed all day. I didn't do anything." Even then, it was hard for me to believe I had spent an entire day on a bed doing nothing. Other than times when I'd been very sick and just slept, all my days had been full of lots of activities.

Tuesday, I awoke feeling refreshed. I showered, dressed, ate breakfast, and went to the supermarket. I'd made a long list of items I needed and was half way through collecting them when I started to cry uncontrollably. I left the carriage with my groceries still in it and ran home. Once back in my apartment, my tears stopped. I did a little cleaning and then headed back to the market, but en route I began crying again. This time, I returned home and stayed there.

That night, Andi called to see how I was. When I told her about my day, she said Rita had spent the day crying and that she had laughed hysterically at everything. By the next day, the three of us were back to normal.

The friendships I made during the summers I spent on Chappaquiddick have not weakened with time. When the book *The Perfect Storm* came out in 1997, and the movie in 2000, Rita, the Dubroffs, and I found ourselves sharing reminiscences of our own storm and giving thanks for our good fortune.

In 2007, as I was about to head off for the Kaisers' St. Patrick's Day party, I learned that my flight had been canceled because of a snowstorm. I ended up on a 6:45 A.M. train to Wilmington, Delaware on Saint Patrick's Day. The express trains were sold out, and this train, which left from Back Bay Station in Boston, was scheduled to take six hours and twenty minutes. It took an extra hour because of problems with lights and switches.

The train had many cars, and every seat was occupied. I sat next to a woman I guessed to be about my age—late 60s, early 70s—and struck up a conversation with her. I quickly learned she was on husband number two, had been a teacher, and is dyslexic. I ended up giving her my card. She looked at it and said, "Lelewer? Stanley Lelewer?"

"Yes, he's my first cousin."

"Brenda?"

"Yes, I know Brenda. She was Stanley's second wife."

"I'm Brenda's best friend, and I'm still in touch with Stanley."

The train had hundreds of passengers on it, and we ended up sitting next to each other. I'm wondering what the probability of that is.

CHAPTER 18
Two Divorces and a New Beginning

By the time I was in my late forties, I was separated from my second husband, David. Both my husbands had been critical of everything I did and were self-involved. Living in that kind of a situation is draining and demoralizing. Divorce, I knew, was not only inevitable, but necessary. With one child married, one working in California and two in college, I found myself alone and truly at loose ends for the first time in my life. Of course, there were still three constants in my life: my father, my mother, and Cristina, who had visited us on many occasions, and with whom Kathy had stayed for a month during the summer between her eighth and ninth grades. With my father and Cristina, I could and did discuss everything. My mother offered the indescribable comfort that comes from knowing that someone loves you—loved you when you were a child, loves you now, and will love you in the future, no matter what happens.

Cristina and I took several trips together. Still, there are only so many trips that one can take, so, when my life hit a low ebb, I entered a six-week program for women who wanted to switch jobs or go into the workforce for the first time. The program wasn't particularly productive, but a potluck dinner party I had for Sarah Lawrence alumnae led to a number of fascinating adventures.

The day of the potluck, I had a bad cold and a temperature close to 100°F. From the bottom of my heart, I wished I had not offered to have the dinner at my apartment. At 10 P.M., I was ushering my last guest, Deborah Hermann, to the door when she said, "I understand you know a lot about dyslexia. Can you tell me about it?"

I felt so awful that I just wanted her to leave and said,

July, 1983, Cristina Lana and Nancy riding to the top of the Mountain of Fire on the Canary Island of Lanzarote

"Sure, perhaps we can have lunch sometime and talk."

"Well, it's really my husband who is interested."

"Fine, have him call me." I gave her the number of the place where I was doing an internship and my home number and shooed her out the door.

A week later I received a phone call at work from a gentleman who identified himself as Dr. Howard Hermann. I had no idea who he was until he said, "My wife met you at the Sarah Lawrence gathering at your home last week. I'm told you know a lot about dyslexia. I'd like to meet you and talk about it. Could I pick you up next Tuesday at 9:00?"

"I'm on an internship and have to be at work at 9:00."

"No, I meant 9:00 P.M."

"That's a bit late. Can we make it 8:00 P.M. and just meet at my apartment?"

"I'll try to make it earlier, but I'm not sure I can. I'd like to take you to MIT and show you the lab."

Tuesday evening, Dr. Hermann called at 8:30 P.M. to say he was going to be late. He arrived at 9:00 P.M. When we reached the Center for Space Research building, he fumbled in his pocket and eventually said, "I didn't bring the right key. Don't worry, there is a lock on a nearby building that I can open with my knife and we can get in that way."

We moved on to another building. With a little finagling, he got the door open, and we proceeded to go up and down stairs and through long, dark corridors until we came to the basement of the Center for Space Research. I must admit that, throughout the walk, I was thinking, "This is not smart. You are with a man about whom you know nothing, he has a knife, you're in dark halls, and no one knows where you are."

Once we arrived, Howard put on the lights, pointed to a large object in the center of the floor, and said, "This is one of the first flight simulators ever made. Would you like to try it?"

"Dr. Hermann, it's 10 P.M.," I replied, "I don't understand. What's that got to do with dyslexia?"

"Nothing."

"So, what do you want to know about dyslexia? I'm dyslexic and have raised dyslexic children. Do you want to test me?"

"No, I know all about you and your work with dyslexic children. I'd like you to work with me on a project studying eye movements in dyslexics. I don't know about dyslexia, and you could help me. I think I could teach you to be a researcher. There's no money for salaries now, but you would learn a lot. After we run the pilot project, we may be able to get NIH funding."

"Can I just waltz into MIT and do research? I have a Liberal Arts degree from Sarah Lawrence and that's it."

"You'd need to turn in your CV and have an interview with Dr. Larry Young, head of the lab."

"What's a CV?"

"Curriculum vitae."

"What's that?"

"It tells what you've done."

"Oh. I have a one-page resume."

"Great. Make it twenty-five pages and you have a CV."

The research sounded interesting, and the program I was in seemed to be leading me nowhere. I decided I would finish the remaining weeks of the program and, at the same time, work on a CV. I called a friend who was a professor at Boston University and asked for help. She came over and, in no time, I had a respectable CV. What I hadn't realized was that my patents, copyrights, and the places where I had lectured could, and should, be listed on my CV. They had not been part of my resume.

In 1983, after an interview with Dr. Larry Young, I became a research affiliate in MIT's Man/Vehicle Lab, Department of Aeronautics and Astronautics. I shared an office with Dr. Hermann who, by that time, was Howard to me, and much to my wonder, with the astronaut Byron Lichtenberg. I quickly realized that Howard is brilliant and, as my first exposure to him proved, occasionally eccentric.

On one of my first days at the lab, Howard arrived after working all day in the Department of Psychiatry at the Veterans Administration hospital, announced that he needed a nap as he was exhausted, and pushed all the papers off his desk onto the floor. The next thing I knew, he was lying on top of his desk in a fetal position, snoring. Fifteen minutes later, he was awake and ready to work.

The day I started as a research affiliate, Howard took me into the room where the research was to be done. One of the technicians asked me, "Do you know how to calibrate the bifurcation paradigm?"

"Not yet," I said.

When we got back to the office I promptly told Howard that I hadn't understood a word the technician had said. Howard laughed and explained that one of the issues the research was designed to examine was whether dyslexics, like normal readers, have a biological preference to look in one particular direction when lights are shown so far on the periphery that both lights can't be seen without moving the eyes from one light to the other. This reaction happens so quickly that people are not conscious of it. To examine the issue, Howard said, a subject's head is secured,

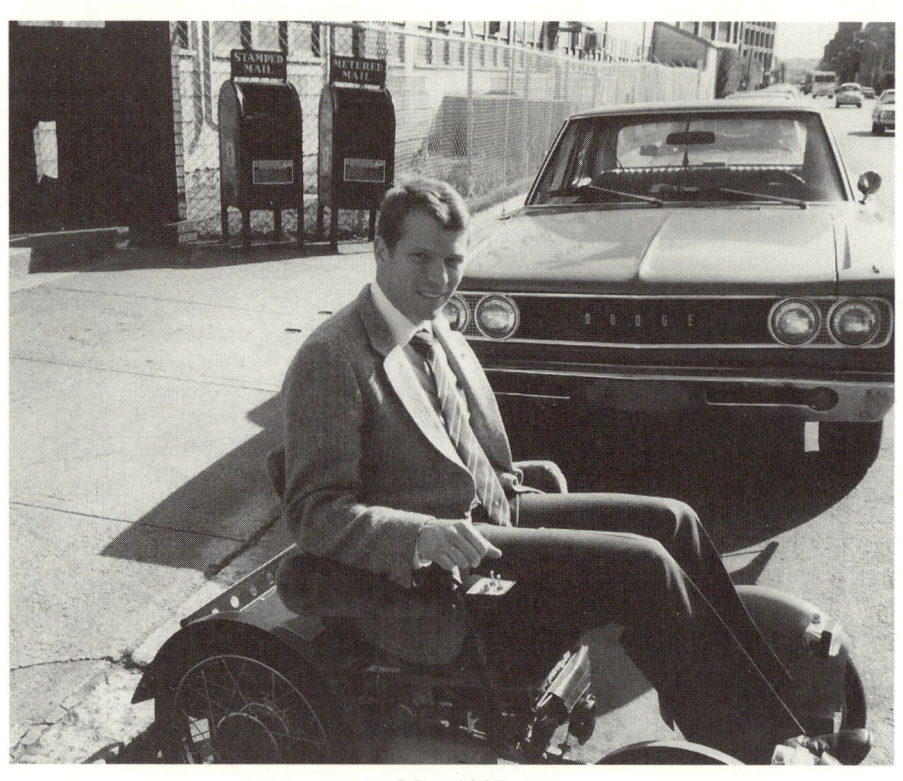

May 1985
Astronaut Byron Lichtenberg riding the Exterior Permobil on Vassar Street at MIT

and the movements of both eyes are recorded as the subject, seated in a dark room, watches a perimeter screen.

Several dyslexics and a control group of normal readers were chosen for the pilot experiment. A center light would appear on the screen. That light would be followed by the projection of either a single light appearing randomly on the left or the right side of the screen or the projection of two lights, one on the left side of the screen and one on the right of the screen. All the lights had the same luminance, and when two lights came on, they were always equal distance from the center light. Over time, our research found dyslexics have a more random choice than normal readers of where they first look when lights are bifurcated (a light on the left and one on the right simultaneously).

Howard was a great teacher and taught me how to be a researcher. In turn, I taught him about dyslexia. Together, we made a great team. He is not good about keeping things organized, but that is my forte. One of my jobs was to file all papers before Howard lost them. In return, Howard, who reads rapidly, would put papers in three piles for me: papers I didn't need to read, papers for which I needed only to read the summary, and papers I needed to read completely.

When we were writing our research, I frequently would ask him how to spell a word. He'd tell me and go right on reading. It was heaven. My spelling is so poor, I sometimes can't find the word I want in the dictionary.

In September, 1986, three years after I began work at MIT, an article entitled "Interhemispheric coordination is compromised in subjects with developmental dyslexia" by Howard T. Hermann, Nancy L. Sonnabend, and Yehoshua Y. Zeevi appeared in *Cortex*. That year also saw the publication in *Annals of Dyslexia* of "Bihemifield Visual Stimulation Reveals Reduced Lateral Bias in Dyslexia" by Howard T. Hermann, Nancy L. Sonnabend and Yehoshua Y. Zeevi. There is no way to describe the thrill or the pride I felt when these articles appeared.

Although I shared a desk with Byron Lichtenberg (a fact that still leaves me rather awed), he was rarely present, and when he was, he was involved in research in the basement that didn't require a desk. Since he wasn't usually around, I was told, when I began work, to put his pictures of outer space and the things he had in the drawers in boxes and take them to the building's storage area. I did so, and a month later a young, handsome man appeared at my desk and asked, "Is this your desk?"

I jumped up and said, "You must be Byron Lichtenberg. If you need the desk, I'll move some place else."

"No, I don't need the desk. I'm just wondering what happened to all my pictures and the stuff that was in the drawers."

"It's all in storage. Do you want me to get it?"

"No. What are you researching?"

When I told him, he laughed. "It's appropriate that we share a desk. You're studying inner space, and I'm studying outer space." And with that, we became friends.

Byron was the first true scientist to become an astronaut. All those before him were astronauts who then learned something about science. During my first year at MIT, Byron was launched into outer space on Space Lab One. Dr. Larry Young was the chief investigator on the experiments Byron carried out during his mission, so all communications were down-linked to our lab. I remember sitting for hours listening to Byron and the others as they carried out their duties while circling the earth every hour and a half. In 1992, after all three of us had left MIT, Byron went up again. This time, he invited me to the launch. It was one of the most dramatic events I've ever experienced. Knowing Byron was on board, listening to the countdown, hearing "You're green to go, God Speed," feeling the ground shake under me like an earthquake reduced me to tears.

I met a number of interesting people during my time at MIT. One day, while I was working in the lab, a large man shuffled into my office. He was grossly overweight, his clothes were disheveled, and his beard was unkempt and showed the remnants of his last meal on it. He poked me in the arm and said, "You Nancy?"

"Yes," I said reluctantly.

"I've been looking for you. I'm having a conference next month at my monastery, Villa Musso, on the Italian Riviera and will be bringing together top scientists from all over the world to discuss dyslexia and learning differences. I'd like you to come."

"Thank you, but I can't get away next month," I replied politely, while thinking, "This guy is a street person and a crazy one at that. How do I get him out of my office?"

He turned to leave and then turned back to say, "Now that I've seen you, you will help me start my wheelchair company in the U.S."

"No, I don't do wheelchairs," I said firmly.

"Sure you do. You'll see."

He ambled out, and I forgot about him. Two nights later, at 3 A.M., my phone rang. I picked it up and heard a foreign language.

"Who is this?"

"Per Udden."

"Who? Speak English."

"Remember, I was in your office a couple of days ago. I want you to come to my conference and start my wheelchair company in the U.S."

"It's 3:00 in the morning. Please don't call me again." I hung up.

The phone rang again immediately. "You're rude. Don't hang up on me."

"Look, I don't know you, and it's 3:00 in the morning."

"It's not 3:00 here."

"If you call me again in the middle of the night, I'll call the police. Now, I'm hanging up."

Over the next several days, as I asked around the lab if anyone knew about a man named Per Udden, Per continued to call me, but at least he called during daytime hours. From colleagues, I learned Per was a Swedish doctor who, along with Axel Wennerblom, an engineer, invented the sticky material that holds a pad to women's underpants.

The two men, who had made the invention while working in the laboratory of Svenska Cellulose AB, sold the license for their invention to Stille-Werner, a company in Sweden. The sanitary pad was called Stilles Sanisept and was sold throughout Europe. Per used some of the money he received for the sale of the license to buy Villa Musso, his Italian monastery, and some to start an electric wheelchair company, Permobil A.B. , in Sweden. At some point during various conversations about Per, I learned he was dyslexic, which, of course, intrigued me.

I did not go to the conference Per first invited me to, but I have gone to many since then in various parts of the world. And I did help him to establish Permobil in the United States. I spent a month in Sweden, learning how Permobil wheelchairs were made and serviced and then became a founding director of Permobil of America. From 1984 to 1987, I served as Permobil of America's clerk and treasurer. In fact, the company's first U.S. office was in my apartment. I would set up appointments, and a technician would come from Sweden once a month to do fittings at various hospitals. The technician would fax information from the fittings back to Sweden, and, by the next day, we would have prices, so we could begin filling out the insurance forms.

As more Permobils were delivered, the technicians from Sweden who serviced the chairs began training local people to service them. So good were the Permobil chairs that, shortly after they began appearing here, U.S. and foreign companies began duplicating their features. Over the years, Permobil electric wheelchairs, with computerized operating systems and many individualized components, have set the standard for modern electric wheelchairs.

It was through my work with Permobil that I met Princess Marianne Bernadotte. During the month that I spent in Sweden learning about Permobil A. B., I was introduced to her. Later, she, Per, and I spent a few days in Wilmington, Delaware with the Kaisers to promote Permobils at the Dupont Institute. Since our first meeting, Princess Marianne and I have shared many memorable adventures, from cruising through the islands of Stockholm's archipelago on her son's boat, to riding the subway at night from the New York theatre district to the World Trade Center, where we were attending a Rodin conference, to a Colorado taxi ride in the worst wreck I have seen since the taxi my parents and I took in Granada. I still remember the day I introduced Marianne to the New York City bus system. We came out of Tiffany's that day only to discover that it was pouring and there were no taxis available.

"Have you ever ridden a public bus?" I asked.

"No."

"Well, you're going to now," I said as I handed her quarters and pushed her in front of me. The bus we got on was already

Top: Dr. Per Udden and Nancy at the President's Committee on the Handicapped
Washington D.C., May 1985
Bottom: Per Udden's Villa Musso on the Italian Rivera

Princess Marianne Bernadotte of Sweden
Picture by Stig Forsberg

quite full. We found ourselves standing in the aisle, squashed between bodies in front and behind us. The driver was one of those who like to accelerate and then jam on the brakes throwing everyone backward and forward with each jerk.

"How do you like riding this bus?" I asked.

"I like my chauffeur-driven limo better."

She got even. One evening, we were walking down the street on the Upper East Side when Marianne noticed people going to an art opening party.

"Come on, let's go," she said.

"We can't just walk in there."

"Sure, we can," she said as she pulled me into the party. We drank champagne, ate hors d'oeuvres, and looked at the pictures. No one even noticed us. As we left, we thanked the man at the door.

Marianne was kind enough to act as the honorary chairperson for the William P. Graves Ovarian Cancer Fund, which helped to fund a pioneering research project begun under the leadership of Dr. Robert C. Knapp, a long time friend of mine. A number of years earlier, in 1977, several Boston medical institutions had joined together in an effort to develop new and better methods for the diagnosis and treatment of ovarian cancer. The CA 125 assay, which is now used to monitor the treatment of patients and to determine recurrence of the disease, was the result of this research.

When the Graves Benefit Committee was looking for an honorary chairperson for the benefit, I offered to ask Marianne because I knew some studies had been done in Sweden. In return, the committee offered to pay for Marianne's round trip ticket. Marianne came, the benefit was a great success, and we had a wonderful time.

Robert C. Knapp, M.D., emeritus director of gynecologic oncology at Brigham and Women's Hospital and William H. Baker professor of gynecology at Harvard Medical School
Picture by Yousuf Karsh

When I became a founding director of Permobil of America, Per sent me to Edward L. Bernays to get some advice on marketing Permobil in this country. Dr. Bernays, whom I came to call Edward, was gracious with his time, helpful, and a fascinating man. There was an entire wall of pictures of him with every president, head of state, and CEO of a major corporation that I could imagine. I learned from others that he was the nephew of Sigmund Freud. Edward also was one of the first to attempt to influence public opinion using the psychology of the subconscious, and many consider him to be the originator of modern public relations. He was named one of the 100 most influential Americans of the twentieth century by Life magazine.

I remember noticing a new painting of him over the fireplace one afternoon and saying, "Edward, that's a wonderful new portrait of you. I like it. Did you just decide to have it painted?"

"No," he said. "It's for the National Gallery in D.C., but there is some rule that they can't hang it until ten years after I die, so I told them they'd have to wait and, in the mean time, I wanted to enjoy it."

Although Edward was beginning to suffer from dementia by the time I had finished writing SOMETHING'S NOT RIGHT, I wanted to get his advice on marketing my book. He must have asked me thirty times in half an hour who my publisher was, however, when I asked him what newspapers were the most important ones in which to be reviewed, he gave the names to me in order of importance. In fact, he answered all my questions perfectly and was a fantastic resource.

Per was a collector of people. Through him I not only met Princess Marianne and Dr. Edward Bernays, but also Dr. Jan Ober of Poland, Bjorg Jacob of Switzerland, and Montserrat Estil-les of Barcelona, Spain. It was because of Per that I was able to work in Frank Duffy's BEAM (Brain Electrical Activity Mapping) laboratory at Harvard Medical School as an associate in neurology and, because of Per, that I could assist in other projects including Heidelise Als' kangaroo box studies.

The Ober 2 eye tracker was one of Per's scientific projects. It was a new eye tracker that Per and Dr. Jan Ober had developed together. When the eye movement project at MIT did not receive funding from the National Institutes of Health, Per paved the way for Jan and me to use the Ober 2 eye tracker with some of the dyslexic youngsters, and their matched controls on which Frank was running BEAM studies. I was grandfathered into the lab as an associate in neurology at Harvard Medical School, and Jan and I ran eye movement studies on Frank's dyslexic population for six weeks. Later Per sent me to Poland to spend a week in Jan's lab in Poznan.

The Ober project led to assisting with a number of projects including some of Heidelise Als'. My job for Heidelise Als' kangaroo-in-a-box studies was to keep the mother and child in the center of each lens as I videotaped their movements. I also administered the WISC-R to eight-year-olds who were a part of Heidelise's longitudinal population of preemies, and spent many months in a room working the computers and keeping one child per day happy and involved as a technician recorded the child's brain waves.

Per was, as far as I know, the first person to bring neurologists, geneticists, specialists in temporal processing, and other medical specialists together to discuss reading, learning differences, and dyslexia. Per and Professor Ragnar Granit founded the Rodin Remediation Academy in 1984 to promote multidisciplinary research on dyslexia and other learning disabilities. Rodin Remediation Academy conferences are by invitation only and usually include about 100 people. Participants present their research findings and then have the opportunity to discuss their work with colleagues from different disciplines as well as different countries.

While traveling in Switzerland, I met Bjorg Jacobs, who was then Per's assistant. Per was out of town and had arranged for her to be my guide. We liked each other right from the start. Since that meeting, we have traveled together to Spain and Norway and roomed together at many other Rodin conferences. Bjorg has visited me in Boston, and we have gotten together in Sarasota, Florida.

In 1994, a Rodin conference held on the island of Malta introduced me to Montserrat Estil-les. As I had studied the program for the conference, I had noticed that one of the women attending the conference, Montserrat Estil-les, was from Spain. Later, after the first day's papers had been given, I spotted Montserrat Estil-les on an excursion boat that we had all boarded. From what I could observe, she didn't seem to speak much English. As the conference was held in English, I asked her in Spanish, "Do you understand what is being said at the conference?"

Thrilled to find someone who spoke her language, she replied in Spanish, "No, I don't understand. I have a clinic for dyslexics in Barcelona and I'm here to learn. Can you come to my room tonight and explain everything that has been said today in Spanish?" That was the beginning of our friendship. That night, and every night until the end of the conference, I translated all that I could remember of the day's events into Spanish for her, and then we would discuss the events and papers in detail. To this day, we keep in close contact. We have visited each other's homes on several occasions and talk by phone and e-mail frequently.

For a while, I had thought my forties were going to be the low point of my life. Instead, they opened the door to a new career and new friends. I went from wife and mother—always mother—to a research affiliate at MIT, where I shared a desk with a brilliant doctor and an astronaut, to a founding director of Permobil of America with friends around the world, to an associate in neurology at Harvard Medical School who attended world renowned conferences on dyslexia and learning differences. My forties were not a low point, but a whole new beginning, offering new worlds to conquer.

Top: Dr. Edward Bernays and Dr. Per Udden in
Nancy's apartment at The Prudential Center
Bottom (Left to Right): Dr. Larry Young and Dr. Howard Hermann,
The Prudential Center, Boston, MA, February 13, 1985

Top left: Dr. Jan Ober of Poland, in California June, 1985.
Top Right: Dr. Heidelise Als
Bottom Left: Montserrat Estil-les, Barcelona, Spain
Bottom Right: Bjorg Jacob, Per Udden's Assistant, Lake Lucerne, Switzerland

CHAPTER 19
Growing Older

I suspect it is hard for most grown children to realize their parents are aging. To their eyes, after all, their parents—no matter how gray they become—are forever "Mom" and "Dad;" those people who bandaged their knees, kissed them goodnight, and thought they were perfect no matter what anyone else said.

I knew that my mother had first become aware of a hearing problem when she struggled to understand what people were saying as she stood in the receiving line at my wedding. At that point, however, I certainly did not think in terms of age. She was only forty-six. Over the next several years—my busy years—she had her hearing checked and got hearing aids. It seemed to me that she was handling the situation just as she had always handled problems. Mother, however, stopped talking on the telephone because of her hearing loss, so all communication was through my father.

It wasn't until I was visiting one year that I realized how adept my parents had become at charades. One morning, my father awakened my mother, who then asked, "How's the weather?" As she wasn't wearing her hearing aids, my father pointed to his eye and then pretended to be dealing cards. Mother immediately understood the weather was "ideal." When she was cooking and the timer rang, my father made two fists and banged them together a couple of times. That meant the timer was ringing. They had developed a language all their own.

Five years after the onset of my mother's hearing problems, she began losing strength in her left leg. My father took her to several doctors in Chicago and the Mayo Clinic. Although they told my parents my mother's leg would not worsen, it continued to deteriorate. Eventually, the doctors speculated that she had had polio as a child and her present problems were a result of that. As my mother had no memory of having the disease, the doctors concluded it had been a very mild case. Gradually, her leg became paralyzed from the knee to the ankle, and Mother wore a brace to support her leg and foot. She once remarked that carrying around the atrophied leg was like carrying around a forty-pound dead weight, but, again, she coped well with her problems.

During the years my mother was dealing with her hearing loss and leg problems, the patience my father exhibited towards her was a good lesson for me. "Your mother," he often said to me, "has many problems. She deals well with them. I'm lucky not to have the problems, and I'm here to help her. She would do the same for me if the situation were reversed."

It was also during my busy years that my father had his first heart attack. Just as I did not think in terms of age for my mother's health issues, I did not think in terms of age when my father had his heart attack. After all, he was only in his fifties at the time.

My father usually called me every Sunday morning whether they were in Winnetka, Highland Park, or Florida. I remember this particular call well. "I played golf yesterday," he said.

"You did? Why? You haven't played in years."

"I wanted to see if I could still play."

"Can you? How did you do?"

"I had a good round, got lucky and sank two approaches."

"So, what was your score?"

"Four over par."

"Oh my, that's incredible."

Three days later, Mother called to tell me my father had a heart attack while playing tennis and was in Highland Park Hospital. I flew from Boston to Chicago immediately. When I arrived at the hospital's intensive care unit, my father was sitting up in bed and attached to a number of monitors. He greeted me with, "You didn't have to come. I'm not going to die this time."

"I'm glad to hear that," I replied. "I think you played golf Saturday because you were having pain on the tennis court and thought you might have to switch back to your old sport." He didn't answer, just gave me a guilty look. If you learn nothing else from having children, you learn how to recognize guilty looks instantly.

The next morning, as I got off the elevator, I saw all the nurses suddenly rush from their station into his room. I joined the rush. There he was, walking in place, next to his bed, with his monitors blaring and the lines on the screens going in every direction.

"Mr. Lelewer, what are you doing?"

"Taking a walk."

"It's not allowed. You must get back in bed immediately."

"You die if you lie in bed."

"Please, Mr. Lelewer, get in bed."

"Okay, the walk is over."

The following day, his monitors were removed, and he was up walking.

In time, my father went back to playing tennis and helping my mother. Eventually, my mother's hearing deteriorated so much that she couldn't hear her own voice without powerful hearing aids. As that happened, she took courses in lip reading and became involved with an organization called Self-Help for the Hard of Hearing (SHHH) now known as the Hearing Loss Association of America. Her proficiency in lip reading led her to teach lip reading at the North Shore Senior Center in Winnetka, Illinois. She also founded a Winnetka chapter of SHHH. Mother headed that chapter for years and eventually founded another chapter in Sarasota, Florida. In 1988, she received the Keystone Award for her work toward establishing SHHH as a national organization. She went on to serve on the SHHH national board and, in 1991, was presented with The Spirit of SHHH Award. In 1996, Mother received the organization's most prestigious award, the Rocky Stone Humanitarian Award, for extraordinary contributions toward furthering the goals of SHHH.

While Mother more than earned the praise and awards she received, they would not have happened without my father's support and encouragement. Many times, Mother wanted to throw in the towel, but giving up was not in my father's vocabulary. When my mother wanted to resign from the board of directors because she no longer felt comfortable traveling alone, my father began to travel with her, sitting in on the board meetings and sometimes participating in the discussions, even though he was never officially a board member. When the SHHH chapters

Sis Lelewer teaching lip reading at the North Shore Senior Center,
Winnetka, Illinois

lacked money, my father organized fundraisers at my parents' home. It was my father who came up with the idea of selling a variety of dried beans in a bag with a poem he had written about SHHH. The poem was attached to the bag by a ribbon. Inside the bag were the dried beans and directions for making bean soup. SHHH members sold the bags to their friends and at senior centers. Although my father's hearing was fine, he was so much a part of the organization that he was given an award at one of the conferences.

In 1978, at age seventy-three, my father finally retired and, despite the seeming contradiction in terms, began to look for something to do. Tennis, golf, and weekly meetings with RO-MEO were not going to be enough for him. ROMEO (Retired Old Men Eating Out) was a luncheon and discussion group that was begun in Highland Park. My father so enjoyed the group that he took the concept with him to Florida and began another group there.

As he searched for new ways to stay busy, he learned the Chicago Art Institute had a pewter collection that had not been cataloged. Since my father had enjoyed going to the Art Institute for years, it seemed only logical for him to volunteer to catalog the collection. He would go into Chicago one or two days a week, clean some of the museum's pieces, and then, through research, identify and catalog them.

As my parents grew older, so did their grandchildren. One by one, my children went to school, attended colleges, took jobs, and married. Kathy married Tom Rowe in a beautiful ceremony followed by dinner and dancing at the Sonesta Hotel in Cambridge, Massachusetts. On a blistering hot March day, Wendy was wed to Michael Erickson at Vizcaya Museum and Gardens in the Coconut Grove District of Miami, Florida.

Top: Kathy Rowe in her Corporate Office, Boston, Massachusetts
Bottom Left: Kathy and Tom Rowe at their wedding in Cambridge, MA (8/30/1981)
Bottom Right: Sis and Joe Lelewer at Kathy and Tom Rowe's wedding.

The ceremony took place in the middle of the gardens on a grass-covered, oval-shaped peninsula, surrounded by a moat of water. Fountains shot water high into the sky.

Eric and Donna Patti were married by a justice of the peace in New Jersey.

Patti married Steven Wagner on a snowy New Year's Eve in St. Ignatius Church at Boston College. Her grandfather—my remarkable father—gave such a moving talk[9] that Father Gee, who was conducting the service, said he wouldn't have given a homily if he'd known how inspirational Mr. Lelewer's words were going to be. The ceremony was followed by a dinner-dance at the Sonesta Hotel in Cambridge. For me, the piece de resistance of the dinner was an entire room filled with desserts.

Neither age nor marriage could ever weaken the bond between my children and their grandparents. Each child and her or his spouse visited my parents frequently. Tom, number one son-in-law, still remembers the first time he met my father and mother, which was before he and Kathy were even married. My father greeted them and immediately began telling jokes. "Do you know the difference between in-laws and outlaws?" he asked. Before Tom could answer, my father said, "Outlaws are wanted" and went right into the next joke. "I was nervous," Tom recalled, "in part because Kathy's family is Jewish and I'm not. But when Great Mama served pork roast for dinner, I figured everything would work out fine."

One visit that Patti and Steven found unforgettable involved a game of tennis at the Bensingers' home. Great Papa, as my father was known to his grandchildren once the great-grandchildren were born, was eighty-five at the time. "We're going to play tennis at Linda Bensinger's," he announced. "After tennis Great Mama will join us at Linda's for a luncheon she's having."

[9] See full text of this speech in Appendix B.

Top: Wendy and Michael Erickson at their wedding (3/25/1984)
Bottom: Wendy Sonnabend Erickson at her wedding, wearing
her mom's wedding dress

December 31, 1989, Patti and Steven Wagner at their wedding

*Top: Nancy and Eric Sonnabend
at Patti and Steven Wagner's wedding (12/31/1989)
Bottom: Barbara Ullman at Patti and Steven Wagner's wedding*

Mrs. Bensinger, who was also 85, greeted them at her front door and told them, "Go hit some balls. I'll join you shortly."

They started hitting balls back and forth on the clay court. Eventually, Linda came out wearing a tennis dress and espadrilles. It was decided that Patti and Steven would be on one team, and Great Papa and Linda on the other. At first, Linda didn't play very well because she forgot to take the cover off her racquet, but once it was off, her game improved greatly. In fact, the old folks killed Patti and Steven. Worrying that the old folks couldn't run, Patti and Steven hit the ball to them. In return, Linda and my father sliced it back or placed it in a part of the court Patti and Steven couldn't reach.

My father's love of tennis never waned. In Florida, he played tennis at 10 A.M. almost every day, at least until he was eighty-nine.

As he grew older, he stopped trying to remember with whom he was playing and simply sat on the stairs at the tennis club until a friend came along. The friend would call out, "Hi, Joe, we're on court 6," or whatever, and off they would go. For the last fifteen years that he played, he was usually the oldest player on the court. On at least one occasion, he played with three men whose ages totaled less than his. As his eighties rolled on, he ceased to be able to run, but he could place his serve well and his drop shot continued to be deadly. He had learned the drop shot from George Lott who had played for the United States in the Davis Cup.

When I was in Florida, my father would play the first set and drive home. I would play the second set and one of his friends then would drive me home. On one such drive home, when my father was in his mid-eighties, one of his friends said to

Christmas 1994, Boston, MA
Joseph Lelewer holding Joseph Wagner
Mina "Sis" Lelewer holding Mina Rowe

Patti and Steven Wagner

me, "Your parents are too old to be living in a house on a canal alone. You should tell them to move into a retirement home."

I repeated the conversation to my father, who said, "Well, we like it here and plan to stay for some time." Thus, a few years later, as he and I watched the sun set one evening, I was surprised when he announced, "Nancy, your parents are old."

"You'll never be old," I said looking at them and seeing no gray hair.

He laughed, "I'm 89 and your mother is 84. We're already there. We feel all right, have all our marbles, but we're old." He went on to another subject, but I'm afraid I wasn't listening. I was still on "old." They didn't seem old to me. As I said, I suspect it is always difficult to realize your parents are aging.

A year later, in 1996, during one of our weekly calls, my father said, "Mom and I are thinking it would make more sense to move into a retirement home near you and the children rather than in Florida or Illinois where we've been looking—if that would be all right with you."

"We'd love it. I'll start looking immediately," I answered. Within the month, I'd selected five possible locations. My parents came, studied each one, and nixed all of them. The one location they loved was in Newton. There were developers seeking a permit to build a retirement home by the name of Lasell Village. My parents loved the location and that it would have its own educational component. It would be a good fit, but it wasn't built, and as my father said, "I'm ninety years old. I need something that's already built." They returned to Highland Park and did nothing about retirement homes for several more years.

Apart from the surgery he had for a double hernia when I was in college, and that mild heart attack when he was in his fifties, my father had managed to avoid hospitals. In July, 1998, however, when he was ninety-two, he felt a pain in his neck followed by progressive numbness down his left side. During our weekly phone conversation, he quipped that he really was a "pain in the neck." When I probed, I learned he had been to an internist and was told he needed an MRI immediately. My father went for the MRI as scheduled, and the next day the neurosurgeon reviewing the scan told my father he needed surgery. My father asked the surgeon how many surgeries of this type he'd done.

The neurosurgeon said, "Three, a forty-two-year-old woman and two others."

My father called the woman and asked her about her experience with the surgeon. "He cut up my face and I'm still in pain. You're ninety-two years old, you're better off just dying" was her response. My father called the surgeon back, "I didn't get a very good recommendation. May I have the names of the other two patients?" The doctor said, "I don't remember their names," and my father promptly called me to discuss what to do next. My response was instantaneous: "You're not going under the knife of that surgeon no matter what. I'll talk to my friend, Jeep."

Dr. Ellison C. Pierce, known to me as "Jeep," was a good friend who is considered by many to be the grandfather of modern anesthesia. He had been head of anesthesiology at the Deaconess Hospital in Boston from 1982 to 1995 and had then become chairman emeritus. After hearing me out, Jeep called a colleague in Chicago who recommended Dr. Steven Ondra. Jeep arranged for Dr. Ondra to see my father and review the MRI the following day at Northwestern Memorial Hospital in Chicago. I passed this information on to my father, who said, "I'd rather have the surgery done at the Highland Park Hospital."

"This is not a surgery any neurosurgeon can do," I said, my words tumbling over each other in my anxiety. "Only five neurosurgeons in the world have performed it. You're lucky that Dr. Ondra happens to be in Chicago. Dad, you must confirm the appointment, pick up the MRI, and see Dr. Ondra tomorrow. I'm flying out to Chicago. I'll be there as soon as I can."

With that, the negotiations began. My father knew I was to visit friends for the weekend on Cape Cod. He didn't want to disrupt my plans. We reached a compromise. He would see Dr. Ondra if I went to the Cape for the weekend.

Friday afternoon, I drove to the Cape. We had just started dinner when my father called, "There's good news and bad news. Dr. Ondra has done this surgery on thirty-five people, he knows the names of all of them, and they're all alive and healthy. He says I can survive the operation. That's the good news. The bad news is he says I'm running out of time and must have the surgery immediately. I have a mass on my spinal cord that either will kill me or leave me a respirator-dependent quadriplegic. He wants me in the hospital at 9 A.M. tomorrow morning so he can operate on me Monday. He is reserving the operating room and canceling his other surgeries for Monday. The operation will take fourteen hours. He leaves on vacation Tuesday morning with his wife and two young children. His assistants will keep a close eye on me. I can't wait for the surgery until he returns."

"Okay," I said. "I'm on my way."

"It isn't necessary."

"Who is going to be with Mom while you are in surgery for fourteen hours and then are in recovery for several hours?"

"You're right. I guess you'd better come."

I returned to Boston and began canceling my appointments for the next three weeks even though I wasn't sure how long I would be away. Would I only be at the hospital, or, assuming my father survived, would I be at home in Highland Park for a while? I remember thinking I needed to cover all possibilities and, therefore, packed a black suit, just in case. When I finished packing, I went to the airport and caught the first plane to Chicago, having never gone to bed. Fortunately, Chicago is an hour behind Boston. I arrived at Northwestern Memorial one minute before my parents walked through the hospital's front door.

Saturday was uneventful. Dad refused to change into the hospital johnny, preferring to sit and lie on the bed in his clothes. Sunday morning, I met Dr. Ondra for the first time when he came in to talk to my father and to order several tests for that day. He was, I discovered, a tall, well-built, handsome man with a wonderful bedside manner. He exuded confidence as he explained the operation in detail. As I have some background in neurology, his explanation left me ill with worry. It is probably just as well that my father didn't understand much of what was said. My mother sat panic stricken in a chair in the corner of the room. I explained to Dr. Ondra that she had not been able to hear what he'd said. He went over, knelt beside her, held her hands in his hands, and, looking straight into her eyes, said, "Your husband will be fine, I promise you."

The operation lasted 14 hours. When my father awoke, he was in intensive care with tubes in him everywhere and a surgical halo screwed into his skull. Surgical halos often are used to stabilize the head when there has been a neck injury. In my father's case, the surgical halo was used to stabilize his head until the plate that had been inserted and the discs that had been fused in the back of his neck could support his head. The halo was screwed into the skull at the right and left front of his forehead and two places at the back of his skull. The halo was then attached to metal posts that rested on shoulder pads that were a part of a continuous piece held together on his chest.

Looking back at my father's hospital experience, all I can say is heaven help those who have no family when they are hospitalized. For the first few days after his surgery, my father could not move his body very well and could not speak because he had an endotracheal tube down his throat. The first night after his surgery, my mother and I stayed with a cousin in the city. The next morning, my father spelled out on a board, "It's true, they awaken you in a hospital to give you sleeping medicine."

It wasn't necessary to say more. The second night, I fixed a bed for my mother on a sofa in a small room at the hospital, and I slept on the floor, so I could check on my father every few hours. By morning, I knew I needed help and called my daughter, Wendy, in California. She immediately flew to Chicago and took the night shifts which allowed my mother and me to get some sleep.

There had been no room in the neurological intensive care unit when my father had his surgery, so he was sent to a cardiac intensive care unit. After six days, he was transferred to a neurological intensive care unit. The unit was in a dirty corner of the hospital, and the nurses there neither wore uniforms nor washed their hands when they came in to deal with tubes, medications, and bedding. Because he had been given the wrong medication once, we constantly checked medications before they were given to him and insisted the nurses wash their hands. That helped, but did not solve all problems. Since the primary concern in a neurological care unit is paralysis, caregivers check for numbness by sticking a patient with a pin. My father was stuck with a pin numerous times, even after we explained the test had already been performed and he was not numb.

At one point, my father was told he needed an MRI. Unfortunately, no one mentioned that the MRI machine was in a building several blocks from my father's room. Fortunately, it was summer, and Wendy was with him and stayed with him when he was put on a stretcher, wheeled outside, and loaded into an ambulance. While Wendy and my father were gone, my mother and I arrived and found his room empty. We searched for a nurse and were told he'd gone for an MRI. When they didn't return for several hours, we began to worry and, again, searched for a nurse to find out why. It had occurred to no one to explain where the MRI was being taken.

After a brief stay in the neurological care unit, my father was moved to a single room near the nursing center for stroke patients. From there, he was to go to the rehabilitation center which was in a building next door to the hospital. He had hoped to be able to stay in his single room over the weekend. He was comfortable there and was quite certain there would be no services offered in rehab over the weekend, however, because of restrictions on how many days a patient could remain in a hospital, that was not permitted. Instead, he was transferred from his comfortable air-conditioned room through a sub-basement tunnel that was a 100°F due to the laundry facility located there to the freezing air-conditioned rehab building. I have to say, there were many times during his stay in the hospital and the rehab center when my father could have caught pneumonia waiting in some drafty hallway for a CAT scan, MRI, or some other test had it not been for some family member who piled on blankets when he was cold and removed them when he was hot.

Every day while he was in the rehab center, at least five staff members and therapists came in to take his medical history. This may have been because sometimes nurses disappeared after a single shift, or it may have been because no one seemed to read what anyone else had written. Almost everyone who entered the room to take my father's history asked him his age, even though it was printed on the chart at the foot of his bed. In fairness, he didn't look his age, and one young nurse, when he told her he was indeed 92, did ask, "Then where are your wrinkles?"

The rehab center's system of transferring patients from their room to classes and back had all the warmth and personal touch of moving a sack of potatoes from point A to point B. In the morning, a nurse would put a daily class schedule on each patient's door where the patient could neither see nor read it. At the noted time, a nurse would collect the patient in a wheelchair, transfer the schedule from the door to the wheelchair, and deposit the patient at the elevator. She would then press the elevator button and leave. Eventually the elevator operator would come, read the schedule, and push the wheelchair into the elevator. The operator would deposit the patient outside the elevator on the appropriate floor, and the patient would wait for the teacher to collect him or her. We found that the nurse who had the responsibility of collecting my father and depositing him at the elevator was late so, he missed most of his classes the first day. After that, I took him to all of his classes.

Because my father's last room in the hospital had been next to the stroke center, the file that went with him to the rehab center stated that he'd had a stroke. At the rehab center, every day for five days, a new young therapist arrived to give him speech therapy. He explained to the first youngster that he'd had surgery, not a stroke, and he didn't need speech therapy. Because, by this time, he knew how the medical bureaucracy functioned, he asked her to please remove his name from all speech therapy lists. The next day, another speech therapist showed up. The third day, when another youngster entered his room and announced she was a speech therapist, he asked her if she wanted him to conduct the class. She didn't get it. On the fifth day, when yet one more speech therapist entered his room, he pushed his mouth to the left and said, "I used to speak out of this side of my mouth" and then pushed his mouth to the right side and said, "Do you think you could teach me to talk out of this side of my mouth?" She got it, and that ended speech therapy.

Dr. Ondra had thought my father would be in the rehab for about three weeks, but after a week, we decided he'd be better off at home. I hired a wheelchair van and driver and we all returned to Highland Park. Six weeks after his surgery, I took my father into Chicago to have the halo removed. Before Dr. Ondra removed the screws, my father handed him the following poem:

> *Forgive me for what I did last night*
> *Was the drink that threw me.*
> *Make me the way I was before.*
> *Please, dear God, unscrew me.*

Attached to the poem, was a signed picture of my father in the halo. Dr. Ondra got a big kick out of the poem and picture and put them in his jacket pocket, right over his heart. My father would have laughed too, but he was too nervous. He feared taking out the screws would hurt. Dr. Ondra and his assistant removed the halo quickly. It didn't hurt.

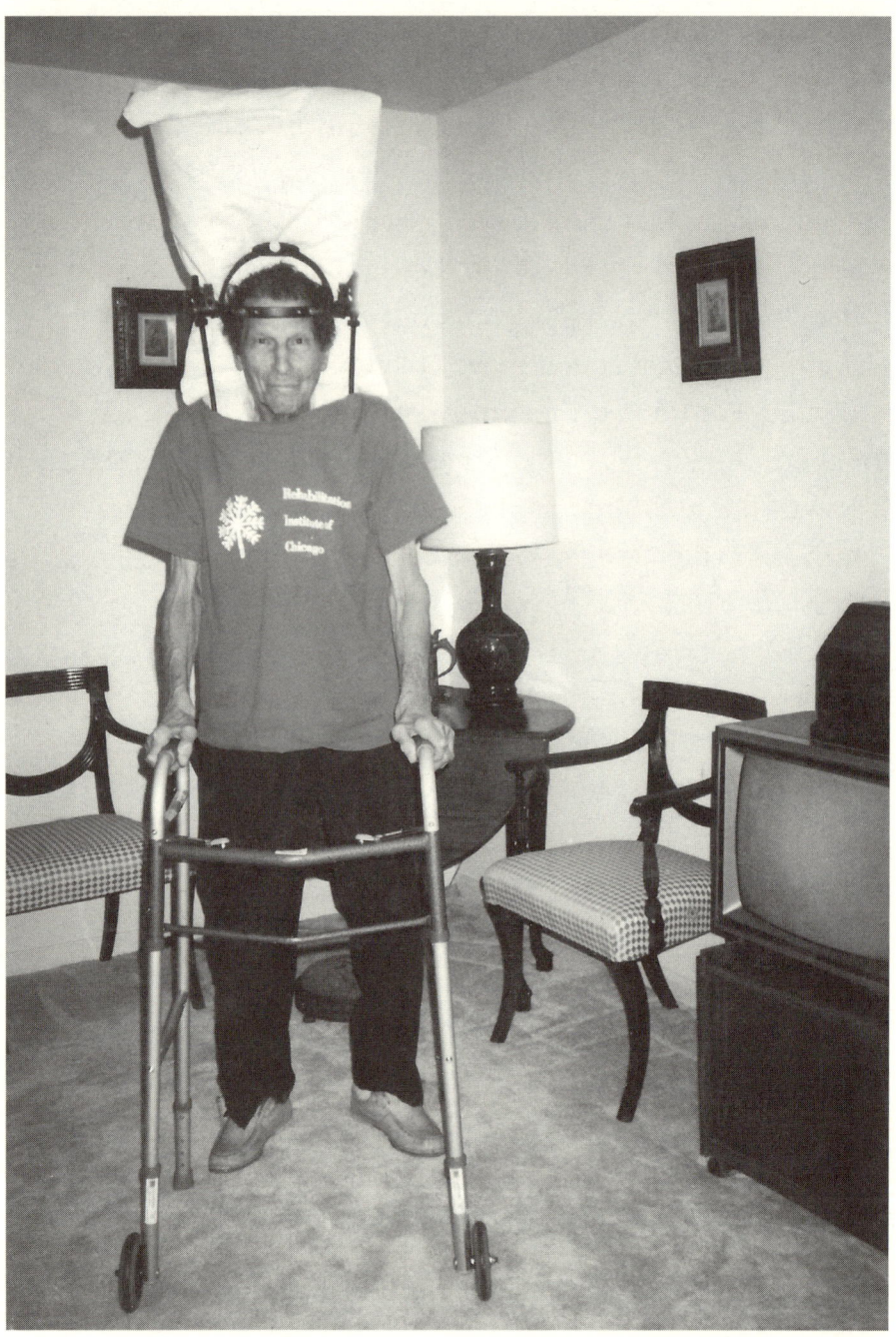

1998: Joe Lelewer with his halo, back in his apartment in Highland Park, Illinois,
after his fourteen-hour spinal cord surgery at age 92
A friend of mine ran into my father in the supermarket while he was still in his halo.
"Mr. Lelewer, is that you?"
"Yes, I've just returned from Mars."

CHAPTER 20
Slowing Down

As the 1990s began, my parents' busy lives continued. Even though my father no longer traveled to Chicago to care for the pewter collection at the Art Institute, he did not have time on his hands. At one point, he said to me, "I can't believe I'm so busy doing nothing. I used to run a business, play tennis, and do most of what I'm doing now, too. How did I ever do it?" He was still in charge of breakfast, made the bed, went shopping with my mother, handled his and her portfolio, as well as the portfolios he had set up for my daughters, advised and educated me on investments and estate planning, and handled all their social arrangements.

No one should ever underestimate the importance of handling social arrangements. After all, it was because of social arrangements—because my father decided to attend his seventieth high school reunion and decided to call a friend to wish her a happy birthday—that an old friendship was rekindled and my parents moved to a retirement home in Newton, Massachusetts.

In May, 1993, the University of Chicago Laboratory School's class of 1923, my father's class, had its seventieth reunion. Letters were sent to the 105 members of the class. Thirty-five could not be found, thirty-five had passed away, and thirty-five responded. Of the thirty-five who responded, nine attended the reunion: six men and three women. Four of the six men—my father, Gerald S. Gidwitz, founder of Helene Curtis Industries, Howard Kahn, a lifelong friend of my father's, and Chuck Walgreen—had eaten lunch and played billiards together at the Boys Club every noon for four years.

As they looked through the school yearbook for 1923, the men had a good laugh over Chuck's selection as "Least likely to succeed." After all, Chuck Walgreen was probably the most successful merchant to come out of the school. Chuck's father had purchased his first store—Walgreen's Drug Store—on the south side of Chicago in 1901. By 1920, he had owned 20 stores and nine years later had grown the chain to 525 stores. After his father's death in 1939 and before passing control on to his son Charles R. Walgreen III in 1969, Chuck continued the expansion. Today, there are almost 5,500 Walgreens operating throughout the country.

After graduation, Chuck and my father lost track of each other. Seventy years later, at the reunion, they met again and found they still enjoyed each other's company. From that point on, they stayed in touch.

Seven years later, at the beginning of the twenty-first century, and once again in the springtime, my parents received an invitation to the Boston birthday party of their friend, Molly Wilson, who was about to become ninety. When my father called to congratulate her, she mentioned that she and her husband Carl were going to move into Lasell Village. My father promptly asked Molly if it had been built yet. She told him some of it was built and some was under construction. As soon as he finished talking to her, my father called me and asked me to go to Lasell Village. If I saw anything I thought they would like, he said, I should put a hold on it, and they would fly out to see it. They were in Boston within a week and purchased the two apartments I had on hold. As the wall between the two hadn't been erected, my parents were able to make modifications.

Lasell's location was perfect. My apartment and my son's in Boston was 15 minutes away. My eldest and youngest daughters and their families also lived within a 15 to 20 minute drive. Still, given my parents' ages of eighty-nine and ninety-four, I knew the move would be a big step for them.

Physically, the move was easy. My mother's nephew, Don Ullman, who was in the moving business, sent a truck with two of his best people to pack the belongings I had not already packed, and to load all the furniture onto the truck. With the help of a floor plan, my father and I worked out where every piece of furniture was to go in the new apartment.

I am sure the move was emotionally difficult for them. After all, my father and mother were leaving Illinois, the state they had lived in their entire lives. For this reason, I tried to make sure they visited all the people and places they knew and loved before they left for Massachusetts.

Shortly before the move, Chuck Walgreen, my father, and I had a delightful lunch together. While reminiscing, Chuck talked about how he had to take a course during the summer after high school graduation to gain admission to the University of Michigan. Once he had completed his sophomore year at the College of Literature, Science and the Arts at the University of Michigan, he had spent a year working for his father's company and had then decided to make it his career. He transferred to the College of Pharmacy and graduated in 1928. Chuck said,

"I became president of Walgreen in 1939, and Dad died a few months later, leaving me with enormous responsibility." This was probably the only serious conversation during the entire two-hour lunch.

One bright Monday morning, my mother, father, and I headed south to Idlewild. I always had wanted to see the two country clubs where my father had won each club's golf championship—Idlewild in 1928 and Ravisloe in 1929. We were standing on the first tee when an elderly man approached us, asking if he could help. My father introduced himself, explained that he had belonged to the club years ago and that his daughter had wanted to see where he'd won the championship. The elderly man said, "Lelewer, any relation to SS?"

"Yes, he was my father."

"I used to caddie for him a long time ago."

We walked a couple of holes on both courses. My father told me they had added a few sand traps to the courses, but he still had a clear mental picture of every hole on both courses.

On the chosen day, after the moving van was packed and on its way, the three of us flew from Chicago to Boston and spent the night at my apartment. The moving van arrived the next morning, the two men who had loaded the truck unloaded it, and my children and I unpacked and put everything away. Within 48 hours, all boxes were gone, the pictures were hung, and my parents' apartment looked exactly like the one in which they had lived in Highland Park. The following evening, my mother, father, and I had dinner with Carl and Molly Wilson, the friends who had told my father Lasell Village was under construction.

My parents were lucky to move into Lasell Village just as the community was opening. Cliques, which form in any community, had not yet had a chance to develop, and everyone

*Summer 2000: Joe Lelewer, age 94, and Sis
Lelewer, age 89, at Idlewild Country Club
where Joe was golf champion in 1928*

was interested in meeting new residents. The dining room offered restaurant-style dining, and the dining room hostess frequently asked couples if they wanted to eat with other couples or if they wanted to be seated at a table for two.

My father's only real complaint was the size of the shrimp that were served as shrimp cocktail. When the village's managers invited residents to a meeting the following year to discuss any concerns they had, my father raised his hand and said, "I've been waiting a year for the shrimp to grow up." He didn't have to say another word. Everyone burst out laughing, and Lasell's management got the hint.

My parents often said that it was the people—the "inmates," as my father would say—at Lasell that made the community so special. The average age was seventy-eight, and most members of the community were in good health. The courses, some of which were offered in conjunction with Lasell College, were intellectually stimulating and offered my father and other participants further opportunities to make friends. Even my mother, with her severe hearing problem, found it easy to make friends. This was, in part, because of the people she met at Lasell and, in part, because my father kept her tuned into much of what was being said and encouraged her to teach lip-reading. With over thirty-five years experience as a lip-reading teacher, Mother was a great teacher, so her students at Lasell benefited and she made friends on her own.

As my parents became acquainted with other residents, my father was often asked, "When did you get married?"

He always replied, "I was born married. I've been married so long I don't remember being single."

My mother would always respond, "Joe may not

remember ever being single, but he hasn't forgotten the names of any of his old girlfriends!"

A few months after their move, my parents' annual migration to Florida took place. As there were no nonstop or direct flights to Sarasota; they had to change planes in Charlotte, North Carolina. By this point, because of balance problems, Mother had been using a walker for some time, and my father was using a cane, so when they called me from Charlotte to tell me their plane to Sarasota had been canceled, I was concerned they would become exhausted navigating the airport. I called Sue, a friend of mine who works for U.S. Air. Earning my eternal gratitude, Sue drove over to the airport, found my parents, got them lunch, and kept them company. Eventually, they caught another flight that was due to arrive in Sarasota after dark. As I sat in my Boston apartment worrying about them finding their car, which had been driven there before they arrived, then driving to Longboat Key, and entering a closed up house, I decided this trip would be the last time they traveled alone.

The following year—2001—right before we all left for Sarasota, my father mentioned, rather casually, that the roof on the house on Longboat Key had caved in. He assured me he had had it fixed. When we arrived at Longboat, I found the roof was still under repair and tiles were everywhere. For whatever reason, I could not get the key to the house to work and, therefore, had to dig around in the dirt for another key hidden in a fake stone. After a five-minute struggle with that key, the front door opened, and I discovered my father had neglected to mention that the roof collapse had led to the collapse of part of the ceiling in the living room and master bedroom. The repair work required was done, but no one had cleaned up.

Draperies were lying on my bed; wet plaster had dripped on the windows, floor, and some furniture; the living room and dining room furniture was stacked to one side; a coat of plaster dust covered everything; and large and small chunks of the old ceiling were everywhere. On top of that, the house was freezing.

As my father tried to turn on the heat, I looked for the garage door remote, so I could park the car in the garage and unload the suitcases. The remote wasn't where it was usually stored. When I couldn't find it, I tried pushing the button in the garage. The double door went up two feet and stopped. I pushed the button again and nothing happened. At that point, I left the car in the driveway with suitcases in it, went back inside, uncovered a love seat for my parents to sit on, and went to work cleaning up the chunks of plaster lying on the floor.

As I went to work, my father turned up the thermostat. Once the chunks of plaster were picked up, I plugged in the vacuum cleaner. It didn't work in a nearby plug or in any other plug, nor did a lamp that I tried. In fact, the electricity wasn't working at all, and the house remained very cold. It was beginning to get dark, so my father and I went next door to borrow a large flashlight and to call the emergency number for the oil company. It seems the bill had not been forwarded to my parents' new home, so my mother hadn't paid it.

After some discussion, we decided the best thing to do was to go to market, buy a few essentials, and then go out for dinner. Once we put the items in the refrigerator and freezer, which ran on gas, as did the hot water heater, we left for dinner. When we returned, my parents climbed in bed with extra blankets to keep warm, and I went to get them each a dish of ice cream. Scooping it was easy; the ice cream was the consistency of thick soup. It took just a moment to discover the refrigerator was warm and the freezer was cool but not cold. I was profoundly grateful that we had reached the end of the day.

The next day, the refrigerator, freezer, and overhead garage door were fixed, and heat and electricity were restored. I made chicken for dinner and invited a single, older woman friend of my parents to join us. After dinner, I put the dishes in the dishwasher, mumbled, "I hope this thing works," and left to take my parents' friend home. Ten minutes later, I arrived back at the house to find my father ankle deep in water, mopping. He had managed to turn the machine off, but not before water had flooded the kitchen and oozed into the dining room. Together, we cleaned up the water, and the following day a repairman fixed the dishwasher.

A few days later, I decided to do some laundry. I'd noticed the sheets on my bed had a funny texture. I discovered the washer went through all its cycles, but without any water on the rinse cycle. As the repairman worked on the washer, I began to wonder what the following year would be like.

In the fall of 2002, I flew to Sarasota with my parents, helped them open the house, and then returned to Boston. I was nervous about leaving them and, during daily phone calls, suggested a couple of times that I should come for a visit for a few days. My father insisted it wasn't necessary, but still, I checked flight schedules. On January 15, I received a call from a visiting nurse who, I learned, saw my parents a couple of times a week to check blood pressure. She said, "Mrs. Sonnabend, your parents are both failing. You need to get to them as soon as possible." I was in Sarasota that afternoon. My parents were surprised to see me. "We're fine," my father told me.

"That's great," I said, "but as long as I'm here, I'll stay for a while."

It was a wise decision on my part. My mother had a doctor's appointment the next day. Because she was deaf, my father went to all appointments with her. This time, I went with them and soon realized the problems we were facing. Mother didn't say a word during the appointment. The doctor spoke quickly. My father asked pertinent questions, but his hand tremor made the notes that he took illegible, even to him, and his short-term memory wasn't what it used to be. Finally, I said to the doctor, "You need to write everything down for my parents." He looked at me as if I'd asked him to speak Croatian.

After a few more appointments with other doctors, it became clear that most of them were not going to bother with my parents because they were old. The exception was their internist, who was wonderful. We changed many of their other doctors over time, but, even so, my parents' treatment was more thorough when I was present because I would insist the doctors put in writing the diagnosis, when the next appointment was, what medications were to be taken, what my parents were supposed to do between visits, and, if blood work or other tests were needed, where they should go for the tests.

By the age of ninety-six, my father had no strength or feeling in his hands or fingers. Bottles were impossible for him to open, so he would have my mother open the bottles and he would switch the medications to larger containers with no lids. He reasoned that, as long as they knew when to take a pill, it didn't matter what the pill was. Thus, he used a black box labeled either Sis or Joe for pills he or my mother had to take at night and a white box labeled either Sis or Joe for pills that had to be taken during the day. Although the idea of color-coding the boxes to the time of day was good, any information about the medications was thrown out when the pills were put in their boxes. I'd been with my parents for a couple of weeks before I discovered my mother had had a heart attack a week or two before my arrival. The discovery was purely accidental. I found one of Mother's empty pill bottles and the literature that went with it. According to the literature, the medication was for a person who had suffered a heart attack. "Dad," I said a bit frantically, "Mom is on the wrong medication. This is for people who have had heart attacks."

"No, it's correct," he answered. "Your Mom did have a heart attack."

"She did? When?"

"About three weeks ago. She was only in the hospital for a few days."

"Don't you think you might have told me?"

"We didn't want to worry you."

A few days after this conversation, I discovered my father had been diagnosed with congestive heart failure. Again, he made light of it. I suspect two forces were at work in his response: denial and the constant parental urge to protect children from hurtful things. I began to hire help for them. By the middle of March 2003, the house was running smoothly, except for weekends for which I simply could not find satisfactory help.

It seems to be a truism that no sooner do you get one problem solved than another one arises. In my case, the problem that arose could have spelled disaster for children who already had problems, their parents, and the adults who wanted to help the children. Early one morning, I received a phone call from the headmaster of a private school for dyslexic and learning disabled boys in Northfield, Massachusetts. I was chairwoman of the school's board of trustees.

"Nancy," the headmaster said, "I'm in New York at a conference with a couple of boys and a colleagian. One of the boys has accused me of sexually touching him."

"Michael," I replied, "that's ridiculous. Forget about it and take them all back to school."

"I can't. The school has already sent a van to collect the boys and the colleagian. It's been reported to the state."

My entire body began to shake. This was a scandal that, when added to the school's sizable debt and lack of endowment, could endanger its existence.

The other trustees, a great lawyer, and I managed to keep the school running, but trying to deal with my parents in Florida and the school in Massachusetts cost me thirty pounds and most of my hearing. There were many lawsuits, and faculty, parents, and staff were constantly calling to find out what was happening and whether the school would continue. At roughly the same time, my father failed his eye test and lost his Florida driver's license. He was upset and displeased with the local registry of motor vehicles. "They're not smart," he protested to me. "They tested my right eye and then my left. I don't drive with one eye at a time!"

I suggested we hire a driver. He wanted none of that. All I could do was make sure I was available to drive him wherever he wanted to go when I was in town and be grateful that my mother still had her license, even though she didn't like to drive at night. I can remember calling from Boston one evening and not being able to reach them until 8 P.M. Needless to say, I was beginning to be frantic.

"Where were you?"

"We went to the club for dinner."

"Dad, you didn't drive, did you?"

"No, your mother drove."

"Where is the chef who has been cooking you dinner every night?"

"She got a job at a club downtown and quit."

"With no notice?"

"She told us yesterday."

"Mom doesn't like to drive after dark. Was it okay?"

"Sort of."

"What does that mean?"

"It was light out when we went. Because it was dark when we came home, Mom was driving very slowly, and the car stalled out. I didn't know a moving car could stall, but it can. She got it started, and we made it home safely. Don't worry."

I flew down the next day. It was clear the winter migration my father had undertaken since childhood was coming to an end.

In the fall of 2003, after some discussion and pleading on my part, my father agreed to spend the winter in Massachusetts. I think my mother was relieved, but I know my father was disappointed, so I was thrilled for him when he received a call from Chuck Walgreen in November.

"Hi, Joe," said Chuck. Chuck and my father had talked on the phone frequently after my parents moved to Lasell, but in 2001, a letter had arrived from Chuck instead of a phone call. He had suffered a stroke, was in the hospital, and would be in a wheelchair for the rest of his life. He told my father that he planned to build a wheelchair-accessible boat. It would, he said, take two years to complete, and he invited my father to fly to

Chicago in June 2003 for the dedication and launching of the boat. My father thought Chuck had lost his mind. They were both 95 and Dad wondered how much time either of them had left. "If you want a boat, Chuck, buy one and retrofit it," my father had said. Chuck, however, knew exactly what he wanted and proceeded to build the first wheelchair-accessible mega-yacht ever built in this country. My father hadn't made it to the Chicago launching in June 2003, and now Chuck said, "I'm on my boat. I just got into Charlestown harbor. We'll be here only until early tomorrow morning, and I hope you'll come see me."

My father hung up and called me. I was scheduled to pick up two of my grandchildren that afternoon and take them to various activities. I decided it would be a more meaningful experience for them to meet Chuck and go on his boat. After several phone calls, we were all in the car headed toward Charlestown with a sheet of elaborate directions.

At the gate, which was locked, we called Chuck, who sent a wheelchair with two men and umbrellas to take us to the boat. We descended a long, steep gangplank in the rain to the floating rafts where the boats were moored. After a ten-minute walk, we reached Chuck's boat. The captain appeared and told my father he'd hoist him onto the boat in the wheelchair. "Don't drop me!" was my father's only comment as he was swung across the water to the yacht in the wheelchair.

Chuck's boat, The Sis W, is a spectacular, 127-foot Burger with a three-deck elevator, magnificent interiors and exteriors, and every technological device imaginable. Joe (age nine), Kristi (almost eleven), my father, and I toured the boat. We had our pictures taken in the main salon with Chuck and his second wife, Jean Campbell, met Chuck's grandson, Casey Pratt, and had a great time. Although Chuck and Dad were ninety-seven, their

Top (Left to Right on sofa): Kristi Wagner, Joe Wagner, Joe Lelewer, Chuck's second wife, Jean Campbell, Nancy Sonnabend and Chuck Walgreen Jr., in wheelchair, on board the SIS W (November 2003)
Bottom: The SIS W, Chuck Walgreen's 127-foot Burger

minds were sharp, and they had plenty to talk about. At one point, Chuck said to Dad, "I'm sorry we don't have time to take you out so you'd know how it feels under power."

Dad replied, "I know how it feels, same as now." They both laughed.

Chuck invited us to stay for dinner, but my mother was alone in the apartment, so we returned to Lasell. Even in their old age, my parents were very much in love, and my father never liked to leave her for too long. I can still remember hearing them giggle late one afternoon when I arrived to visit them in their apartment. I reached the bedroom door just in time to see them fall onto their king-size bed in each other's arms.

"What are you doing, and what is so funny?" I asked.

When my father finally stopped laughing, he said, "Neither of us has much balance any more so if we want to kiss we come into the bedroom and stand at the foot of the bed. That way, when we fall we don't get hurt."

With that, they both began to laugh again.

CHAPTER 21
Into the Good Night:
The Celebration of Life Services

The move to Lasell Village brought my parents some pleasures they had not been able to enjoy when they lived in Illinois. Many of their grandchildren and great-grandchildren were only minutes away, so "Great Papa" and "Great Mama" (as my father and mother were called) could and did enjoy ballet recitals, birthday parties, and all the other major events of their great-grandchildren's lives. Still, there was no question that the years were adding up. In the middle of my father's ninety-seventh year, he said, "I've stopped reading the death notices because I'm afraid I might find myself in them!"

His health had always been good, but that year things began to get a bit dicey. He told me he was beginning to wonder how his ninety-eighth year would be. Just a few days into it, we got the unwelcome answer. My mother was hospitalized, and, from there on, things began to unravel. My father found he had little energy because of his deteriorating heart, and commonplace tasks, such as dressing, became difficult for him. He said to me, "Ninety-eight is not a good year, just go directly from ninety-seven to ninety-nine when you get there."

Still, he was thrilled when, in September 2004, I was chosen to receive the Alice Garside Award from the Massachusetts Branch of the International Dyslexia Association (MABIDA). The award is given annually to honor an individual who has made an outstanding contribution to the field of dyslexia. The presentation was to be made at the association's annual dinner on September 17, 2004 at the MIT Faculty Club. My father and mother were to be among the guests at the dinner. The morning of the presentation, my father dressed slowly, and I helped him with his socks and shoes. Although he made it into the dining room, he ate little. "I need to take a nap," he said and lay down on the Trat sleeper. I sat on the floor next to him reading a book while he dozed.

At 1 P.M., I awakened him and said, "Lunch time." He said he wasn't hungry and wanted to go back to sleep. I brought him half a sandwich and a glass of milk. He took a few bites and lay back down. I studied his face for a moment and then said, "Dad, you are too sick to go tonight."

He looked as if he were going to cry, an expression I'd never before seen on his face. "I want to be there to see you get the award."

"I know," I replied, "and I want you there. But you can hardly hold your head up. It just seems very unlikely that, in a few hours, you'll be able to sit in a car for half an hour to get to Cambridge, get from the car to the dinner, and then sit through the meal, the guest speaker, my award, and another half hour's drive home. I'll ask Tom Rowe [my son-in-law] to videotape the

Isabel Wesley, President of the Massachusetts Branch of the International Dyslexia Association presented the Alice H. Garside Award to Nancy Lelewer Sonnabend at the MIT Faculty Club, Cambridge, MA. September 17, 2004

evening, and you'll see everything in a day or two. Should I ask Mom if she wants to go without you?"

"No," he answered. "You make that decision and tell her."

"I don't think she'll be happy without you there, and she's so deaf, she won't hear a word anyone is saying. I'm not taking her."

During the afternoon, I practiced my acceptance speech. As I practiced, he listened carefully and, of course, said the speech was great. I gave my mother a printed copy of it, and when she finished reading it, she smiled.

Three of my children, their spouses, my granddaughter Kristi, and several friends of mine were among those at the dinner. Kristi interviewed many of the attendees as Tom videotaped them. He then videotaped the president's presentation of the award, a large pewter plate with my name and the date engraved on it, and a huge armful of flowers. He also videotaped my acceptance speech, which I dedicated to my parents. Two days later, I saw my father smile widely as he watched the tape.

Looking back, it seems as if October and November of that year were designed to bring my parents as much pleasure as possible and to give those of us who were participants in their lives indelible memories. On October 12, Joe Wagner, my parents' great-grandson, celebrated his tenth birthday. For his party, which his great-grandparents and I attended, Joe invited a few of his friends to participate in a karate lesson. Joe had taken karate lessons from Rocky DiRico for a number of years, and Rocky had even had him help teach some of the younger boys. My parents and I watched the lesson and were greatly impressed by Rocky, who not only teaches the moves of karate, but also its philosophy. Joe, who thought the world of his great-grandfather, was close to Rocky and had told him of my father's interest in the White Sox and his memory of the team's early players. Shortly after Joe's birthday, Rocky purchased and gave Joe a book containing cards and pictures of Shoeless Joe Jackson, one of the really great White Sox players my father had seen when he was young. Joe was thrilled and rushed to show his "Great Papa" the book. My father was touched by Rocky's gesture and, on October 26, 2004, wrote the following note to him, which he asked Joe to deliver along with a pewter candleholder:

> *Dear Rocky,*
> *The enclosed early English chamber stick (candle-holder) is part of my wife's and my pewter collection that we have put together over our 72 years of married life. We are most appreciative of your mentor-*

*ship of our great-grandson, Joe Wagner, and want
you to have this light as a memento from us as you
are a guiding light to young Joe.*

Sincerely,
Joseph Lelewer

Rocky's response was almost immediate:

Dear Mr. Lelewer,
*Over the years, I have received many gifts from
students, however, the beautiful English Chamber
Stick, along with your gracious and thoughtful letter
is perhaps the most appreciated because of the meaning of them.*

*My heartfelt thanks to you for your kind words and
generosity.*

Rocky DiRico

Joe, who has been taught social graces, wrote the following note thanking my parents for his birthday gift and for their
gift to Rocky:

Dear Great Mama and Great Papa,
*Thank you . . . also for your very thoughtful gift
to my karate teacher, Rocky. That was very nice of
you. He has been very nice to me and I like spend-
ing Thursday afternoons with him. I hope to get my
black belt sometime in the near future. I will show it*

to you as soon as I get it.
I love you and hope to see you soon.
Love,
Joe

The last family gathering to be attended by both my parents was the tenth birthday of their great-granddaughter, Mina Caroline Rowe, who was named after my mother and is the eldest child of my eldest child, Kathy. Mina, whose birthday was on November 5, knew it was difficult for her great-grandparents to get in and out of cars, so asked if she could have her party at her great-grandparents' apartment. In honor of the occasion, there was a birthday tablecloth, balloons, candy, gourmet food, many presents, and her great-grandparents.

After dinner, Kathy asked, "Papa, What were the two most important events in your life?"

The answer came in a flash: "When I got my first bike and first car."

"But, Papa, weren't marrying Great Mama and having Mom more important than getting a bike and a car?"

"They were very important to me, but not the most important."

"Why?"

"Because the bike and car gave me freedom and speed."

For a man who loved freedom and speed, he was singularly devoted to caring for the people who were important to him. A few weeks before he died, my father said to me, "I'm so sorry I can no longer take care of you."

I pointed out that it was unprecedented for a father to take care of his daughter for nearly seventy years and that I was happy to take care of him now, so he should live a long time. He looked

at me, smiled, and said, "I'm trying." It was a very typical response. My father never was one to throw his hands up in the air
and announce there was nothing that could be done. The day after he told me the doctor had told him he was dying, he said, "It's
hard living when you don't have a future. On the other hand, no
one knows what the future holds, so the important thing is what
you do with each day."

As a part of doing something with each day, he went to
classes at Lasell right up to the end of his life. His favorite professor was Joe Aieta. A week before my father died, I pushed
his wheelchair into Joe's classroom, just a few minutes late. Joe
promptly stopped what he was doing and said, "Joe's here.
You've made my day."

Things might have become physically difficult for my father, but his mind was still sharp. "And you've made mine," he
shot back.

For Thanksgiving that year, Stephen, my former husband, and his wife took Eric, Kathy, Patti and their spouses, plus
Wendy's husband and all eight of our grandchildren on a cruise
out of Miami. Wendy came to Boston to spend Thanksgiving
with my parents and me. Before they left, Kathy and Patti, perhaps recognizing how fragile their grandfather had become, said
to me, "Call if you need to, and we'll get off the ship and fly
home."

It had become clear during the year that both my parents
now needed at least some help twenty-four hours a day. My
mother had a fabulous woman named Rosetta during the day
and a not so wonderful woman at night. My father had Fred,
a strong but gentle man, from 9 A.M. to 9 P.M. I had hoped my
father would sleep in his own apartment at night with the assis-
tance of my mother's night aide. There was only one bathroom in

the apartment my father could use, as it was small and had been fitted with grips to help him steady himself. We discovered my mother's night aid was too heavy to help him into that bathroom, therefore, because my father often had to get up at night, and because I couldn't handle him by myself, he had to sleep in Lasell House, the nursing section of Lasell Village. I know my father hated being in the nursing section at night, as every morning he would complain about what had gone on the previous night, and he wasn't one to complain. To this day, I wish I had found a more satisfactory solution for him.

Thanksgiving morning, I brought him his breakfast—hot cereal, warm coffee cake, and hot coffee with plenty of cream and sugar—all either easy to chew or requiring no chewing at all. The food in Lasell House was typical of the food in most nursing units: cold coffee, cold scrambled eggs, rock-hard cold toast, or rubbery pancakes. (My father once remarked after trying one of the pancakes, "Remind me to congratulate the chef. This is the best recipe for rubber I have ever tasted!") In theory, sugar and cream were not permitted, but after a certain age, quality of life is more important than quantity.

He didn't eat much, just said that he needed to go back to sleep. When lunchtime came, he called the apartment to say he was skipping lunch, "I need to sleep some more, but I'll be down for dinner and to watch a TV program with Mama."

Since Wendy and I were to have dinner with my friends, the Volks, I prepared Thanksgiving dinner and had everything arranged for my parents before we left. By 5 P.M., my father and his aide were in the apartment. My father was dressed in a dinner jacket and my mother was wearing one of her St. John outfits. I will forever carry in my mind the image of my mother and father sitting side by side in their wheelchairs, holding hands and watching television. After we left, Mother's evening aide served them Thanksgiving dinner at the dining room table they'd purchased sixty-seven years ago when they'd first moved to Highland Park.

After dinner, I dropped Wendy off at her friend's home, where she had been staying, and returned to Lasell Village. I went first to check on my father. He had a strange expression on his face, one I hadn't seen before, that made me uneasy. I kissed him gently, not wanting to awaken him, then found the head nurse, told her I was worried, and asked her to keep a close eye on him. From there, I went to their apartment. Exhausted, I decided to spend the night and promptly went to sleep on the Trat sleeper. The next thing I knew Mother's aide was awakening me, "The phone's for you."

"This is Rachel, Nancy. Your father just passed away. Do you want to come up now or wait until morning?"

"I'm not coming up. I want to remember Dad alive. I will send Mom's night helper up with some clothes in which to dress him."

I hung up and then called Wendy on her cell phone. I don't know how I would have managed without her. She changed her flight and joined me at the apartment. Together, we made a list of what needed to be done: call the crematorium, fill in the obituary my father had previously written, break the news to my mother, tell the rest of the family, notify the newspapers, arrange a celebration of life service, and get in touch with the Florida bank that was to handle the filing of my father's estate papers.

As we knew the rest of the family would be at sea all day Friday, we decided not to contact them until Saturday morning. There seemed no point in awakening my mother, who usually slept until 11 A.M., with news that would break her heart, so we decided not to tell her until lunchtime. I called the crematorium, discussed details of the cremation according to instructions my father had left me, and asked them to pick him up. Wendy made arrangements to hold the celebration of life service in the ballroom Monday afternoon. After that, we went to my apartment in Boston to access my father's obituary on my computer, updated it, and sent it to the various newspapers my father had listed in his instructions to me.

We then returned to my parents' apartment, and, just before lunch, I wrote on a white board for my mother, "I'm sorry, Mom. Dad died last night." She stared at me and didn't say a word. I wrote, "You knew he was very ill. It was his heart. It just finally stopped beating. He didn't suffer." She shook her head up and down. She had not participated in conversations for some time by then, so I was not surprised when she said nothing throughout lunch. Later in the afternoon, Rosetta took her for a walk in her wheelchair. When they returned, my mother said, "It's hard not having Papa here." That was the first and last thing she ever said about him. I never saw her cry.

There are sorrows that run so deep there are no words or tears for them. I suspect she spent that afternoon remembering the little things, the gestures, a look, the turn of his head that had been a part of her life for seventy-two years. In a drawer next to her bed, Mother kept a stack of notes that my father had written to her over the years. He wasn't big on buying cards. He preferred to use the back of advertisements or a scrap of paper to tell her of his devotion. The following are a few from the stack.

To Mina—What a lucky day this is for me—You finally said yes 65 years ago. Happy Valentine's Day, I love you. T. A. J. [My father often signed notes to my mother, T. A. J., short for Terrible, Awful Joe, or T. A. M., Terrible Awful Me.]

To My Darling Wife—70 years with you seems like 7. I love you. T. A. J.

I promise—no more ½ ass quips—just love me.

My best Birthday present is having you.

Dearest Mina—I am so happy you married me. You were and are a soothing influence and a tower of strength. And you looked so pretty and happy as you slept this AM—So I just had to tell you and thank you—I am lucky.

My love is to you. T. A. M.

Dearest—I loved you at first sight, I always have, I always shall. T. A J.

87 will always love 83 even when she gets old.

Saturday morning, Wendy reached Kathy and the rest of the family in Key Biscayne. The minute Wendy told Kathy about Great Papa's death, Kathy broke down completely. Her husband, Tom, took the phone to find out what had happened. A few minutes later, Patti called in tears. I'm told everyone in the family was crying. By Saturday night, the entire family had gathered at my parents' apartment to make the final arrangements for my father. We decided to tell people at Lasell Village that the family would be at the apartment Sunday afternoon from 4 to 6 P.M., and that there would be a celebration of life service on Monday, November 29, 2004 from 4 to 6 P.M. in the ballroom. Kathy took charge of arranging for refreshments and help for both afternoons. Wendy handled the announcements and worked with Lasell Village personnel.

About 100 people attended my father's celebration of life service. My daughter-in-law, Donna, drove Eric's and her daughters, Rachel and Olivia, from Pennsylvania to participate in the service. Together, the girls—Olivia on the violin and Rachel on the flute—played "Melody for Strings" by Arthur Rubinstein. Next, Rachel played "Handel's Sonata in A minor, Adagio." My children, their children, and my father's friends all spoke during the ceremony[10].

As each child and friend spoke, my father seemed to stand before me smiling, sometimes laughing, listening carefully, and always ready to offer encouragement or a lecture as needed. Regardless of how old my father was, he was always young. Yes, he matured from his youthful, wild days, but he was always looking ahead. Ruth Sacks, who had her first film credit at age eighty-five, once said, "Age lets us see farther, youth lets us see brighter. Those who have both are blessed." My father had both right up until his last breath. He was fun, and I worshiped him as far back as I can remember. That never changed.

For a number of years, my children and I, when we allowed ourselves to think about it at all, had rather hoped that Great Papa, my father, would out-live Great Mama because we thought that it would be easier for her. Although, it wasn't to be, she lived only two and a half months after his death. My three

---

[10] The full text of some speeches from this service are in Appendix C.

daughters and I were with my mother when she took her last breath on February 11, 2005.

I was still in shock over my father's death when Mother passed away. Her death was a different kind of loss for me, but still great. Now, I would never have the kind of conversation with my mother that I'd always wanted to have. Our family repeated everything we'd done two and a half months earlier. We had a sitting in my parents' apartment on Sunday, February 13, 2005 and a celebration of life ceremony in the ballroom on Monday, February 14. Much of the family was there, and, once again, both family and friends spoke during the service.

I spoke of my mother's achievements, awards, relationship with my father, and the love in my childhood home. "Today is Valentine's Day," I noted at the end. "Seventy-three years ago today, also on Valentine's Day, my parents became engaged. They had over seventy-two wonderful years together and learned to adapt to one another. I found a Valentine's Day card Mom gave Dad many years ago. On the cover it reads, 'A Valentine for my husband.' On page two, 'Lots of women marry a guy and then try to change him, but not me, Honey! I love you just the way you are ...' Page three, 'BUT DON'T GET WORSE! HAPPY VALENTINE'S DAY.' Signed, 'I do love you, Sis.'"

The ceremony was followed by a lovely reception organized by Kathy in my parents' apartment. The service was elegant, and the flowers were beautiful. It was indeed a fitting tribute to my mother.

Sometime after my parents died, a Braeside classmate of mine, Beth Jacobs Boyle, sent me her thoughts about them:

I think your Dad glowed. Sometimes he seemed

to twinkle. I wouldn't have said it this way as a child; now I see him as a man without pretension. When we met again in 1995, I felt that we knew each other. Almost none of the fathers paid anything close to real attention to us kids. We weren't 'people'—almost another foreign species. Not so with your Dad. But in truth, those other dads, I am sure of this, did not for the most part truly connect with their peers either. They had their interests. They weren't entirely empty suits. But they were stunted, many of them. Not your Dad. I was so happy to see both your parents that summer day in front of Braeside School at the reunion. I had grown up and, without hesitation, I asked your Dad, "So, now we are Sis and Joe and Beth, right?" It would not have occurred to me to ask any other parent that. And indeed, I had always liked and admired Mrs. Davidow, but we had no connection person to person. So I was, in the child that I had been, happy to see Mrs. Davidow and to see her well. . . It didn't occur to me, nor did it vex me, that we would not share a mutual moment.

Your mother to me was always gracious, but distant. Even my memories of the two of them have your father, present and in focus –your mother as if through a veil. You said there was lots of laughter in your home. I cannot recall having heard your mother laugh. In sum, I think your father had/was a deep font of love.

I would never dispute Beth's memories of my father, but after my mother died, we created a card to send out in response to the condolence notes and donations to charities we received. I think this card perhaps best describes my mother:

A woman of style and grace
A radiant smile,
With warmth and quiet dignity.

Joe and Sis Lelewer

Joseph David Lelewer
(3/30/1906–11/26/2004)

Mina "Sis" Ullman Lelewer
1/24/1911 to 2/11/2005

CHAPTER 22
Travels with My Grandchildren

When I was fourteen, my grandma, Myrtle Lelewer, took me by train to Banff in the Canadian Rockies. During the train ride, I learned all about the early years of my father and his brother and a great deal about my grandmother. For some reason—probably because it seems impossible they could ever be interested in anything but their families—grandchildren find it difficult to imagine that their grandparents have much of a life. I learned that Grandma gave a great deal of time to Unaghinger Orden Treue Schwestern (United Order of True Sisters), (UOTS), a secret charitable organization that was dedicated to working with cancer patients. The organization had been founded by women of German Jewish ancestry in 1847 and continues to this day. In fact, Grandma was honored for fifty years of service to UOTS Johanna Lodge #9, the first midwestern chapter of the organization. She was also a director of the Sinai Temple Sisterhood.

Grandma was adept at cards and, during the trip, taught me how to play both gin rummy and canasta. By the end of it, I

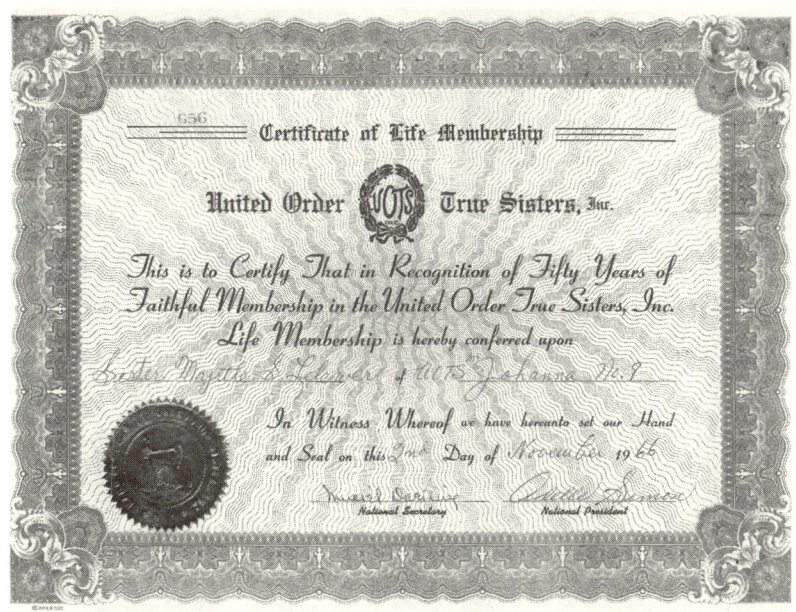

Life membership conferred upon Myrtle Lelewer by UOTS Johanna Lodge #9

had become a decent adversary for her. As we played, we would peer out the train windows. Every curve of the track would bring to our eyes new scenes of lakes, trees, or majestic mountains, sometimes in full sun, sometimes in shadow. I'm not sure we took a camera with us, but the scenes are etched deep within my memory, so it doesn't matter. Whenever something spectacular came into view, I would feel some unspoken connection between Grandma and me.

At dinnertime, I would sit across from Grandma at a white, cloth-covered table set with shiny silverware. Free to choose whatever I wished, I would carefully unfold a large, white napkin, place it on my lap, and peruse the menu. Usually, I wanted steak or roast beef or barbecued chicken. Grandma and I would chat away as we ate. We always seemed to have something to say to each other. After dinner, a uniformed porter would make up the two beds in our sleeping compartment. Before I climbed to my upper berth, Grandma and I would sit on her berth and peer out at the scenery. In the full moon, the mountains and trees were bathed in an eerie soft blanket of light.

Grandma splurged on this trip. In every hotel, we had rooms with spectacular views. I still remember the double rainbow Grandma and I spotted together over the deep-green water of Lake Louise. It was as though our room at the Banff Hotel offered a once-in-a-lifetime view of the lake and, in its water, a reflection of the mountain behind it.

It was magical and completely unforgettable. For a part of the trip, we joined a tour, and I still vividly recall seeing the amazing Athabasca Ice Fields. As we explored the area, the guide kept urging us to stay with him. I was a teenager and tended to wander a bit on my own until he finally said, "There are numerous hidden crevasses in the ice; most aren't easy to detect until you fall through." From that moment on, I became his shadow.

The only drawback to our trip, as far as I could see, was the lack of people my age. With the exception of me, a good-looking, nineteen-year-old boy and a beautiful, buxom eighteen-year-old girl, all of the people on the tour were adults. If I harbored any thoughts of companionship with the boy or girl, I was soon disappointed. The boy and girl bonded, and I became invisible to them. I remember feeling rather left out, but not saying anything to Grandma. Then, one day, while Grandma and I were sitting at the hotel pool, a handsome young man came over to us, smiled graciously at Grandma, introduced himself, and then bent toward me. "I've noticed you at the pool before. There is a restaurant at this hotel where there's dancing. I'm wondering if your grandmother would allow you to dine there with me tonight? "

I felt my cheeks burn as I looked at Grandma. "It's just fine with me," she said with a pleasant smile, "as long as you don't leave the hotel and do get back to the room by 11 P.M."

I have to admit, this was more exciting to me than all the beautiful views we had seen. Tom was tall, easy to talk to, and a good dancer. We covered the whole floor with our jitterbugging. He was also very polite. At 11 P.M. on the dot, he and I reached my door and said goodnight. Grandma greeted me as I entered, and I floated off to bed.

Years went by, but I never forgot that magical trip and the unexpected dinner date. When I became a grandmother for the first time, I told my father that I hoped some day I could take each of my grandchildren on a trip like the one Grandma and I took. My father smiled and said, "I guess it's okay if you know now. My mother wanted you to have a good time and worried about the two teenagers who were ignoring you. The ones you didn't mention to her. She decided you needed a date and found that handsome young man, asked him to take you out, and paid for the dinners. She also told him he was not to lay a hand on you or to tell you she had arranged the date. She laid down the law about how the evening should progress: 'Have a nice conversation with my granddaughter, eat dinner, dance, and bring her home by 11.' She had dinner in her room, so she wouldn't bump into you downstairs."

As my grandchildren[11] arrived and began to grow up, I wondered what I would do to give each one of them one trip that would bring them as much pleasure as my grandmother's trip had brought me. It took a bit of time and planning, but it began one day when I called my daughter, Wendy, and told her I would like to take Kelly, her eldest daughter and my eldest granddaughter, to China. That evening, Kelly called me and exclaimed, "Mama! I'm going to China with you and I can hardly

---

[11] Pictures of all eight grandchildren are in Appendix D.

Nancy Sonnabend with her granddaughter, Kelly Erickson, in China, 2005

get my mind wrapped around the idea!" In the fall of 2005, Kelly flew from San Francisco, and I departed from Boston. We met in the baggage claim area of the Beijing airport and rushed into each other's arms.

We saw the historic sights of Beijing, walked along the Great Wall, and spent a day in Xian viewing the 2,000-year-old, life-sized terra cotta warriors, archers, infantrymen, and horses that guarded the tomb of Emperor Qin Shi Huang. From Xian, we moved on to Chongqing. We arrived at night and were surprised to find an enormous city in the middle of farmland along the Yangtze River. The city seemed to have more skyscrapers than Manhattan, and its center was busier than Times Square. On Chongqing's waterfront, we boarded a ship for three days on the Yangtze River and toured the Three Gorges Dam, China's largest construction project since the Great Wall. It is, in fact, the largest hydroelectric project in the world. As we traveled, we saw how the river's rising water level had led to the flooding of villages and homes along its banks. It was estimated that the project would force the relocation of up to 4 million people. On the third night, we went through the dam's locks and, the following day, toured the dam itself. Next, we moved on to Shanghai for more sightseeing, a trip to its knockoff market, a great Chinese acrobatic performance, and a night view of Shanghai from the Cloud 9 Bar on the eighty-seventh floor of the Grand Hyatt Hotel, the highest and best place to see the city completely illuminated.

I was amazed by the changes that had taken place in the country since I first saw it in 1979. Back then, there were few cars in the cities and no high rises in Shanghai. Men and women wore light blue Mao jackets. Individuality seemed frowned upon, and contact with Westerners was limited. On this visit, we were invited to spend time with a family in their home. It was Kelly's favorite experience during the trip because it exposed her to the multi-generations living together, and the pride the elders took in their children. Today, there are super highways with three or more lanes in each direction and traffic jams at rush hour. Gone are the drab hotels constructed by the Russians with thick walls and bathrooms that did not function. In their place are five-star hotels with health clubs, swimming pools, and tennis courts. The Shanghai of 1979 is now a residential area. Across the river, a new Shanghai has been built with magnificent buildings, shops, discos, and restaurants.

It was an incredible trip that left both of us with wonderful memories of sights and sounds and time spent together. It was my first "grandchild trip."

My second grandchild trip occurred in August 2006. A small group put together by Judy Karp, a friend of mine who runs such trips, Joe, my grandson, and I went to Kenya on a safari.

When I made arrangements for that trip, I told Judy that I wanted to fly business class to Kenya and I wanted Joe to be in the seat next to mine. Since turning seventy, I've made it a habit to fly business class for overnight flights. In the past, I always flew economy, which meant I didn't sleep at all and inevitably felt sick the first day or two of a trip. I finally decided it was worth the extra money to be able to lie flat and sleep, and, if I'm going to do that, so are my grandchildren when they travel with me.

When Joe and I checked into Virgin Atlantic, we discovered that he was in 3A and I was in 4A. I hoped that when we boarded I could swap an A seat for a B seat. What I didn't know is that Virgin Atlantic does not have a business class, only a first class, or, as it is known, upper class. In Virgin Atlantic's upper class, the reclining seats are large and include all the area that would normally be taken up by seats A, B, and C. Thus, when Joe was in 3A and I was in 4A, we were side by side. Each seat has a smaller seat at its foot, which can be used as a footrest or as a seat for another person who is sharing a meal. Stored along one side of each seat is a table that two people can comfortably sit at to eat. Each seat also has its own TV that swings out with the push of a button and offers over 100 movies. After dinner, Joe and I were given pajamas, our chairs were flipped over making them into beds, a bed pad and pillow were placed on each, and a large, down sleeping bag was placed on the bed pad. Once we were in bed, the flight attendant loosely secured a seat belt around each of us. If I hadn't been so busy being a practical grandmother the next morning at breakfast, I would have joined Joe's chorus of "This is so cool!" Instead, I assumed my practical grandmother role and said, "Don't get used to it. I've never flown like this before and we may never again, but it's certainly nice."

There were sixteen of us on the safari. Joe, who was almost twelve years old, was the only youngster and, in everyone's eyes, he was worth his weight in gold. He was first to spot animals, he could fix cameras quickly, and he helped fellow travelers send e-mails home. Joe has always loved animals and, like his great-grandfather before him, he was enchanted by every animal he saw. When I think back on our trip, I see Joe with his camera in front of his face all day going click, click, click. He got the best pictures of anyone in the group.

Because it is the best way to see everything, we traveled by van from place to place, often bouncing from the ditch on one side of a dirt road to the ditch on the other side of the road.

It didn't seem to matter greatly which side of the road the van traveled on. If I ever had a moment's doubt about the ability of our driver/guide, it disappeared the day our van was charged by an enormous male elephant. We had been taking pictures

*Top: Nancy Sonnabend and Joe Wagner having dinner in Upper
Class on Virgin Atlantic while crossing the Atlantic, August 2006
Bottom: Joseph Wagner trying on the hat of a Maasai in Kenya, August 2006*

from the van of the bull elephant, his mate, and their baby. He was on the right side of the path and she and the baby were on the left side. All of a sudden, he raised his trunk, let out a terrible bellow and charged the side of the van that Judy and Joe were on. Those two leapt to the other side of the van, and our driver/ guide gunned the van. The elephant missed us by only a foot or two.

As a part of our tour, we visited two native villages deep in the bush, and Joe learned how to make a fire with two sticks. In both villages, the homes were made from cow dung, and there were, of course, no bathroom facilities. In fact, throughout the trip, bathroom facilities during the day were typical third-world facilities, thus hand sanitizer was a necessity. For villagers, paper of any kind, or even a change of clothes, are an unheard of luxury. The village school we visited had no books. Joe learned women had limited choices and female circumcision is a fact of life. Still, the villagers we met seemed to be happy to share what they had with strangers. At one village, the women, all wearing colorful lengths of cloth that they wrapped around themselves, somewhat like sarongs, put their bead necklaces on us so we could wear them while we were there. I remember thinking, "How remarkable. This is all they own other than the cloth covering them, and the first thing they do is share their one possession with us." My father had once told me that we could learn a lot from the people of Africa, and, as I listened to the school children in one village sing, I knew he was right.

In one of the villages, Joe and I were invited into one of the homes. While there, Joe admired some animal teeth the owner had hanging around his neck, so I bought a rope with a lion's tooth on it for Joe, who put it around his neck. A day later we learned it was illegal to buy lions' teeth.

There seemed to be no end to our adventures. Joe and I crossed the equator, and even went up in a hot air balloon. On our last day in Kenya, we left the group and spent time with Onesmo and his American wife, Linda, at their home in Tagoni, which is about thirty minutes from Nairobi. I had learned of Onesmo from a friend who had written about him for a writing class that we both had taken. Through intelligence, hard work, and good luck, Onesmo, who was born and grew up in a small village in Kenya, had received a scholarship to Harvard College. After graduating, he had attended Harvard Medical School, where he had met and married Linda. They had stayed in the United States for a few years and then moved to Kenya, where they raised their three children. Each child has graduated from a university in the United States. Today, Onesmo specializes in malaria research and Linda teaches. When I had mentioned I was going to Kenya with my grandson, my friend in the writing class had passed the word to another friend who had passed the word to Onesmo, and, so, on our last day, we spent the afternoon in Tagoni, walking around their magnificent grounds, seeing their animals, and eating a delicious dinner at their home. It was the perfect ending to our trip.

Security at the Nairobi airport when we arrived that evening was at an all-time high. A few days prior to our departure, the plot to blow up planes from Heathrow over the Atlantic had been uncovered, and British authorities feared there were some in the group who had not been apprehended. We had to be at the airport in Nairobi more than three hours before departure, and the only thing we could carry onto the plane was a clear plastic bag containing passport, keys, money, yellow health card, and medications. We packed the camera and film and prayed the pictures wouldn't be ruined. We packed our books, but it didn't

Top: Nancy Sonnabend and Joe Wagner on the Equator, Kenya, August 2006
Bottom: Nancy Sonnabend, Onesmo ole-Moiyoi, Linda ole-Moiyoi, Joe Wagner
Tagoni, Kenya 8/13/2006

occur to me that Joe would not be allowed to take the journal he kept while we were in Kenya on the plane with him. Unfortunately, security people seized the journal and put it in the trash.

We landed at Heathrow at 6 A.M. The airport was mobbed with people from canceled and delayed flights. Joe and I were fortunate that the upper class lounge of Virgin Atlantic was available to us. It is a huge area with several large televisions, many computers, a restaurant that is free of charge, a person to shine shoes, and a hair salon for men and women. Joe had his hair washed and cut, and I had mine washed and blown dry, and neither one of us was presented with a bill. To help pass the time, I took a nap on a sofa, and Joe swung back and forth in one of the lounge's big chairs. Since twelve-year-olds almost always have a boundless supply of energy, he also watched television, and sent an e-mail to his mother telling her that we were at Heathrow and that I felt it was probably one of the safest times to fly because the security level was so high. Our flight to Boston finally took off twelve hours later, at 6 P.M. It was strange to be on a flight without a single piece of carry-on luggage or book in the entire plane. I know Joe's parents were happy and relieved to see us come through the doors of the international terminal at Logan.

The third grandchild trip was with my granddaughter Rachel. She is Eric's elder daughter and was sixteen at the time. The two of us took a fifteen-day excursion to India. In January 2007, we joined fourteen other people and, led by a Travcoa guide, set out to see as much of India as we could in the time we had. The visual, culinary, spiritual, and cultural experiences fulfilled just about every fantasy that the word *India* could conjure in our imaginations. From the rose-pink capital of Rajasthan to Jodhpur, the "Blue City," we explored ancient forts and palaces, towering monuments and dazzling shrines. Ranthambhore National Park, where the Aravuli and Vindhya mountain ranges meet, introduced us to India's extraordinary flora and remarkable array of wildlife including tigers.

In New Delhi, or Delhi, the capital of India, we toured the sights with our group and then spent Sunday afternoon and evening with Satia, an Indian Muslim, who is related to the husband of Rachel's flute teacher. Satia took us shopping in the oldest section of Delhi, showed us the embassies, took us to a mall that was packed with people shopping on the first several floors and, on the top two floors, with people waiting to get into the various movie theaters and bars located there. The mall was so crowded that it looked like the malls the day before Christmas in the United States. Satia told us all the malls were like this on Sundays. She also took us to the new subway and insisted we take a ride. The subway station required passengers to go through security, was immaculately clean—no graffiti anywhere—and I could scarcely feel the train move.

Even if we had not already been dazzled by Rajasthan, Jodhpur, or New Delhi, the Taj Mahal in Agra would have made the trip more than worthwhile. It is truly a magnificent piece of architecture. In Udaipur, we took a sunset cruise around the lake at the Lake Palace Hotel. Men in blue jackets and white pants with red turbans and sashes at their waists rowed the boat while Rachel played the flute.

When our tour ended, Rachel and I flew to Chennai to spend an afternoon and evening with an Indian Hindu family who are relatives of Rachel's neighbor in Pennsylvania. The couple and their sixteen-year-old daughter, who was exactly the same size and shape as Rachel, met us at the airport with a van and driver and took us to their home where we had lunch. Although there was a servant in the kitchen, the wife served the meal and did not eat until we were finished. The family followed the Indian custom of eating everything with the fingers of their right hand, but thoughtfully provided Rachel and me with a knife, fork, and spoon.

I listened while Rachel and our hosts' daughter talked.

"Do you play an instrument?" Rachel asked.

"No."

"Do you have an orchestra or band at your school?"

"We don't have music at my school."

"Do you do a sport?"

"No, we don't have sports at my school."

"What would a typical school day be like for you?"

"I get up and go to school. I come home and do homework."

"Do you go to parties or dances?"

"No, I've never been to a party or a dance."

"What do you do on the weekends?"

"On the weekends, I have a lot of homework, so I study."

"Your parents said their marriage was arranged. How do you feel about arranged marriages?"

"My parents will arrange my marriage when the time is right. That's fine with me."

It was a fascinating afternoon, and, after we left, Rachel said to me, "Oh, Mama, I'm so glad I'm an American."

Following in the footsteps of a multitude of grandmothers and grandfathers before me, I said, "Yes, life is good for you, but life in the United States has gotten too soft for many Americans. You will have to compete with children from India, China, and other Asian countries where all they do is study. Because many of these students are better prepared academically than U.S. students, more and more are being accepted in American

Top: January 2007, Rachel and Nancy Sonnabend at the Taj Mahal, Agra, India
Bottom: Rachel and Nancy Sonnabend riding an elephant
at Amber Fort, Jaipur, India

universities. Of course, all work and no play is not healthy either. There needs to be a balance." We then went back to enjoying our trip.

My fourth grandchild trip in the spring of 2008 was quite different from the first three. Eric's younger daughter, Olivia, who was then sixteen, is a happy-go-lucky teenager, interested in makeup, her hair, clothing, cheerleading, beaches, and attractive boys. Museums, monuments, and adults in anything but small doses are not among her favorite things, thus, I was still mulling over what we should do when my daughter Patti suggested that Olivia and I join her family on a cruise to the Greek Islands. The ship also would spend a day in Dubrovnik, Croatia, and another day in Kusadasi, Turkey. We would have several hours in London on the first and last days of the trip, as well as a night and part of two days in Venice and Rome. Furthermore, the ship's promotional material stated there would be many teenage activities on board. It sounded ideal.

When the time came, we boarded the Emerald Princess and walked into a whole new world. The ship was enormous, immaculate, and beautifully decorated. There were five swimming pools, seven jacuzzis and deck chairs galore. In the stern of the ship, behind and above one of the largest pools, there was an enormous screen where movies were shown at night and during the day. At night, the lounge chairs were covered with a padded material, and blankets were distributed to the audience so no one would be cold while watching the movie under the stars. We learned that bags of warm popcorn were passed out at the beginning of each movie. As the movie progressed, warm chocolate chip cookies with milk were served. There were 2,700 children and adults, 500 teenagers between the ages of 13 to 19, and about 1,200 employees on board. Clearly, Olivia and her cousins Kristi, who was 15, and Joe, who was 13, were going to have a wonderful time.

We had three cabins in a row. Olivia and I shared one cabin, Kristi and her brother, Joe, shared the cabin next to ours, and Patti and Steven, their parents, shared the cabin next to Kristi and Joe's. Our cabin had at least ten feet of closet space, plenty of drawers and shelves, two comfortable twin beds, and enough space between the beds for a night table and lamp. Suitcases were stored under the beds, and each room had a full bath. It was all quite different from my trip to Europe for my junior year abroad.

Both breakfast and lunch were huge buffets where you could choose whatever you wanted. Dinner was in a large, formal dining room. Sometimes we ate as a family and other times Kristi and Olivia would have dinner with friends, while Joe would swim or play basketball or golf and get something to eat on the run. There were places to get pizza or a hamburger and fries, and there was 24-hour room service. There also were two specialty restaurants, an Italian restaurant and a Steak House.

Olivia and Kristi immediately met a variety of seventeen-year-old boys from England, Canada, and Georgia. The girls were much in demand and, as a result, spent several hours before dinner every night deciding on the appropriate dress for the evening and doing their makeup and hair. I have to admit, it was fun watching their efforts, particularly since Olivia would fix my hair for me every night. It was just heaven to have my own hairdresser. One night, Kristi even did my makeup and, for the first time in my life, I wore mascara. Most evenings Kristi and Olivia ended up in the jacuzzi, watching a movie with the guys, or on the dance floor.

Joe met the captain's daughter who gave him coupons to

The Emerald Princess cruise ship, Summer 2008

Olivia Sonnabend with Olivia products in the Greek Islands

Olivia Sonnabend. Dessert in the steak house on the Emerald Princess,
Summer 2008

Left to Right: Steven Wagner, Patti Wagner, Olivia Sonnabend, Joe Wagner, Kristi Wagner and Nancy Sonnabend at the Parthenon

the food stations, thus providing him with cheeseburgers and sundaes whenever he wanted at no charge. Patti, Steven, and I had a relaxing and wonderful time together. The ship's photographers took lots of pictures that we enjoyed looking at every night, and the ship's employees met our every need, and always with a smile. It was the perfect trip, made even better by my purchase of a magnificent carpet for my living room in Kusadasi, Turkey.

Before we had boarded the ship, we had signed up for a few day excursions which usually included sightseeing in the morning and a beach or shopping trip in a small town in the afternoon.

It was during one of these excursions that I found a carpet for my living room. I was so thrilled with it after it arrived I bought another for my front hall from one of their sales people a few weeks later. Every time I enter my apartment or cross my front hall now, it brings back happy memories.

The fifth grandchild trip was the first two weeks of July 2009 with Mina Rowe, Kathy's daughter. It was a repeat of the trip to China I had taken with Kelly four years earlier, but we saw more this time.

When our plane landed in Beijing, we were told no one could disembark. Several masked, medical personnel boarded the plane and aimed a gadget at each of our foreheads to measure our temperatures. Two passengers with temperatures above what they deemed acceptable were removed. Then, the rest of us were allowed to leave the plane. The Chinese were concerned about the spread of Swine Flu and they were isolating anyone suspected of having it.

We were met by our young Chinese guide, Rebecca, who was waiting for us with a sign with our names on it. Her driver picked us up and quickly drove us directly to the Olympic Village. En route, Rebecca wrote our names and those of our family in Chinese characters. She also told us she had been lucky to attend one event at the Beijing Olympics.

We were impressed by the inside and outside of the Bird's Nest and the Water Cube. The Bird's Nest seats 100,000 people, has a retractable roof, and is where the opening and closing ceremonies took place for the 2008 Olympics. The Water Cube also is an enormous building which houses the Olympic swimming pool, diving platforms, springboards and a practice pool. The spectator seats are high above the pool and were designed to look like waves. In the center of the long sidewall is an opening

Mina and Nancy on the Great Wall, Beijing, China

that resembles an entrance to a cave and the walls are decorated with replicas of vines and foliage.

Mina and I also saw the huge park in Chongqing with its spectacular view of the city and Chongqing's business center called "Monument," which is similar to New York City's Times Square. Greater Chongqing is the largest city in the world with a population of 32,000,000 people. It's an important shipping port, as it lies at the intersection of the Jialing and Yangtze rivers.

Other high lights of the trip were our visits to the Viking River Cruise Elementary School and our visit to the Wuhan Museum, where we attended a Bells of Wuhan concert. At the school, the children danced and played the drums for us. Then, we went into a classroom and each child chose one of us to sit at his or her desk. My Chinese student companion took great pride in showing me her notebook, which showed she was learning the words *door* and *window*, and to count to six in English. She gave me a colored stick with origami design on each end and two other gifts, a box and a bird she had made out of paper. I gave her my card with my name on it and showed her a book I had authored, which had my picture in it that I'd brought for the head of the school. She was thrilled to see my picture and my name on both the book and the card I left with her.

The 2400-year-old bells in Wuhan each emit two tones, depending on where it is struck. The originals are on display and we were treated to a concert of ancient music on replica bells. Also in the Wuhan Museum, we saw two skulls of Paleolithic Homo erectus that are believed to date back one million years.

Our last day was in Shanghai, my favorite city in China. We did a lot of shopping in back alleys of old Shanghai, where I wasn't sure we were always safe, but it was productive and great fun. In the afternoon, we went to the knock-off market. That night,

Left to Right: Mina Rowe, our guide Shirley and Nancy at Monument, the center of downtown Chongqing, China

we had a farewell dinner, attended the amazing Acrobat Show, and went to Cloud Nine, a bar at the top of the Grand Hyatt Hotel, for the best view of the city. China has become commercial, but it still is an exciting place to visit.

I seem to have inherited a curiosity about other people and places from my father. I have been lucky enough to be able to satisfy that curiosity and, at the same time, travel with my family.

While my travels with my grandchildren are among my most treasured memories, there have been other fascinating trips.

On Friday, February 15, 2008, nine family members[12] (five adults, four children, ages nine to fifteen, who were on February school break) and another couple, Jon and Marcie Pucker, with their fifteen-year-old son, Oliver, flew from Boston to Lima, Peru. When we left, we had no idea we were about to get caught up in a general strike that left us taking a long bus ride with armed guards through the mountains to a small seaside town, but then, you can't always predict what will happen when you travel.

When we arrived in Lima Friday night, we went straight to our hotel. We spent Saturday touring the city and relaxing at the Sonesta Hotel El Olivar pool. Sunday, we flew to Cusco, boarded a private bus with a guide, stopped along the way to see the impressive fort of Sacsayhuaman, as well as three other sights, and arrived late in the afternoon at the Sonesta Posada del Inca in Sacred Valley. Monday, we spent the day in the Urubamba Valley seeing the Ollantaytambo Fortress, walking through the ancient salt mines of Maras, and ascending and descending the terraces of Moray. Tuesday, we boarded the PeruRail train and traveled

---

[12] Kathy, Tom, Mina, Hattie Rowe; Patti, Steven, Kristi, Joe Wagner; Nancy Sonnabend

in a vistadome car to Machu Picchu. There we were greeted by a guide who took us by bus to the archeological complex.

Machu Picchu was built by the Incas during the fourteenth century. Since it is at an elevation of about 10,000 feet, we all had taken altitude pills so we could climb about the complex, which includes many agricultural terraces, several plazas and buildings, without feeling ill. I was impressed by the size of the complex, the solar clock, the calendar, and the enormity of some of the stones.

On our way back to Cusco late that afternoon, our guide announced there would be a general strike in the city on Thursday. Peru is divided into three self-governing sections, a small southern section, a middle section, which is made up of Cusco and Machu Picchu, and the northern section, which consists of the city of Lima. A third of the population of Peru lives in Lima, and, at that point, Lima was trying to gain control of all of Peru. The strike only involved Cusco, and was to protest Lima's attempt to control the area. A particularly hot issue for the people of Cusco was Lima's desire to build high-rise buildings there and in the areas surrounding Machu Picchu. Because of the strike, our guide suggested including all of the activities planned for Thursday on our Wednesday schedule. We agreed, although a bit reluctantly, because our guidebooks and friends had warned us that Cusco's 12,000-foot altitude makes many tourists sick on their first day there.

We asked our guide how long the strike would last. "Three days," she said. As we were to fly to Lima on Friday, we asked if the airport would be affected, and were told it would not be.

On Thursday, thousands of people marched past our hotel, which was only a short block from the Plaza de Armas where

Top Picture: February 2008, Peru (Pictured Left to Right)
Back Row: Kathy Rowe, Nancy Sonnabend, Tom Rowe, Patti Wagner, Jon Pucker,
Marcie Pucker, Steven Wagner
Middle Row: Oliver Pucker, Kristi Wagner, Hattie Rowe, Joe Wagner, Mina Rowe
Front Row: Peruvian children with their animals

Bottom Picture: Hattie Ullman Rowe feeding the Llama

Top (Left to Right): Nancy Sonnabend, Steven Wagner, Patti Wagner
at Machu Pichu

Bottom: Machu Pichu

Strikers in Cusco, February 2008

many shops are located, and where much of the strike took place. The police were out in force, and we saw people being beaten. All the shops and restaurants in the city were closed. If you wanted to enter a shop, you had to bang on the door. The owner would open the door a crack and, if there weren't too many strikers in the area, pull you inside. The protesters lit fires in the streets and set off firecrackers that sounded like gunfire.

At noon, we learned the airport was closed and called our guide, who said a few flights had managed to go to Lima that morning before the protesters shut the airport down at 8 A.M. She suggested that we should get to the airport by 5:30 A.M. Friday morning. It seemed unlikely to me that twelve people, all going standby, would be able to get on a single plane, but we were at the airport Friday at 5:30 A.M. The weather was bad, nothing took off, and protesters closed the airport again. At that point, we returned to the hotel with our guide to discuss our options.

There was no train from Cusco to any town with an airport. The roads were blocked during the day, and people who attempted to leave the city were being taken out of their cars, put in trucks, and driven back to the city. We asked about a private plane, but there were none available. If we wanted to go north to Lima, we were told we would have to leave at midnight, and it would take twenty hours to drive through the mountains and the heavy rain at night. Assuming we would not be turned back by protesters if we left after midnight, we asked if there was an airport nearby that could be reached by bus. We learned Arequipa, a small seaside town eight to ten hours south of Cusco, had an airport with flights to Lima.

We booked a flight scheduled to leave midday Saturday for the twelve and put the $8.00 per person change fee for the tickets on Jon Pucker's credit card. We hired a bus, two drivers, an armed guard, and a guide. Friday night we went to bed early, and boarded the bus at midnight. We each brought along a pillow and a blanket. After about five miles, we changed buses and continued our journey. Eight hours later, we were still in the mountains and the rain hadn't stopped.

We arrived in Arequipa at 10:20 A.M. Saturday morning. As soon as the bus stopped, the armed guard got out and boarded a taxi, which then drove off. "Where's he going?" I asked.

"To the airport," our guide replied. "We don't know the way so we'll follow the taxi."

Ten minutes later, we entered the airport. I was the first of our group to reach the ticket agent. She looked at my passport and told me I had a reservation on the plane, but couldn't take the flight because I hadn't paid the $8.00 fee to change my ticket. I called to Jon Pucker who came forward to discuss the matter with the ticket agent. The agent insisted the charge for all the tickets had not gone through and could not be made at the airport. As she was adamant, Jon grabbed a taxi, and went into town to put the charge through again. After some further discussion, the agent agreed to tag our luggage and print out boarding passes. She would hold the luggage and boarding passes until Jon returned. Finally, Jon returned, our baggage disappeared down the chute, we were given our boarding passes, and we got on the plane, which immediately took off.

Looking back, the pre-Inca and Inca ruins were fascinating, feeding the alpacas and llamas was fun, the salt fields were interesting, the shopping was terrific, but the strike was, without a doubt, the most exciting part of the trip.

There is another group of trips that also brought me great pleasure. For three summers over the last twelve years, my children, grandchildren, and I have had the extraordinary good fortune to spend a week in July or August on two islands in Maine that are owned by my son-in-law, Michael Erickson, and several of his relatives. Michael's grandfather, Arioch Wentworth Erickson, purchased the islands in 1912 with the intent of building a house on one of the islands. Over the next two years, the Main House, as it is called, was constructed. The house has a number of large bedrooms, many with their own bath, a huge living room with an enormous fireplace, spectacular views, a kitchen/bar area, and a separate laundry area. In the front of the house, a large wooden deck with a hammock and tables and chairs runs the length of the house and, in the back, there are two smaller decks and an encased outdoor shower.

Grass leads from the Main House down to what is known as the Cook House. On the first floor, there is a small kitchen with three storage areas, a bathroom, and a dining room that seats about twenty. On the second floor, there are sleeping quarters. The Cook House originally was brought over to the island to house the laborers who were working on the Main House. Once the Main House was completed, Michael's grandparents decided to continue using the Cook House as their kitchen and dining area.

There are three other buildings on the island: a large boathouse where the materials needed to maintain the other buildings are kept and where boats can be repaired; a smaller boathouse, which originally was used as a place to repair small boats, but has been converted into living quarters with a kitchen, living room, dining room, bath downstairs and a bedroom upstairs; and the caretaker's house. The island's dock was built in 1977 to make the task of getting people on and off the island easier.

The first time I stayed on the island, Kelly, my grand-daughter, was a baby. The island's electrical system was powered by a generator and provided about five hours of electricity per night. I was reading a book before going to sleep my first night there when the generator shut down. As I had been warned about it, I grabbed my flashlight and planned to continue reading . . . and I did . . . for about five minutes. At that point, batteries in my flashlight died and I attempted to sleep. Unfortunately, the mattress was far too soft for me, so I made a bed for myself on the floor. The next day, someone placed a piece of plywood between the bed's mattress and box spring, which made it possible for me to sleep on it.

Since that trip, many of the box springs and mattresses have been replaced and things have become a lot less rustic. In 2003, electricity became available twenty-four hours a day, and in 2008, the old refrigerator, which was powered by propane gas, was replaced. Now, ice cream remains frozen when placed in the freezer, which means we can have ice cream on the pies we make from the islands' abundant supply of raspberries and blackberries. In 2008, the Cook House also became the proud possessor of a toaster oven, so we no longer need to make toast by inserting a long-handled fork into a piece of bread and holding it over the gas stove.

The islands are beautiful. Everyone has space to do whatever he or she wants. There is no television, so the children swim, run, pick raspberries, gather mussels, go boating, hit golf balls, play volleyball, read, sunbathe, paint fingernails, and walk on the rocks along the outer edge of the islands. Breakfast and lunch are eaten whenever and wherever. For dinners, we usually post a list indicating who is responsible for cooking and who is on clean-up duty. We buy lobsters from the lobstermen fishing off the coast, and typically have lobster dinner two nights a week. We also cook out on the stones, and the children make s'mores. After dinner, the kids sing, dance, play games, and generally enjoy themselves. For all too short a period, we step back to a simpler time, and I have the unalloyed joy of having all my children together and all my grandchildren happy with one another.

Top: The Island Dock and Small Boat House
Bottom: The Cook House and Main House on the Island

Top Picture: July 1999, Sonnabend Reunion on the Island, Maine (L toR)
Back Row: Brett Erickson, Kristi Wagner, Kelly Erickson, Nancy Sonnabend
Bottom Row: Hattie Rowe, Joe Wagner, Mina Rowe, Olivia Sonnabend
and Rachel Sonnabend

Bottom Picture: July 1999, Hattie Rowe having a bath on the Island, Maine

Top: Erickson Family on the Island, Maine, July 1999
(Left to Right): Brett, Wendy, Michael and Kelly
Bottom: Sonnabend Family on the Island, Maine July, 1999
(Left to Right): Eric, Olivia, Donna and Rachel

Top: August 2001, On the Island in Maine
(Left to Right): Patti Wagner, Nancy Sonnabend, Wendy Erickson
Bottom: August 2001, leaving the Island in Maine
(Left to Right): Joe Wagner, Nancy Sonnabend, Kristi, Patti and Steven Wagner

Nancy Lelewer Sonnabend's family on the Island, Maine, August 2004

Top Row (Left to Right): Denise Farrell, Eric Sonnabend,
Joe Wagner (9 years), Steven Wagner

Middle Row (Left to Right): Tom Rowe, Kristi Wagner (11 years),
Isabella Sanseverino (8 years) Brett Erickson (13 years), Nancy Lelewer Sonnabend,
Rachel Sonnabend (14 years), Dana Wright (10 years), Michael Erickson

Bottom Row (Left to Right):
Evan Wright (17 months), Donna Sonnabend Wright, Mina Rowe (9 years),
Kathy Rowe, Patti Wagner, Olivia Sonnabend (12 years), Wendy Erickson,
Kelly Erickson (15 years), Hattie Rowe (6 years)

Top Row (Left to Right): Kristi Sonnabend Wagner, sophomore, Weston High School, Weston, MA; Kelly Sonnabend Erickson, sophomore, Dartmouth College, Hanover, NH; Mina Caroline Rowe, eighth grade, Thurston Middle School, Weston, MA; Joe Sonnabend Wagner, eighth grade, Weston Middle School, Weston, MA.

Bottom Row (Left to Right): Hattie Ullman Rowe, fifth grade, Martha Jones School, Westwood, MA; Rachel Lauren Sonnabend, freshman, La Salle University, Phila-delphia, PA; Nancy Lelewer Sonnabend, called "Mama" by my grandchildren, three courses at Harvard Institute for Learning in Retirement (HILR); Olivia Hanna Sonnabend, junior, Delaware County Christian School, Newtown Square, PA; Brett Lelewer Erickson, Senior, Redwood High School, Larkspur, CA.

Picture taken August 2008 on the Island
Schools and grades as of September 2008

August 2008, Brett Erickson and Olivia Sonnabend cheerleading on the Island

EPILOGUE
Time Past, Time Present, Time Future

Sometimes, foreign language teachers try to explain tenses to their students by pointing out that every day we speak of things in the past (time past), of things in the present or today (time present), and of things yet to come (time future). As I packed up my parents' apartment after my mother's death, I found myself thinking about time past, time present, and what the future might hold.

My parents lived their lives by a code of helping others and building for the future. The foundation of their code lay in the teachings of Grandpa SS, who passed on to my father what he had learned from Great-Grandfather David's precepts, which had been written in 1910 as part of his autobiography.

"Let it be your aim in life, when children grow up, that you can impart to them some instructions I gave you, with more valuable hints added, gathered in by your own experiences. If you do this, your

life and the lives of your descendants will be happy, prosperous and respected in the community, and the memory of the founder thereof will be blessed."

"Let your life be such that no one can say you wronged him. Be a help to your fellow man. There is no one so poor he cannot be of help to somebody less fortunate. You did not know poverty but I did."

"If you are an employer, be generous to all who are deserving."

"Give encouragement to those lacking in spirit and lagging behind in the race of life. Is the weed in the garden responsible that it is not a flower with beauty and fragrance?"

"Let your life be a good example for others to follow and not as a person who like a thistle, is shunned by everybody. It is there where wealth is a curse."

"Happiness consists only when you make others happy."

"Don't do acts of kindness for the sake of getting gratitude in return. Don't be disappointed if you can't get it."

"Are you paying, or have you always paid your debts, for good will and kindness rendered you?"

"Don't let disappointments in others make you lose confidence in mankind. The majority of people are good, at least I found that so."

"The world is like a mirror; as you look into it, it gives you your own reflection in return."

"Don't put your signature to anything before being fully aware what you are signing. You'll not walk on ice before testing its strength."

"A man is part of the community where he lives, and shall be identified in social and public matters appertaining to the welfare of the community. It is for your own improvement."

"Charitable institutions, to give comfort to the sick, the helpless and the unfortunate, have a claim on you."

"Keep out of courts. Don't sue and don't be sued."

"Through life's journey there is a time to work and a time to play. Don't neglect either, and have them balance. Nature demands it. Work six days and rest the seventh, for pleasure and recreation that you may live long and enjoy what the Lord has given."

"Don't be old during the time when you are young. Every decade in a man's life has its enjoyments. Don't let it pass, but use it in moderation."

"Happiness springs not from a large fortune but from temperate habits and simple wishes."

"The abundance of pleasure ceases to be a pleasure and generally ends in pain, like a bitter taste following the eating of too much sweets. The poor enjoy the sweets more than the rich because they eat them very sparingly."

"May providence never give my children abundance in such a manner that they are puzzled in the morning to know how to spend the day in hunting for pleasures. There is where unhappiness begins and life loses its real charm. Like the flower when it has reached its full bloom, it begins to wither."

"Use thy youth so that you may have comfort to

remember it. Use it as the springtime, which soon departs and wherein you ought to plant and sow all provisions for a long and happy life."

I suppose there are some who will say that my great-grandfather's precepts are not particularly unique. This may be true, but what was unique was the degree to which they became the bedrock of my grandfather and father's lives. I can only hope that I have followed Great-Grandfather David's precepts as well as my father did.

My father used to say that my eldest daughter, Kathy, "made all the right decisions for the wrong reasons." Perhaps he could have said the same thing about my marriages. I did not make wise choices in the men I married. But, out of my second marriage came new friends and a new career, and out of my first marriage came my children. Nothing, absolutely nothing, in my life has been more fulfilling or rewarding than being a mother. I loved the role when my children were young; I love the role now that my children have grown. As for grandchildren, well, as I have said, they are a special bonus, the icing on the cake! Certainly, I found raising children with dyslexia and attention deficit disorder a challenge in the sixties and seventies, but it was a challenge that brought me many friends, taught me a great deal, answered some questions that had haunted me since my childhood, and left me happy with life.

Years ago, when my parents moved from Highland Park to Winnetka and my mother threw out the school papers I had treasured from elementary school through college, the scrapbook of ribbons I had won in various sports, and my diplomas, I was crushed. Now I wonder what I would do with them if I still had them. Perhaps once in a while I would look at them and savor the memory of those days, but probably not. After all, everything they represented is a part of me now. The papers showed only that I worked hard, the diplomas only that I graduated, the ribbons only that I won. They do not show the love my family surrounded me with, the friends that I have made over the years, or the accomplishments, both big and little, that have filled my days.

These days I find myself attached to those pieces of furniture I have purchased or inherited, my mother's engagement ring, some items I have collected on my travels, and the family photographs on my grandmother's piano and in my bedroom. My other treasures include a 1946 chalk drawing that I made for my father's fortieth birthday and the Igor portraits of my children.

The Igor portraits began as a gift to my father for his sixtieth birthday. In 1965, I was chatting with my parents.

"What would you like for your birthday?" I had asked my father.

"An Igor."

"Not in our house," my mother had responded immediately. I hadn't a clue what an Igor was, but, given my mother's response, suggested we go to Plan B.

A week later, I entered an art gallery in New York City and noticed along one wall stylized paintings of girls just entering puberty. Each girl was nude from the waist up. I went over to have a closer look. They were all signed "Igor." The gallery owner told me Igor was a Russian artist currently living in New York. He gave me Igor's phone number, and shortly thereafter, Igor, carrying several more paintings of nude girls, met me at the Plaza, where I was staying.

"I'm not interested in those. Can you paint portraits?"

Kathy Sonnabend by Igor

Wendy Sonnabend by Igor

Eric Sonnabend by Igor

Patti Sonnabend by Igor

"Yes."

"I have two daughters, seven and eight, who I would like you to paint, with their clothes on, provided the price is right and you'll come to Boston."

"Do you have scotch?"

"Yes."

We settled on a date and a price. I remember worrying that he would be drunk the entire weekend. He wasn't, but he did consume a great deal of scotch.

Both my parents were thrilled with my father's birthday present.

A few years later, Igor called. "You have two other children. Don't you think I should paint them too?" After several calls, I finally gave in, and Igor came, painted, and drank scotch again. My parents and I used to swap two pictures each year.

The chalk drawing also was a birthday present for my father. My parents were away for the weekend and I wanted to make something special for his birthday, so I got my easel, set it up in the driveway, and drew our home. Considering that I was eleven and the only art lessons I had had were at school, it turned out well. On the back I wrote "For Daddy on your fortieth birthday. I hope we will always be just as happy together and never have any cross words. I will remember you even after you die. Love, Nancy Ullman Lelewer." My parents had the picture framed with a piece of glass on the back so that what was written there would be visible to anyone who looked.

My mother's engagement ring, which my father redesigned at her request to look more important and unusual, rarely leaves my finger. Wherever I go I receive compliments on its beauty. It is a link to my past, as is, as strange as it may seem, my love of football.

508 Sheridan Road by Nancy Ullman Lelewer

My father taught me to love the game when I was a child. I have been frozen to the bone when I was a student at football games at Northwestern University and, as an adult, at New England Patriot games, even with the little heating packets in my gloves, but I still think the coldest games of all were the Thanksgiving Day Peoria Central High School games I attended when we visited Nana and Popeye. Since 1960, I have been fortunate enough to have fabulous season tickets to the Patriots games. I have seen the Patriots play at Fenway Park, Harvard Stadium, Boston College Alumni Stadium, Boston University, and Foxborough, first at Shaefer Stadium and now at Gillette Stadium. It has been my special joy to introduce two more generations to this sport loved by my father and me.

There is not a day that goes by that I do not think of my parents. If I found it difficult to talk to my mother, I never doubted that she loved me. My father was a man of extraordinary warmth, enduring wisdom, and great humor. My father, my mother, and all of my relatives held me securely in their hearts and filled my days with laughter. The Lelewer men of whatever generation had a way of looking toward the light of a situation. They told wonderful stories, smiled, and laughed. They enjoyed life, lived it to the fullest, and carried the people they loved along in the current of their joy. Their coda has enriched my life immeasurably.

My father spent hundreds of hours with me plowing through numerous files and going over his financial and estate papers. There were two files about which he said, "Those can wait, you don't have to bother with them now." Two years after his death, I finally had time to open the files. In them, I found my father's birth certificate, graduation programs from elementary and high school, my parents' wedding invitation, an envelope from the Lelewer stores, sales contracts for the properties my parents had bought and/or sold during their marriage, various pictures and a poem, Death is Nothing at All. The poem had a note attached to it. "For Baby, I thought you might like to have this. Love, Papa" My father didn't believe in an afterlife, "Dust to dust," as it states in Judaism. Thus, he omitted the four lines after "Why should I be out of mind because I am out of sight?" and concluded with the last line, "All is well." I include it here as he gave it to me so that others, too, can know that all is well.

Death Is Nothing at All
By Henry Scott Holland (1847-1918),
Canon of St. Paul's Cathedral

Death is nothing at all.
I have only slipped away into the next room.
I am I and you are you.
Whatever we were to each other,
that we still are.
Call me by my old familiar name.
Speak to me in the easy way
which you always used.
Put no difference in your tone.
Wear no forced air of solemnity or sorrow.
Laugh as we always laughed
at the little jokes we enjoyed together.
Play, smile, think of me, pray for me.
Let my name be ever the household word
that it always was.
Let it be spoken without affect,
without the trace of a shadow on it.
Life means all that it ever meant.
It is the same that it ever was.
There is absolutely unbroken continuity.
Why should I be out of mind
because I am out of sight?
. . . .
All is well.

AFTERWORD
Traditions Continue

My father loved athletics and we had many happy hours participating in them. This joy was passed along to my children who all played various sports. It seems with each generation someone performs on a higher level than the previous generation. My father was golf champion of two clubs. My tennis partner and I won the New England Regional Collegiate Doubles Championship our sophomore year at Sarah Lawrence. My daughter, Wendy, was a member of Harvard's Women's Squash Team, which competed in the Howe Cup Championships and was a member of the Harvard Women's Soccer Team, which also went to the national championship. The grandchildren are already more impressive.

*Kelly's Erickson's team competed in the U.S. Volleyball Junior Olympics' 14 &
Under Open Division in June, 2003 and placed 10th. Her team competed in the U.S.
Volleyball Junior Olympics' 15 & Under Open Division the following year and tied
for 27th place.*

*Kelly Erickson, sixth from left, receiving the bronze medal
with her lightweight eight crew.*

*June, 2006, Kelly's crew placed 3rd in the U.S. Rowing Youth National Women's
Lightweight Eight event. Her crew placed 2nd in the same event the following year.
Kelly subsequently rowed on Dartmouth's Women's Freshman Crew.*

*Brett Erickson's team competed in the U.S. Volleyball Junior Olympics' 13 &
Under Open Division in June, 2004 and tied for 53rd place. At the end of her high
school freshman volleyball season, Brett won the "Break Out" award given to the
most improved player. The following year, Brett was the only starting sophomore
on Redwood High School's varsity volleyball team, which tied for 3rd in Division II
(i.e., schools with more than 1,500 students) of the Northern California Volleyball
Championship. Brett subsequently switched to crew and, in her senior year, her
Marin Rowing Association Women's JV Eight won their event at the San Diego
Crew Classic. She was recruited by Boston College and joined their women's crew
team in September, 2009. Brett rowed in the Head of the Charles as well as many
other regattas for BC this year.*

Rachel Sonnabend participated in crew, field hockey, track and cross-country in high school.

Rachel Sonnabend has studied ballet and piano for many years, but her real passion during much of elementary and high school was the flute.

Olivia Sonnabend played third singles in high school on the varsity tennis team junior year (2008) and first singles her senior year (2009). She won the MVP award both years.

In high school, Olivia Sonnabend also did track, cross country and cheerleading. She plays the violin, sings and has studied ballet.

Kristi Wagner played baseball, basketball and soccer in middle school. In high school, she played JV basketball as a freshman and, as a sophomore, played varsity, won a letter and won the Most Improved Player Award. Kristi is #22, wearing a nose guard because her nose was broken during varsity practice. As a junior Kristi is the starting center on Weston's varsity basketball team.

June, 2009, Harsha Lake, Batavia, Ohio. U.S. National Championships
Wayland/Weston Women's Varsity Four consisted of Kristi Wagner, stroke,
(wearing white hat on far left), three other sophomores and one junior. During the
last race, one rower had an asthmatic attack at the half way mark while they were
leading. Even being the youngest boat in their division, and with only three girls
finishing the race, they finished 12th in the nation. In June, 2008, Kristi, then a
freshman, also rowed in the U.S. Youth National Championships in a Wayland/
Weston Women's Varsity Four with four seniors. The boat placed 11th in the nation.
Kristi was one of 34 girls out of the entire U.S. invited to
Development Camp for crew. She attended 6/2009.

Top: 2009 Kristi Wagner during her junior year in high school in the boat she stroked at the Head of the Charles that came in 7th place.
Picture courtesy Sport Graphics.
Bottom: 2008 Kristi Wagner, wearing a white hat, rowing in the Head of the Charles her sophomore year. Her boat placed 15th. By the end of her sophomore year, Kristi had earned three varsity crew letters.
Picture courtesy Row 2k Media.

Joe Wagner (# 11) plays baseball, soccer, basketball, and golf. In middle school, Joe made the "A" core team in soccer, basketball and baseball. His baseball team won the championship of all the surrounding towns when he was in sixth grade. He went to karate camp and won outstanding camper. His soccer teams have usually made it to the finals and he was generally one of the highest scorers. Entering high school, Joe and one other freshmen made the varsity golf team and both earned varsity letters. Joe also made the freshman basketball team.

Joe Wagner playing baseball, June, 2009

At the 2006 Cheerleading Regional Competition, Mina Rowe's squad placed third.
Her cheerleading squad also placed third in 2007 and
fourth in 2008 at the regional competitions.
(Mina is second from left of the four girls with one leg near the ground.)

As a high school freshman, Mina made the varsity cheerleading team and
the varsity cheerleading competition team.

Over the years, she also has done a lot of dance. Her favorite sport is basketball.

June, 2009, Mina playing for the Ducks, an Amateur Athletic Union (AAU) spring basketball team. Mina also made her high school freshman basketball team.

Cheerleader Hattie Ullman Rowe

Hattie's cheerleading squad placed first in their division competition and second in the tri-regional division competition.

Spring, 2008, Hattie Ullman Rowe with the ball playing soccer.
Hattie also plays baseball and is on a competition dance team.

APPENDIX A
Cristina Lana's impact on other family members

Cristina impacted the lives of my eldest daughter, Kathy, my youngest daughter, Patti, and her daughter, Kristi.

Because Kathy is dyslexic and was struggling in school, I was determined to have her with Cristina in Spain where she could learn the Spanish language and a different culture. Kathy and I spent three weeks with Cristina in August of 1972 sightseeing and relaxing on Spain's northern beaches.

The summer of 1973, Kathy, Cristina, and I enjoyed a week on Spain's eastern shore before going to Cristina's home in Alpadreti, a very small pueblo. We were joined there by two of Cristina's nieces who were close to Kathy's age. The plan was for Kathy to stay with Cristina and for me to return home. Kathy didn't think much of Alpadreti. There were no stores, no paved streets, and no TV. There was only a radio with two stations in Spanish, one telephone in the town—and it wasn't in Cristina's home—and the flat, rocky plateau known as La Mancha which was all one could see in every direction. No one in the pueblo spoke a word of English.

"What am I supposed to do here?" she asked me.

I looked out the window and saw about twenty kids, more or less her age, running around with smiles on their faces. I said, "Go outdoors, find out what they are doing, and join them."

She said, "How can you leave me here? Now I know you hate me."

The next day I left her in hysterics hanging onto Cristina. I watched from the rear of the train as their image grew smaller and smaller, and prayed I'd made the right decision. I returned to the U.S. and heard nothing for two weeks. Then, Kathy's first letter arrived.

"Mom," she wrote, "We've been to the Prado Museum and I've seen the most fantastic pictures painted by Valazquez and Goya. I've also been to Toledo and seen the elongated paintings of El Greco. We are going to a bullfight. I'm so excited. The kids here are great. I'm having lots of fun. Love, Kathy"

Kathy learned Spanish, to dance Flamenco, and about Spanish art and culture. She had one of the best summers of her life.

Cristina came several times to visit our family. She always came laden with presents. On one trip, she brought my daughter, Patti, who was three, an enormous doll with a small suitcase full of clothing for the doll. Patti was enamored with the doll and carried it every place she went.

Patti said, "This is my doll, Cristina, and when I have my first real baby, I will name her Cristina." Long after she outgrew the doll, she continued to say that she would name her first child Cristina.

We used to tease her. "What if you have a boy first, or your husband doesn't like the name?" Even after she was married,

Kathy learning Flamenco during her month with Cristina in Spain

I asked if her husband knew that their first child would be a girl and that her name would be Cristina?

Patti said, "No, I'll tell him when the time is right."

Patti and Steven's first child was a girl and they named her Kristina after Cristina Lana and the doll. We call her Kristi.

Left to Right: Cristina, Kathy, Patti and Wendy in my bed in Brookline, MA

APPENDIX B
A Man of Many Titles:
Joseph Lelewer's talk at the wedding of Patti
Sonnabend and Steven Wagner, December 31, 1989

I am Joseph Lelewer, holder of many titles. But, before I delve into them, I want to thank Patti, the beautiful bride, for wanting me to say a few words and also to thank Steven and Father Gee for giving me the privilege of participating in this sacred ceremony.

Now back to titles.

1: I was known as 'Seward and Myrtle Lelewer's son.' This I cherished because I truly loved and revered my parents—something I have observed missing in some of my friends.

2: I got extra lucky and married Sis Ullman and soon became known as 'Sis's husband'– a nice, nice title because of her charm and accomplishments before and after a severe hearing loss.

3: Nancy, mother of the bride, was born, so I became 'Nancy's father' to her friends. This pretty and talented lady was the easiest child to raise and continues to be her own reward for us.

4: You see me as 'Patti's grandfather'—you too will find her easy to love as I do.

5: Amongst the one-year-olds and younger I am known as 'Kelly Erickson's great-grandfather.' Maybe, in time, this circle will be enlarged.

My grandchildren always expect a lecture when they see me and I wouldn't disappoint them. So tonight, before I retire back to all my worthy titles, I'll share with you the words of the general secretary of the Church Missionary Society of the Church of England:

> 'There is need for a deep humility, by which we remember that God has not left himself without a witness in any nation at any time. When we approach the man of another faith than our own, it will be in a spirit of expectancy to find out how God has been speaking to him and what new understandings of the grace and love of God we may ourselves discover in this encounter. Our first task in approaching another people, another culture, another religion, is to take off our shoes, for the place we are approaching is holy.'

Thank you and may the Jewish Year 5750, now three months old, see you in health, happiness and with peace in our world.

APPENDIX C
Speeches from My Father's Celebration of Life Service

My father couldn't resist calling his grandchildren by number, as well as by name. Thus, Kathy was #1, Wendy, #2, Eric, #3, and Patti, #4. Their spouses were also #1, #2, #3, and #4, and their children were #1A, #1B, #2A, #2B, and so on. The kids loved it, and often would say when they called, "Hi, Papa, this is #1," or whatever number they were.

Kathy: My name is Kathy Rowe, and I'm Joe's #1 granddaughter. I wrote this letter two and a half years ago in honor of my grandparents' seventieth wedding anniversary and want to share it with you today.

'Dear Mama and Papa,

It's quite amazing that you are celebrating your 70th wedding Anniversary. CONGRATULATIONS!

Through my life you have both always been there for me, as my friend, my sounding board, my inspiration.

Some of my fondest memories of our years together are of visiting Highland Park "all by myself," loving the paths and the stream behind your house, playing with Sally Benjamin, celebrating my birthday at McDonalds, walks with Papa, getting my daily dose of advice, enjoying chocolate sodas, cooking, "making everything pretty" with Mama, cocktail hour with warm fires, being the waitress at your parties, walking down the hall with my arms crossed as the house was freshly painted, watching home movies of Mom, back to school shopping with Mama, modeling all my beautiful clothes for Papa, PANCAKES!!, Ferry Hall … "the dorms are brand new," said Mama! "Yes," I said, "40 years ago" … bringing friends to your house for cozy dinners, getting my learner's permit with Mama and speeding home!, BEINLICH'S!!, "I'll have a bloody Mary, please," the excitement of Mama and Papa coming to visit!!, and, oh, my corner office—"not bad for a little shit"!!! I could go on and on.

Mostly, I remember so many private moments, sitting at breakfast or in the den where I could always tell you both anything.

I do truly appreciate all you have done for me. You have both given me so much, and I love you very much. Happy, Happy Anniversary!

With love, Kathy'

Wendy: Hi. I'm Wendy Erickson, Joe's second granddaughter. 'Nothing trivial, I hope,' was a typical response of my grandfather when someone sneezed or coughed. 'Awful,' was one common answer of his when asked, 'How are you?'

The unexpected was frequently heard coming from Papa. With the twinkle in his eye and his lighthearted banter, he could converse with anyone and put them at ease. Several years ago, he called me early one weekend morning. I was just getting out of bed and not feeling particularly chatty. When I told Papa that I was tired and not really up to talking, he said, 'Then we will have a moment of silence.' His comment made me laugh, and we then went on to have a most enjoyable conversation.

My grandparents have both been a special part of my life. Starting when I was five years old, I flew by myself from Boston to Chicago to visit with them every summer for a week. There, I had the pleasure of having both of my grandparents all to myself. I fondly remember tennis outings with Papa, trips to the arboretum, relaxing over cocktails each evening, and his relish of a good meal. I never knew a couple that were beloved by so many people.

My grandfather had unique and special qualities that made him a great role model and mentor. While we will miss him dearly, he lives on in the hearts of all of us who loved him and were so lucky to have him in our lives.

Eric: 'This is #3,' I would say when phoning my grandfather from Boston to Chicago, Florida, or Lasell Village. Papa was quick to recognize which kid was on the phone, in part because I'm the only male of the four grandchildren. 'Hi Eric . . .' As soon as I heard Papa speak, I knew I was in trouble from the tone of his voice. I felt a lecture coming on. Papa always gave me something to think about in his lectures, which were his way of showing he cared deeply about me.

There was something very warm and safe about being in the company of Papa. I noticed, too, that when Papa greeted somebody for the first time, he was devastatingly charming and polite, always putting people at ease, and within a few minutes, endearing and commanding easily the respect of whomever he just met, leaving an indelible impression forever.

I always looked forward to a visit, whether it was in Chicago, Florida, or Lasell Village. Papa had an incredible memory, and his storytelling kept me wanting to hear more. I knew once the lecture was finished, we would move onto a new joke or a story about some interesting event in his life or a discussion about world politics.

One of the many warm memories I have of Papa was a visit to Chicago during the fall. Papa and I, early in the morning, went through his neighborhood collecting leaves. Later, we glued each leaf to a page in a scrapbook and Papa helped me label each leaf according to the tree from which it had come. Having one-on-one time with Papa was special.

Papa had amazing timing and ability to tell a joke. One of my favorite jokes Papa told me is one I recently retold to a group of motorcycle enthusiasts I encountered while on a bike myself at a stop at Dunkin' Donuts:

A truck driver goes into a diner for breakfast and sits at the counter to order two easy-over eggs, toast, sausage and a cup of coffee. Two bikers enter the diner and sit beside the truck driver at the counter, one on each side of him. When the truck driver's breakfast is served, one of the bikers takes his two easy-over eggs, toast, and sausage. The other biker takes the truck driver's cup of coffee.

The truck driver politely asks the waitress for the bill, pays the cashier, and leaves the diner. The biker, looking up at the waitress and his biker friend, says, 'He's not much of a man.'

The waitress says, 'He's not much of a truck driver either. He just backed over two motorcycles.'

Patti: Hi. My name is Patti Wagner, and I am Sis and Joe's youngest grandchild. It's an incredible honor to be their granddaughter. I have only met people who think they are wonderful, and I always feel proud to listen to their praise about them. I feel so lucky that I was able to enjoy them both for my 41 years and witness and feel the love they always had for each other. Not only were they always holding hands, they were always telling me how lucky they were to have each other. They appreciated each day they had together.

As you all know and have heard from many of my family's speeches, my grandfather had a wonderful sense of humor. Many memories come to mind, but I will share one of my favorites.

When I was ten years old, I was visiting my grandparents in Chicago, which I did each summer. I was tall for my age, with especially large feet, and I complained a lot about having such big feet. One morning during that visit, I ran into my grandparent's bedroom screaming, 'Mama, Papa, a mouse just ran over my foot!'

Papa said, 'Oh dear, that mouse must be exhausted!'

Martin Braver is a certified public accountant and the founder of Braver and Company, the thirteenth largest accounting company in Massachusetts. He was head of the finance committee at Lasell Village and a friend of my father. Martin visited my father every day after he became ill, but the day of my father's service, Martin was ill. The following day, he came to my parents' apartment and handed me the talk he'd intended to give at the service.

Martin Braver: When I was contemplating what I would say this afternoon, I had a small panic attack. After all, I didn't know Joe for very long. I knew that he came from Chicago's Highland Park. He didn't know my friends from Highland Park. I knew that he owned and operated men's hat stores, and I knew that he loved Florida. But then I paused, because suddenly I felt as though I knew him all my life. I realized that in the few years that we sat with each other, that we joked with each other, that we confided in each other, and that we argued with each other, we had developed a bond—that we had become fast friends.

I thought of one of the first conversations that I had with Joe. It was, of course, about the Village finances. He came seeking me out; he wanted to talk to that Braver fellow who is supposed to know all about the Village finances. I'll never forget that first encounter. I did know his age of 94, and I expected that I could just tell him in general terms that the finances were not so good and not so bad, that there are expenses that have to be reviewed and that as time goes on, I would obtain more information. This young gentleman would have none of that.

The first thing he asked me was how many full-time equivalent employees we had. I guesstimated, and he then asked me how much the payroll was. I guesstimated that also, and before I could get another word out of my mouth, he said to me, 'Well that's an average salary per person of (whatever it is).' Now, mind you, he didn't have a calculator, he didn't write it down on a piece of paper—he calculated it in his head in about 10 seconds. That was my introduction to Joe Lelewer.

His humor was legendary. You could be sure that you would learn a new joke whenever you ate with Joe. And even though his beloved 'Sis' couldn't hear, he made sure that she 'heard' the joke. He saw to it that she read his lips. It was a treat to have an evening meal with Joe and Sis. They were in great demand as dinner companions, and you had to make a date way in advance.

Joe taught me something—he taught me to keep alive—to keep a smile on my face—to help cheer up those who need cheering up. He taught me the meaning of friendship—he was my friend and let me know it.

Joe made me a better person, and I keep asking myself these past few days what would it have been like if I hadn't met Joe Lelewer?

Here was a man who loved his wife (as he would say, 'I was born married'), loved his daughter Nancy, loved his family and loved his friends. It is an honor and a privilege to be called 'his friend.' I will certainly miss him. And those days when I feel blue, I'll think of Joe and remember his humor and his smile—that will cheer me up. May the Lord have mercy on his soul. Amen.

APPENDIX D
My Grandchildren

Kelly Erickson, Spring, 2007

Rachel Sonnabend, Spring, 2008

Brett Erickson, Spring, 2008

Olivia Sonnabend, July, 2009

Kristi Wagner, January, 2007
Portrait by Roger Pelissier

Joe Wagner, Summer, 2008

Mina Rowe, Spring, 2008

Hattie Rowe, Spring, 2008

About the Author

Nancy Lelewer Sonnabend lives in Boston's Back Bay. She is the creator of games and a calendar designed to help children understand space and time, and the co-author of journal articles dealing with learning differences based on her research at MIT and Harvard Medical School. Her first book, an autobiography entitled *SOMETHING'S NOT RIGHT: One Family's Struggle With Learning Disabilities*, was published under her maiden name and won a Parent's Choice Commendation. In 2007, her short story, *Sue and Gracie* was published in Harvard's *HILR Review*. Although she has many interests, her real passions are her family, travel, and helping those with learning differences and Asperger's Syndrome.